BIOTYPES

ALSO BY JOAN AREHART-TREICHEL
Poisons and Toxins
Immunity—How Our Bodies Resist Disease
Trace Elements, How They Help and Harm Us

BIO TYPES

THE CRITICAL LINK BETWEEN YOUR PERSONALITY AND YOUR HEALTH

JOAN AREHART-TREICHEL

Times
BOOKS

Published by TIME BOOKS, a division of
Quadrangle/The New York Times Book Co., Inc.
Three Park Avenue, New York, N.Y. 10016

Published simultaneously in Canada by
Fitzhenry & Whiteside, Ltd., Toronto

Library of Congress Cataloging in Publication Data
Arehart-Treichel, Joan.
    Biotypes, the critical link between your personality
and your health.
    Bibliography: p. 207
    Includes index.
    1. Medicine, Psychosomatic. 2. Personality.
3. Health. I. Title. [DNLM: 1. Personality—
Popular works. 2. Psychophysiology—Popular
works. 3. Psychosomatic medicine—Popular works.
4. Attitude to health—Popular works. BF698.9.B5
A679b]
RC49.A73   616.08   79-51433
ISBN 0-8129-0840-6

Manufactured in the United States of America

In memory
of my mother—
for whom this book arrived
unfortunately too late

ACKNOWLEDGMENTS

ALTHOUGH THIS BOOK IS BASED on the research of hundreds of scientists and would not have been possible without them, I am particularly grateful to those investigators who took time to vet various chapters in the book for me:

Aaron T. Beck, M.D., professor, Department of Psychiatry, University of Pennsylvania, Philadelphia, Pennsylvania; Seymour Diamond, M.D., director, Diamond Headache Clinic, Chicago, Illinois; Karen R. Duszynski, B.A., research coordinator, the Precursors Study, the Johns Hopkins University School of Medicine, Baltimore, Maryland; Thomas F. Garrity, Ph.D., associate professor, Department of Behavioral Science, University of Kentucky College of Medicine, Lexington, Kentucky; Stephen Goldston, Ed.D., M.S.P.H., coordinator for primary prevention programs, National Institute of Mental Health, Rockville, Maryland; Gaston de Grâce, Ph.D., School of Psychology, Université Laval, Québec, Canada; Lawrence LeShan, Ph.D., experimental and clinical psychologist, New York City; John W. Mason, M.D., professor, Department of Psychiatry, Yale University School of Medicine, New Haven, Connecticut; Aaron Paley, M.D., director, Department of Behavioral Sciences, National Jewish Hospital and Research Center, Denver, Colorado; Ray H. Rosenman, M.D., director, Harold Brunn Institute, Mount Zion Hospital and Medical Center, San Francisco, California; Richard D. Smith, M.D., John Muir Memorial Hospital, Walnut Creek, California; T. Flint Sparks, M.A., research coordinator, Cancer Counseling and Research Center, Fort Worth, Texas; Caroline Bedell Thomas, M.D., professor emeritus of medicine and director, the Precursors Study, the Johns Hopkins University School of Medicine, Baltimore, Maryland; Ingrid Waldron, Ph.D., associate professor, Department of Biology, University of Pennsylvania, Philadelphia; Ralph C. Williams, Jr., M.D., professor and chairman, the University of New Mexico School of Medicine, Albuquerque, New Mexico.

PREFACE

MY FIRST EXPOSURE TO THE fascinating link between personality and health came on a snowy winter's day in 1975 when, as medical editor for *Science News* magazine, I interviewed Claus and Marjorie Bahnson, a husband-wife psychologist team in Philadelphia, about their research on personality and cancer susceptibility. During the next several years I came across still more quiet but significantly expanding research findings on personality and health, notably the long-term study results of Dr. Caroline Thomas of Johns Hopkins University School of Medicine in Baltimore, linking certain personality traits early in life with susceptibility to heart attacks, cancer, mental disease, or suicide some years later. Meanwhile, I was beginning to understand the larger implications of the fact that not only are we largely responsible for our own health, but we also have considerable control over it. That is, if we are sick, then we can call on our minds to help us get well; we can reshape even our thoughts, emotions, and behaviors to ensure continued good health; and it's even possible that we can rear our children to be virtually disease-free throughout their lives.

During the mid 1970s, Americans were becoming increasingly interested in preventive medicine, holistic medicine, life-style medicine. They were eating healthier diets, giving up smoking, exercising more. They were thirsty for guidance on how to live healthier lives. Hence this book on the latest research findings on personality and health—both the "bad" news (we are responsible for our own health far more than we realize) and the good news (since we are largely responsible for our own health, we can also do something about it and at the same time shape our children's future health as well). This is a "how to" book in the deepest sense. I've tried to include only information that is practical, mostly things we can all do on our own and at relatively small cost.

My motivation in undertaking this book was also to some degree personal. My mother, a long-time victim of rheumatoid arthritis, possessed a number of traits of the rheumatoid arthritis personality. In fact, she even agreed with me that this was the case. So I hoped that a book on personality and disease would benefit her especially. My hope was not realized, though, for my mother died from the disease while my book was in progress, and, ironically, the book became a great boon to my own health instead. It provided me with a means of working through my grief, and of avenging my mother for the excruciating pain she suffered by trying to help people in similar circumstances. The research material I gathered made me realize what a powerful disease predisposer grief is, and that I should take especially good care of myself during the months of mourning. It made me aware of what a great hedge against illness family and friends are, particularly when one is suffering the loss of a loved one. Research results even taught me that it was not too soon to start preparing my infant daughter for my own death some day, and that a sound preparation could greatly benefit her health in the years to come.

Thus, research material which I initially culled for others ended up profoundly changing my own outlook and behavior. I hope that the results presented here will also deeply benefit the reader.

JOAN AREHART-TREICHEL

Sherwood Forest, Maryland
August, 1979

CONTENTS

BIOTYPES

INTRODUCTION
BIOTYPES AND HEALTH

DURING THE PAST DECADE we have become increasingly conscious of our own behaviors and especially of the negative behaviors that are obstacles to the lives we want to lead. We have learned behavior modification techniques to deal with problems as diverse as nail-biting, stuttering, grave sexual dysfunctions, even serious antisocial delinquency and crime. We have become familiar with the concept of stress, the toll that it can take on a person's well-being and the fact that we can modify our reactions to it. Yet ill health still threatens many of us in spite of this knowledge, and in spite of such wonders of modern medicine as vaccines, antibiotics, microsurgery, and CAT scans.

We're all now familiar also with the concept of psychosomatic medicine. The word "psychosomatic" is derived from two Greek words—*psyche* (soul) and *soma* (body)—and indicates the influence of mind on body and physical health. Psychosomatic medicine goes back to ancient times. In A.D. 200 the Greek philosopher and physician Galen estimated that some 60 percent of his patients suffered symptoms derived from emotional rather than organic origin. The two greatest representatives of seventeenth-century medicine, Thomas Sydenham and William Harvey, were proponents of psychosomatic medicine. In his paper on hysteria, Sydenham stated that hysteria symptoms may simulate almost all forms of organic diseases. He asserted that hysterical hemiplegia may proceed from "some violent commotion of the mind" and spoke of hysterical headaches that ended in vomiting. In his *De Motu Cordis*, he wrote, "Every affection of the mind that is attended with either pain or pleasure, hope or fear, is the case of agitation whose influence extends to the heart."

In the same vein Harvey wrote:

/ 3

> ... what indeed is more deserving of attention than the fact that in al-
> most every affection, appetite, hope or fear, our body suffers, the counte-
> nance changes, and the blood appears to course hither and thither? In
> anger the eyes are fiery and pupils contracted; in modesty the cheeks are
> suffused with blushes; in fear, and under a sense of infamy and of
> shame, the face is pale, but the ears burn as if for the evil they heard or
> were to hear; in lust how quickly is the member distended with blood
> and erected!

The term "psychosomatic" was used for the first time by a German
psychiatrist named Johann Christian Heinroth, in his *Lehrbuch der
Stoerungen des Seelenlebens*. And the father of psychoanalysis, Sig-
mund Freud, showed in 1895 that specific unconscious mental events
could be symbolically expressed in the "body language" of somatic
symptoms.

We know that stress can lead to physical as well as to mental breakdown. What a number of medical and behavioral studies are now revealing, however, is that a physical breakdown under stress does not
necessarily occur only because of "horizontal" causes imposed from
outside a person—such as genes, infections, and environmental agents
combined with physical exhaustion or physical trauma—but often
also for the same reasons that provoke mental breakdowns, that is, because of "vertical" causes, or the life experiences, thoughts, emotions,
behaviors, and personality structure of a patient. Medical and behavioral studies reveal that there are particular personality types—"biotypes"—that in times of stress break down in specific and predictable
ways. These breakdowns are manifested in life-threatening or chronically uncomfortable conditions, ranging from the blatantly physical—
cancer, heart disease, ulcers, migraines, asthma, and hay fever—to the
more mental—depression, suicide, criminality, sex disorders, drug
abuse. In fact, biotypes are emerging for a range of diseases and disorders that most of us would never suspect of having a psychological
input—accident-proneness, infectious diseases, chronic low-back
pain, sleep disorders, temporary blindness, temporary deafness, urinary tract infections, Parkinson's disease, multiple sclerosis, or pur-
pora (a bruising and bleeding of the skin remotely resembling religious
stigmata).

Each biotype can be identified by certain experiences, traits, or behaviors. The migraine biotype, for instance, tends to be excessively
dutiful, with the resultant effects of exhaustion, frustration, unfulfillment, or guilt; he tends to repress negative emotions and to suffer from
immaturity and insecurity. The tension headache biotype, in contrast,

is apt to be chronically angry and despondent and to translate these negative emotions into muscle tautness and thus into tension headaches. The cluster headache biotype is likely to be, like the migraine and tension headache personalities, conscientious and tense but also extremely reserved and self-sufficient. As for those who are suicidal, they are often idealistic and intelligent but depressed, and will kill themselves when hopelessness engulfs them. Stressful experiences at birth may help set the stage for schizophrenia later in life, particularly when combined with disturbed parenting. The schizophrenic biotype also tends to be nervous, tense, depressed, and angry—even more than the suicide biotype—and so on.

Whereas biotypes differ, certain common experiences and traits also run strikingly through them. These patterns suggest that there are a group of personality characteristics that predispose people to illness in general. The typical profile that has emerged is one of a person who experiences psychological trauma early in life, such as loss of a parent, or suffocating overprotection, or neglect. This trauma fills him with a sense of helplessness or even hopelessness and for the rest of his life erodes his self-image. Yet he tends to repress his troubled thoughts and emotions with a Pollyanna outlook on life and to compensate for his insecurity and unhappiness with self-sacrificing works, excess strivings for order and cleanliness, and other types of obsessive-compulsive behaviors. If later in life he experiences a stressful event, often the loss of a loved one, his deep-seated sense of helplessness or hopelessness is reactivated. All his efforts to repress such thoughts and emotions and to engage in defensive behaviors fail to shield him. As his mental defenses are lowered, so are his bodily defenses, and illness moves in. This process may take anywhere from three weeks up to ten years after the triggering stress, depending on the kind of illness.

Thus a powerful predictive element emerges from this research and provides the basis for this book. Various chapters deal with those biotypes that tend to lead to the illnesses that most commonly, or seriously, afflict people, although there are undoubtedly as many biotypes as there are illnesses. These findings are at the frontier of medical research and, not surprisingly, are highly controversial. One reason is that while "horizontal" causes of disease—genetic, infectious, and chemical—can be visualized, isolated, or otherwise physically demonstrated to result in illness, scientists still are not sure what thoughts, emotions, and behaviors actually are in physical terms, and thus cannot definitively demonstrate that they cause illness. In other words, whereas investigators can inject a cancer virus or chemical carcinogen into a rat and show that it gets cancer as a result, they can't shoot thought emotions or behavior into a rat and show that it also triggers cancer.

Another reason these findings are highly controversial is that they derive largely from retrospective studies. Such investigations generally examine the personalities of individuals with a specific disease and the personalities of healthy persons matched for age, socioeconomic status, or other variables to see whether the former share more personality characteristics than do the healthy control population. If this is the case, the scientists conducting the studies generally conclude that characteristics shared by the sick subjects probably preexisted prior to their illness and helped cause it. The weakness of such investigations is that there is a chance that traits found to be peculiar to persons with a particular disease might have resulted from their having the disease rather than the traits having helped cause the disease. An example will make the point:

Retrospective studies conducted during the past forty years suggest that many asthma victims have a dominating mother and ineffective father and that such parental traits may have helped set the stage for their illness. A 1975 investigation, for instance, started with an editorial letter being placed in three leading newspapers in the Boston area. The letter called for volunteers to participate in a study examining high-risk factors in asthma sufferers ages six to eleven. Some two hundred parents of such children responded to the letter. The researchers then selected twenty-one asthmatic boys from the volunteer families and carefully matched them with nineteen nonasthmatic boys (because childhood asthma is twice as common among boys as girls). Both the subjects and their mothers were then psychologically tested. Attachment patterns between the mothers and their sons were especially probed. As the investigators reported in *Annals of Allergy* in 1976, the asthmatic boys were significantly more overprotected and indulged by their mothers than were the nonasthmatic boys, suggesting that maternal overprotection and overindulgence can help set up a child for asthma. However, it is possible that the opposite is the case instead, that mothers of asthmatic boys start overprotecting and overindulging them only after they get the disease, not before. In that instance, personality traits would be the result of disease, not the cause.

Even with this weakness, though, hundreds of retrospective studies strongly suggest a causal link between personality and disease. This link is also starting to be substantiated by a scientifically more watertight type of investigation known as the prospective study. In a pro-

spective study the thoughts, emotions, behaviors, or life events of subjects are recorded when they are healthy, and then later, when any of
these subjects succumb to disease, their personality traits are compared to those of subjects who continue to stay well. If the sick subjects are found to have shared, before they got sick, a number of
characteristics which the healthy subjects did not, an investigator can
then safely conclude that those traits predated their disease and probably helped predispose them to it.

These prospective studies are also being buttressed by studies revealing how early life experiences, thoughts, emotions, and behaviors
can alter the body so that it falls prey to different illnesses and how
personality changes might conspire with horizontal disease causes to
alter the body and thus set the stage for disease. Rat pups deprived of
enriching early-life experiences such as handling and stimulation have
been found to have lower levels of disease-protecting antibodies later
in life than have rats not so deprived. Helplessness, which is a powerful predisposer to illness, has been shown to impair the body's immune
system, wheras the opposite emotion—a belief that one can cope—
does not have this effect. Depression and grief, two other well-documented predisposers to disease, have likewise been shown to depress
the immune system. Powerful negative emotions, which are the ultimate stressors that can switch on so many diseases, have been shown
to act on the hypothalamus in the brain and then to notify the body's
sympathetic nervous system, the brain's pituitary gland, and the
body's immune system. Psychological stress has been demonstrated to
increase susceptibility of mice injected with a cancer virus to cancer.
Psychological stress is known to raise levels of cholesterol in the
bloodstream—a major heart attack risk factor. Anxiety has been found
to increase the production of stomach acid—an ulcer risk factor. Psychological stress is known to trigger asthma attacks via the vagus
nerve. Rheumatoid factors—presumably rheumatoid arthritis risk factors—have been found to increase in the blood of healthy football
players after an emotionally charged game. When mice were inoculated with a virus, the virus did not cause disease, but when the mice
were inoculated with a virus and psychologically stressed, the virus
did cause infection.

By now you are probably alarmed by the idea of biotypes and by the
notion that you can predict your own disease susceptibility. But all is
by no means lost! You can manage your biotype. You can improve
your health by modifying your biotype. Even more crucial, you can
modify your biotype preventively. You can learn to nurture yourself

and your children in such a way that you will all remain free of illness. This is potent good news indeed, since the general belief, both among the public and the medical community, is that disease can only be treated with conventional therapies, such as drugs and surgery, and that it can only be prevented, if at all, with conventional public health measures such as sanitation, vaccines, and removing toxic chemicals from the environment. True, life-style medicine, such as giving up smoking, eating a better diet, and exercising more, is gaining a foothold, but there are many other ways by which you can favorably influence your health. Thus an ample part of this book will be devoted to the evidence documenting the effectiveness of personality management in preventing and treating disease and to the many personality changes you can implement to safeguard your health and the health of your children.

But suppose you do succeed in keeping your children and yourself healthy in your younger and middle years. Won't you still fall prey to disease later in life? Don't people's immune systems deteriorate with chronological aging and leave them more vulnerable to disease than when they were young? Not necessarily. There are people in select areas of the world, such as the Caucasus Mountains of the Soviet Union and the Andes Mountains of South America, who live well into their nineties or even hundreds. There are some 13,000 Americans who are one hundred years old. The key to those persons' exceptional lifespans and health appears to reside more in their personalities than in their genes, physiques, or environments. In fact, their personalities very much resemble those of younger, healthy persons.

For instance, a major source of Caucasian centenarians' health and longevity appears to be their profound involvement with life from an early age right up to the time they die. Helpless, hopeless, disease-prone persons they are not! As for the Andes centenarians, they too are deeply engaged in vigorous physical work, are dynamic in their movements, and are passionate in their lovemaking. A 1973 Special Task Force to the Secretary for the U.S. Department of Health, Education and Welfare found that the strongest predictors of longevity are job satisfaction and overall happiness. Individual case histories, too, underscore the profound importance of enthrallment with life in warding off illness in later years. Still other evidence suggests that keeping negative stresses to a minimum and living a moderate lifestyle promote healthful longevity. Thus biotype management that can keep you and your family healthy when younger should also help you achieve a healthy old age.

This book, then, seeks to show that by managing your and your family's biotypes, you can dramatically improve or safeguard your health. This is a testament of hope and encouragement: You *can* take charge of your own health!

1
THE
CANCER
BIOTYPE

How CAN SOMETHING SO remote in time and essentially psychological as early life experience predispose a person to a disease as voraciously organic as cancer? The link sounds improbable, yet increasing scientific evidence has been underscoring it. Indeed, of the various thoughts, emotions, behaviors, and life events that have been often shown to characterize the lives of individuals who fall heir to cancer and which appear to play a greater or lesser role in their disease susceptibility, a traumatic childhood may well be the most crucial.

For the past quarter-century, for instance, Dr. Lawrence LeShan, an experimental and clinical psychologist in New York City, has been pursuing a most unorthodox cancer research path, one which numerous research centers derided and refused to fund until the Institute of Applied Biology courageously took him on. He has interviewed, tested, and investigated with intense individual psychotherapy some five hundred cancer patients and has compared them to physically healthy persons of the same age, sex, and social class to see whether he could unmask any thoughts, emotions, behaviors, or life events that might predispose people to cancer.

One of the discoveries he has made is most startling: cancer patients have had a disturbed childhood far more often than control subjects have had. Early in life they lost a parent or sibling through death or experienced an unhappy home environment, particularly cold or neglectful parents. This emotional distress appears to have brought them pain and a profound sense of loneliness and desertion.

The lives of several cancer victims taken from other sources illustrate Dr. LeShan's findings. Eleanor S. of Peoria, Illinois, was a lovely, gracious woman in the minds of those who knew her. Yet she died from a long, ugly bout with cancer at age fifty-five. Although some other persons in her family had also died from cancer, suggesting that Eleanor might have had a genetic predisposition toward the disease, Eleanor had also experienced a turbulent childhood. Both of her parents had died by the time she was fifteen years old, and she was then raised by a possessive, jealous uncle, who kept her from marrying the young doctor she loved.

Another victim was Brennan G. of Rochester, New York, an exceptionally bright young man who had gone through Columbia University on a scholarship. Brennan came down with lung cancer at the age of thirty-five. Although his mother had died of cancer, suggesting that he had a genetic predisposition toward the disease, Brennan had also experienced a difficult childhood that might have opened him toward a malignancy later in life. His father had been a handyman who was bitter over his modest station in life and who took his frustrations out in drinking and in beating his children. In spite of the best medical treatment, Brennan slowly succumbed to his cancer and died at the tragically young age of thirty-eight.

Then there was Sybil C. of Washington, D.C., who died from a brain tumor at age seventy-one. Sybil's childhood had likewise been distressing. Her father had committed suicide while she was an adolescent. She blamed her mother, an extremely dominating woman, for driving her father toward his death. Sybil had never gotten along well with her mother. The two of them clashed more and more, and her mother evicted her from home when she was only seventeen.

Still tougher evidence that an anguished childhood can pave the way for cancer comes from a prospective study of cancer victims that has been ongoing since the 1940s, under the direction of Dr. Caroline Thomas of Johns Hopkins Medical Institutions in Baltimore. Actually, Dr. Thomas launched her investigation to see whether personality traits, behaviors, and early life events, among other more physical characteristics, predispose people to heart attacks later in life.

She collected exhaustive data on seventeen successive classes of medical students at Johns Hopkins, altogether some 1,337 young, healthy subjects. Today many of them have reached middle age, and they include some fifty who have gotten cancer. So Dr. Thomas has also examined data collected on them to see whether early life traits, behaviors, or experiences likewise create an ambience for cancer.

Many of the cancer victims had reported lack of closeness to parents harking back to their childhood. Thirty percent indicated that their fathers had not been steady, warm, or companionable, compared to only 9.5 percent of healthy subjects. Dr. Peter E., for example, had been the son of a prominent medical man, was brought up in cultivated surroundings, and had attended an Ivy League university—conditions that should have assured his later success and happiness. Yet his parents had not shown him much affection as a child. Shortly before his fortieth birthday he had a seizure and was found to have an inoperable cancer. He died six months later.

Still another significant finding from Dr. Thomas's study suggests that birth order as well as early life experiences influences cancer susceptibility. In one report, 50 percent of her heart attack subjects, 39 percent of her mental illness subjects, and 20 percent of her healthy subjects had been only children; yet *none* of her cancer victims had. These results argue that being an only child is the other side of the coin from a traumatic childhood; that is, that it can help protect against cancer.

What might the protective factor be? During the late-nineteenth century a British scientist, Sir Francis Galton, observed that there was a disproportionately large number of only children among English scientists and that this was due in part to parents treating only children differently. Since then other researchers, among them the psychologist Dr. Alfred Adler, have also noted the different treatment accorded only children by their parents. Dr. Adler has written: "Whenever I have studied adults, I have found impressions left on them by their early childhood and lasting forever. The position in the family leaves an indelible stamp upon the type of life." Thus we see that being an only child exerts a profound influence on personality development.

But what does the only child receive psychologically that protects him against cancer? It is lavish parental attention and affection. The reputation that only children have of being pampered and spoiled is not without basis. So, just as being deprived of parental love can increase one's vulnerability to cancer, excessive love can protect one against cancer. And only children are especially safeguarded because they get all the love that their parents have to offer to offspring.

Now how about children with brothers and sisters? How much cancer defense do they receive through parental attention? Until other siblings come along, firstborns receive the same love that only children do. Thus they are probably more protected against cancer than are their brothers and sisters but not to the same degree as only children. Babies of the family often also get more than their share of parental inputs, which probably gives them an extra edge against cancer as well. It's the middle children who often receive less than their portion of parental notice and who, from this vantage, are undoubtedly the least protected against cancer. Still another critical factor that can determine whether one will be protected or vulnerable to cancer later in life is how long one remains the baby of the family.

During his 1960s research, Dr. LeShan suspected that the length of time a person remains the youngest child might influence his later susceptibility to cancer. The reason was simple: the birth of a younger sibling, with the consequent perceived loss of parental energy and time, is a traumatic event for the elder child. Other things being equal, the earlier this occurs, the greater the trauma. The scientist further reasoned that the more severe this painful event, the more likely it is for the elder sibling to view relationships as dangerous and anxiety-provoking. If such early frustration is indeed linked with the later appearance of cancer, then one could expect a correlation between the shortness of time an individual was the youngest child and his later development of cancer.

To test this hypothesis, Dr. LeShan decided to study two hundred families that had been carefully evaluated from a medical standpoint and that had at least one cancer victim among their offspring. Twins, only children, and youngest children were excluded. Noncancerous progeny from the same families were used as controls in order to minimize the influence of genetic predisposition, diet, chemicals, radiation, viruses, or some other cancer cause than the psyche.

Results showed that persons with cancer tended to have had a shorter period of being the youngest child than their cancer-free siblings, especially with another brother or sister often arriving before they reached two years of age.

Comparable results were also obtained in an ancillary study of seventy-five female subjects—twenty-five with breast cancer, twenty-five with benign breast tumors, and twenty-five healthy ones. Again, the cancer patients tended to have had less time being the youngest in the family.

Whether or not a person is breast-fed as an infant may also play a role in later cancer susceptibility, some scientists feel. A New York physician, Dr. Gotthard Booth, speculated in 1969, for instance, that the decline in breast feeding from the 1850s (Industrial Revolution) on into the 1960s may have been one reason why cancer rose so considerably among Americans during those years. "That the predisposition for cancer results partly from modern childrearing practices," he asserted, "is most strongly suggested by the fact that, within the last 25 years, childhood cancer, formerly a rare event, has become the second-ranking cause of death in childhood."

How might nursing protect against cancer and bottle feeding make one more vulnerable to it? With breast feeding, the New York physician explains, babies develop symbiotic adult object relationships, which is psychologically healthy. Bottle feeding, by contrast, he contends, gives too little attention to a baby's psychological needs and too much to his physical needs, hence making him an "anal" type, in psychoanalytical terms. In turn there is evidence that cancer-prone persons are anal personalities, as we shall show. Interestingly, women who nurse their babies are apparently better protected against cancer than are those that do not. Some researchers suspect that the protection lies in milk production. An alternate hypothesis is that nonnursing women were themselves deprived of cancer-protecting love in childhood and hence do not have it in their psychological makeups to nurse their own children.

Taking all these results together, one can conclude that the more attention one receives as a child and especially as an infant, the more likely he is to be protected from cancer. That 50 percent of heart attack subjects and 39 percent of mental illness subjects were only children, however, shows that excessive parental inputs may be a double-edged sword; that is, while lavish parental attention may help protect a person against cancer, it may predispose him to these other diseases instead. (More about this possibility in the next chapter.)

Animal studies, too, reinforce the resounding impact of lack of attention during infancy, loneliness during childhood, and early life stress on later susceptibility to malignancies.

Rats subjected to handling, electrical shock, or neither during the first three weeks of life were injected with tumors at sixty days of age. Those exposed to shock for three weeks did not differ from control rats in the rate of cancer growth, but those that had been handled for three weeks developed tumors much later than did the other two groups. When rats were hand-stroked ten minutes a day for three weeks beginning at age twenty-two days and were then given tumor implants at the age of forty-five days, they lived longer than did control rats who were not stroked but who were injected with tumors at the same age. Female mice isolated in separate cages from four to twenty weeks of age developed breast cancer earlier than did female mice housed eight to a cage during the same period. In young mice put into four types of environments—cages with fifty animals each, cages partitioned in ten sections with five animals to a section, glass jars containing five animals each, and pots holding one animal each—cancer developed in only 2 percent of the animals living fifty together, in 56 and 67 percent of those living five together, and in 84 percent of those living alone in a pot. With rat pups separated from their mothers at the normal weaning age or earlier and then injected with tumors, those that had been weaned abnormally early died more from cancer than did those that had been weaned at a normal age.

And as for early life stress and later cancer development, usually 80 to 100 percent of a strain of mice known as the C3H/HE strain carry a cancer virus that causes breast cancer eight to eighteen months after birth. By putting some of these mice in a stressful environment and others in a protected one, it was found that 92 percent of the former got cancer, whereas only 7 percent of the latter did.

How may prospective cancer victims react to the emotional scars left by a traumatic childhood? They tend to blame themselves for what has happened and not to respect their own accomplishments. They often regard themselves as "stupid," "lazy," "mediocre," or "destructive," although other people do not see them that way. They seem to have acquired a profound helplessness and hopelessness about ever achieving any meaning or validity in their lives, a death wish if you will, that indubitably spurs them along their course to bodily disease. They can be terrifyingly alone, in despair of themselves in the existential sense chillingly described by the nineteenth-century Danish theologian and philosopher Soren Kierkegaard.

In a study of fifty-one women admitted to the hospital for biopsies following cervical smears suspiciously like cancer, those who had cervical cancer were predicted on the basis of whether they had felt hopeless about life during the preceding six months. Diagnosis made on this basis was highly significant. In another study, thirty cancer patients were given a Rorschach test, where a subject interprets inkblot designs in terms that reveal intellectual and emotional factors. After contemplating inkblots, the patients made a number of references to falling apart, being mutilated or cut up, and weird references to death. Particularly impressive were numerous morbid images offered by a sixteen-year-old boy who was not aware that he was seriously ill. Some of the patients' interpretations of the Rorschachs suggested that they were even unconsciously fantasizing about the tumors growing in their bodies. For instance, several cancer patients gave rare responses to the inside parts of the inkblots, referring to self-propagating activities on a primitive level. When these patients interpreted blots as budding potatoes, bulbs, onions, or flowers, the plants were perceived to unfold in a bizarre way. Some patient responses even depicted new islands growing in the ocean, which was really the white space of the Rorschach card.

Even before individuals come down with cancer, though, they tend to interpret Rorschachs in a rather morbid manner. Dr. Thomas's prospective study shows that whereas healthy subjects tended to see clouds, insects, or a piece of fried chicken in an inkblot, prospective cancer victims tended to see pathological images, such as tumors, death, parasites, or bacteria. A typically ominous response from a student who later developed cancer was "a dead man seen from the feet."

"The meaning of these findings," Dr. Thomas admits, "is still highly speculative. Are such responses a reflection of unconscious dreads and morbid fears which, in some individuals, are ever-present stresses undermining the biological guardians of general resistance [to disease]?"

In most depressed persons there is still a ray of hope. Not so with the cancer personality, other scientists have found. His outlook is bleaker than that. And even if he achieves material success, it gives him little satisfaction. Comments from some of LeShan's patients below hint at the dark thoughts and murky emotions that had been smoldering in cancer victims years before they came down with disease:

> You know how it is with a house with no insulation and with cracks in the walls? The more heat you put in, the more leaks out. You can never get it warm. I always knew that was how it was with me in life. I had to keep putting out and putting out, and there was never any reflection back towards me.

> It's as if all my life I've been climbing a very steep mountain. It's very hard work. Every now and then there are ledges that I can rest on for a little bit and maybe even enjoy myself a little, but I've got to keep climbing, and the mountain has no top.

> I found I hated working for the union. It was too late to go back to music, although I tried. I knew I'd have to stay in the business end for good. There was no way out no matter what I did.

> If the rock drops on the egg—poor egg. If the egg drops on the rock— poor egg.

The cancer biotype also believes he doesn't deserve love and will often erect great barriers to keep others from loving him. As one cancer victim said: "It's no wonder no man ever loved me. They were all too tired after climbing over all that barbed wire to get at me." In fact, the cancer personality may be so convinced that he is unworthy of love that he actually denies someone else's love of him. Let's take the case of Virginia T., a cancer victim who was also a stunningly lovely woman. Many men of high caliber had been attracted to her, had courted her, and had even proposed to her. She accepted none of them. Then she met a married man with whom she wanted to have an affair. After they became involved, he wanted to divorce his wife in order to marry Virginia. Instead of welcoming his suggestion, she interpreted it as a rejection of her as a woman, as one more example of all the rejections she had suffered!

But how aware are cancer biotypes of their sad thoughts and emotions? Some evidence suggests that they are quite aware of them and react to them with depression.

The Roman physician and anatomist Galen along with the Greek Hippocrates were the most important physicians and medical scientists of all antiquity. Galen brought to medicine clinical acuity, therapeutic skill, and, above all, a sharply critical and analytical attitude. His views held sway over Western medicine for almost fourteen hundred years, from the time he lived (A.D. 130–200) to A.D 1700.

Galen's observations of human anatomy, health, and disease fill volumes, and in one of these, entitled *De Tumoribus Naturum Praeter,* he wrote that melancholic persons are prone to tumors, or swellings, or what the Greeks called *oncos.* How did Galen define melancholy? He, like Hippocrates, believed that four elements—fire, earth, water, and air—constitute matter and that these are represented in the human body by four humors—blood, yellow bile, black bile, and phlegm. Unlike Hippocrates, however, he restated these humors so that they represented four kinds of human temperament. Persons with a predominance of phlegm would be phlegmatic—slow, stolid, impassive. Those with a predominance of blood would be sanguine—sturdy, cheerful, confident, optimistic. Those with mostly yellow bile would be choleric—hot-tempered, irascible—and those with mostly black bile would be melancholic—depressed and sad.

The four elements have by now grown to some one hundred plus; the human body is now known to consist of cells, tissues, organs, and systems rather than humors; more than four temperaments are now recognized; and human temperament is today thought to hold more sway over the body than vice versa. Nevertheless, Galen's four temperaments are still accepted by medical scientists as having certain validity. Moreover, the words "melancholic," "sanguine," "phlegmatic," and "choleric" continue to be defined in English-language dictionaries just as Galen once defined them. Thus, even though Galen may have mistakenly attributed human temperaments to the wrong causes, he may well have accurately diagnosed patients with melancholic temperaments and correctly noted that such persons were especially prone to tumors.

Nor was Galen the only doctor to link depression with cancer. Similar observations were being made during the Renaissance by a French surgeon named Ambroise Paré and in the nineteenth century by a leading German pathologist, Carl Rokitansky. Additional scientific links between melancholy and tumors have emerged in more recent years, suggesting that cancer victims are anally oriented personalities who have not progressed beyond an early phase of personality development characterized by a preoccupation with feces. One patient, for example, reported a dream in which he found a large pile of feces in the toilet that first turned into bread and then into a bear that chased him. What does the anal personality have to do with cancer and depression? Some researchers feel that anal personalities also tend to be depressed personalities.

On the other hand, substantial evidence implies that cancer biotypes tend to subconsciously repress rather than consciously react to their despondency—in fact, that they go so far as to act as if they have no problems in life. To those around them, even to people close to them, they seem to be coping perfectly well. Cathy F. was diagnosed for an inoperable lung cancer, had never smoked, and during the thirty previous years had lived in a quiet district free of atmospheric pollution, suggesting that chemical carcinogens could be ruled out as the cause of her cancer. She attempted to give the picture of a happy, carefree person. A more searching interrogation, however, revealed that she had deep-seated emotional conflicts about her aged and ailing parents and also about her sister. She was not aware of these emotions until they were unveiled.

Cancer patients usually repress their despair with a stoic lack of bitterness, or as the poet Elizabeth Barrett Browning would have put it, "I tell you, hopeless grief is passionless." Cancer victims also generally demonstrate less psychic anxiety—such as worrying a lot, nervousness, and lack of concentration—than do other disease subjects. And they rate lower than other disease patients on the kind of anxiety that takes itself out in muscle tension, nervous stomach, shakiness, perspiration, or other somatic expression. In fact, they even tend to repress in childhood such outlets as bedwetting, stammering, or temper tantrums.

"Cancer patients," says Dr. Claus Bahnson, of the Eastern Pennsylvania Psychiatric Institute in Philadelphia and one of today's leading investigators into the psychological causes of cancer, "are truly more unaware of their anxiety than are other patients and normal controls, probably due to unconscious repression rather than to misrepresentation. In other words, they do not have fewer problems than other people do, but they cope with them with denial, resulting in the characteristic 'Pollyanna' outlook with which they often astonish their interviewers."

Another hint of the emotional repression so frequently exhibited by cancer and potential cancer victims is their tendency to recall few dreams. In a 1974 study, for instance, fifty-nine patients—thirty-one later diagnosed for lung cancer and twenty-eight for other lung diseases—were asked about various aspects of their life-styles, including how many dreams they recalled each night. Those later diagnosed for cancer tended to recall far fewer dreams than did those who were later diagnosed for other diseases.

Emotional repression, however, isn't the only means by which the cancer or potential cancer patient copes with entrenched psychological trauma. He may also visualize himself as being strong of both body and character, undoubtedly in order to counter feelings of insecurity that stem from his bleak childhood. For instance, studies of cancer patients versus other disease patients and healthy subjects show that cancer patients have the greatest perception of their own bodily strength and physical health and the least sensation of being pushed or controlled by external demands. As Danish-born Claus Bahnson puts it: "With a background of disappointment in early family relationships, the cancer personality finds the world a dangerous place to be and believes that everyone is out for himself. And in order to sustain those attitudes, he must see himself as strong and possessing physical endurance. Only those with grit survive."

In his effort to repress self-destructive desires, the cancer biotype also functions normally in society—in fact, exceptionally so. We now know that cancer biotypes tend to comply with the wishes and demands of others. They are decent, thoughtful people. They consider the wishes and needs of others right and their own desires woefully wrong. They give incredibly more than they receive. A prime example is Phillip J., an engineer, who appeared to be leading a happy and successful life. He lived with his attractive wife and three children in a luxurious suburban home, and his position in his father's firm assured him a secure future. But Phillip was not really living the life he wanted. As a child, he showed exceptional musical ability but was timid and withdrawn and found it difficult to communicate his true desires. As he grew older, he became an engineer to satisfy his father and even married the girl his mother picked out for him. As a result, he hated work as an engineer and his marriage was devoid of hope and empty of personal satisfaction. At age thirty-five he contracted a massive brain tumor.

Conscientiousness and marital stability are two other traits that are common to cancer-prone persons. So, too, are a defensively high view of one's ethical self, and religiosity, and a sense of citizenship. Compared to heart attack patients and healthy subjects, cancer patients scored highest on commitment, religiosity, and authoritarianism and least on stress at work and conflict with authority.

The tendency of the cancer biotype to project the image of a strong, well-adjusted, and helpful individual may, in fact, explain why some studies have found him more extroverted than introverted. Women with breast cancer demonstrated an extraordinary amount of extroversion. Cancer patients tend to be considerably more extroverted than control subjects, studies show.

Other researchers, however, have found the cancer-prone individual to be more introverted than extroverted. His authoritarian commitment to being a good, dependable citizen, they caution, expresses a brand of individualism that should not be confused with sociability and open friendliness. Also, lung cancer patients are found to be less active socially than are patients with other lung diseases.

Is this paradoxical disparity in findings about extroversion and introversion the fault of inadequate study designs? Probably not. Rather, it's undoubtedly the result of the cancer biotype's own confusion over whether he is inner- or outer-world directed. This perplexity has been tersely underscored by some recent research results.

Back in 1951 Dr. Thomas started including a "draw a person" test in her prospective study of various disease personalities. She decided to include it since it was easy to administer and not psychologically threatening to her subjects. In essence, a subject was required to draw a person of the same sex as himself and also a person of the opposite sex.

By 1970 over a hundred of Dr. Thomas's subjects—now middle-aged physicians—had succumbed to cancer or another disease. So Dr. Thomas was in a position to see whether the figures these disease victims had drawn years earlier as young, healthy medical students might have predicted their later susceptibility to a particular disease. In brief, would the drawings made by the victims in each disease group resemble each other in some way? Would they somehow differ from the drawings that had been made by subjects who were still healthy?

Then came the challenge of interpreting the drawings. Should Dr. Thomas and the psychologist who helped her with the study consider both figures drawn by a subject or only the figure of the same sex as the subject? The position of the figure on the page? The facial expression? Since the psychologist had long been convinced that the stance of a figure reflects an artist's view of life, they decided to examine this quality alone.

More specifically, they decided that if a student had drawn a figure with arms hanging loosely at its side, it would express the student's uncommitted attitude toward life—that is, that he had not committed himself to a definite way of dealing with incoming stimuli. In contrast, if a student had drawn a figure with arms extended outward, he would have had a built-in pattern of response so that he would invite more and more input. On the other hand, if a student had made a figure whose arms were not extended, it would indicate that the student was a closed system—afraid to reach out in life. Finally, if a student designed a figure with one arm out and one not extended, it would suggest that the student was neither closed in on himself nor extended toward the outside world. The question now was: could any of these stances have predicted susceptibility to a particular disease?

Indeed they could have. Control subjects, those who were still in good health in 1970, produced twice as many figures with arms hanging loosely at their sides as did subjects who had fallen prey to various diseases, and these results were highly significant statistically. So, in youth, healthy subjects appear to have an uncommitted attitude toward life. Figures made by students who later succumbed to heart disease, in contrast, showed both arms extended nearly twice as often as did figures made by the healthy subjects, suggesting that heart-attack-prone persons invite too many inputs in life. Individuals who succumbed to suicide or mental illness frequently made figures with a withdrawn pose—say, with arms crossed or otherwise touching the body—suggesting that they had been afraid to reach out in life, especially when they needed help. Victims of emotional disturbances had often designed figures engaged in bizarre movements, reflecting their emotional problems. And as for the cancer victims, they had drawn figures with one arm out and one arm toward the body *five* times as often as had healthy subjects. Thus we see that the cancer-prone person takes an ambivalent attitude toward life. He is uncertain over whether he is inner- or outer-directed.

Several traits frequently found by other scientists among cancer and potential cancer victims are also of interest, such as an unsatisfactory sex life, frustration of one's sex role, and dissatisfaction with one's work.

Cervical cancer occurs most often in women who are highly motivated sexually but who do not achieve orgasm because of their need for autonomy, and some research suggests that prostate cancer particularly occurs in men who engage in lovemaking short of intercourse.

Cancer patients report less satisfactory sex lives than do control subjects, and women who have never nursed children experience a higher cancer rate than do those who have. Similar findings are also emerging from animal studies. If female mice are deprived of male mice, they are more prone to cancer than are females who have access to males. When female mice were prevented from nursing, many of them developed breast cancer. In other words, sex problems may not only help set the stage for cancer but encourage the cancer to zero in on sexual organs of psychological concern.

Finally, how might these various traits and behaviors, so common among cancer biotypes, conspire to switch on a malignancy? Dr. LeShan's findings show us that a person may have a sense of loss and hopelessness stemming from childhood, and later in life another individual or a situation gives him an opportunity to find meaning in life. The investment seems safe. It gives him a reason for living. But if he loses this investment, all the despair stemming from his childhood wells up in him again and is compounded, and he is unable to find a substitute. Deprivation and dejection appear to be his eternal doom. And there he stays, waiting without hope. The stress is too much for his body to take; disease moves relentlessly in. Cancer may strike anywhere from six months up to ten years after a cancer biotype experiences a major personal loss and is unable to find a substitute.

The case of a young cancer victim named Dan R. illustrates this psychological and disease progression that so often underlies the lives of cancer patients. Dan had lost his father at age five, which had made him feel terribly alone in life, especially since his mother had been pregnant with another child at the time. In his adolescence, however, Dan obtained a new lease on life. He became passionately interested in science and joined various science clubs in high school. By his junior year he had become a fully accepted member of a group of students working on scientific experiments. Dan joined his friends regularly and spent evenings in their cellar labs. He felt truly alive, decided to become an engineer, had found a raison d'être. But once he graduated from high school he felt he must support his mother and took a well-paying job as a truck driver. He tried to keep up his scientific interests and friends, but it was difficult. As time went on, life lost its interest for him. The loneliness and despair he felt over the loss of his father engulfed him more fully than ever before. Four years after graduating from high school, Dan learned that he had Hodgkin's disease—cancer of the lymph nodes.

The way in which childhood trauma, a renewed lease on life, and then a loss of that investment can trigger cancer is also seen in the case of Amy. As a young child Amy had been loved and protected. But when Amy was seven, her father left Europe to come to America and took the older children with him. Amy and her mother remained behind for several years before they too came to the United States. This separation from her father left Amy with a lasting sense of emotional desertion, but she covered her despair by trying to find, as she put it, "some good in everyone."

Amy later married a weak, somewhat inadequate man and spent her life caring for him and their four children, not only as mother and housekeeper but often as sole wage earner. Once when her son Bobby broke his leg, she even carried him to school on her back. Amy had found a meaning, a purpose in life. After her husband died, she successfully raised their children, and all four went into highly intellectual careers. Once her last son no longer needed her, though, she no longer had any purpose in life. She tried various occupations and hobbies but could not get really interested in any of them. Her children thought she had found peace. But actually the profound loneliness and hopelessness she knew when her father left for America had overwhelmed her with renewed vigor. A year after she stopped keeping house for her youngest son, she developed breast cancer.

Still a third person who illustrates how childhood trauma can be sublimated with a purpose later in life and then resurface to cause cancer when that purpose no longer exists is Sybil of Washington, D.C., mentioned earlier. After Sybil's mother evicted her from home at age seventeen, to make her own way in the world, Sybil became a teacher and met an Ivy League lawyer, whom she married. Sybil was happy during her forty years of marriage, even though her husband was twenty years her senior and she had to care for him after he had a stroke. When Sybil was sixty-six her husband died. Even though they had had a good life together, had raised a son who became a state senator, and her husband had left her enough money to travel around the world a few times, Sybil kept saying, "I must find somewhere to put down my roots." In essence, she had lost her roots—the man she loved. Five years later she died from a brain tumor.

Still other studies underscore the way adverse life events spark malignancies. Let's take defeats in the lives of thirty-two cancer patients. Thirty of the thirty-two patients had developed cancer up to four years after one or several major losses—death of or separation from a loved one, loss of a job, a fall in self-esteem, inability of a wife to have children, lack of hope of having a grandchild, a change in home, and so forth. Sixteen of these thirty patients had suffered three or more such losses within the same time span. A repeat study a decade later on sixty-one cancer patients produced the same striking results. Fifty-seven of the sixty-one patients were adjusting to one or more personal losses that had arisen during the four years prior to the onset of cancer.

In yet another study, adverse life events among both lung cancer patients and patients with other lung diseases were examined. Both groups had experienced a number of personal losses prior to coming down with their diseases, but such losses appeared to be of a more longstanding nature among cancer patients—say up to ten years before the appearance of a malignancy. But in studying fifty-one women with suspicious cervical smears, researchers predicted that cancer would be present in those patients who had responded with feelings of despair to a life event during the previous six months. They predicted that eighteen of the women had cancer and thirty-three did not. They made thirty-six correct predictions out of fifty-one. Eleven out of the eighteen had it, and twenty-five of the thirty-three did not. And the life events that they found to be the most significant antecedents to cancer included the following: a family member with a major illness (the cancer victim's attitude was, "I should have worked harder and taken care of the sick one"); the husband was unfaithful (the cancer patient's stance was, "I should have left him, but I couldn't because of the children, and I also thought he needed me"); the husband rejected the patient's goal (the cancer patient's position was, "I tried everything, and I have failed").

But some of the toughest evidence that specific life events can pull the cancer trigger comes from a study with three different sets of identical twins where one twin in each set came down with leukemia, but the other twin did not. Hence it was possible to separate out any genetic contributions to cancer from personality and behavioral ones.

Let's look at the first family studied, the Norman S. family of Allentown, Pennsylvania. Only three months after Norman's wife, Dorothy, gave birth to twins, whom they named Larry and Jerry, Norman died from a stroke. Since Dorothy also had a daughter, she decided to keep the daughter and to turn the twins over to her parents to raise. The grandparents were delighted since they had never had any sons of their own. During childhood Larry and Jerry also frequently visited their mother and sister.

When Larry and Jerry turned eleven, however, their grandmother died, and at age thirteen, their grandfather. So they returned to living with their mother and sister. After they graduated from high school, Jerry went off to college in Pittsburgh. Larry married, followed Jerry to

Pittsburgh, and took a menial job there in order to support his wife and himself. Soon, however, Larry found that he was traveling in circles that were different from those of his twin. Feeling left out, he and his wife moved back to Allentown.

Then Jerry married. Larry felt that this marriage was final evidence that he and his twin were going separate ways—a keen disappointment to him. Then Larry's wife gave birth to a girl; he was upset that it wasn't a son. Several months later he had an attack of priapism—persistent erection of the penis—which is not due to sexual desire but to disease. He was diagnosed for leukemia and died three years later.

Family number two were Carl and Rosslyn P. of upstate New York. Rosslyn became pregnant with twins, but Carl died before they were born. However, she soon married a farmer in the area, Robert S., and she and the twins—John and Tom—moved to his farm.

While John and Tom were in high school, the state informed the family that an expressway was to be built through their farm. The entire family was angry and apprehensive and fought back. But a year later, expressway construction began and slowly encroached on the farm. The twins' stepfather developed a bleeding stomach ulcer. By the time the twins were seventeen, the farm was actually taken over, with road crews moving in equipment and occupying the land.

As is common among northern New York State farm families, John and Tom had been given a plot of land that they could work and harvest and from which they could keep the profit. It happened that the land that was taken by the expressway included John's land but not Tom's. The twins were disturbed, and Tom offered to share his plot with John.

John refused, countering that their stepfather had dealt with the loss of much of his land and that he, John, could deal with the loss of his. Early in his seventeenth year, John developed a nosebleed, was tired, and showed enlargement of the lymph nodes. He went to the hospital three weeks later and was diagnosed for acute leukemia. He died within two weeks.

Family number three, Linus and Carol P. of Bridgeport, Connecticut, had twins named Peter and Frank. When the twins were eight, however, Carol and Linus separated since Linus had become an alcoholic, and while the twins were in high school their parents started divorce proceedings. Not long afterward, Peter became tired and lethargic. He could no longer run as fast as Frank could; his vision became blurred.

A few months later, their parents' divorce became final. Carol felt that the twins accepted it but sensed that Peter was more troubled by the divorce than Frank was. Then Peter developed acute blurring vision. He was hospitalized and diagnosed for acute leukemia. Although he had an initial remission, he died three years later.

Each of these cancer cases was shown to have developed in a setting that was psychologically stressful for the entire family but especially for the affected twin, and thus this psychological stress probably helped spark cancer. The adverse life events that probably triggered Larry's leukemia were his twin achieving a more advanced education than he did, his twin marrying, and having a daughter instead of a son. John, on the other hand, appeared to develop cancer in the wake of distress over losing his land. As for Peter, his disease appears to have been sparked by his parents divorcing.

Unfortunately, the assessment of these cases did not include determining whether the victims had also suffered a sense of loss and helplessness in early childhood, emotions that might have alchemized their psychological trauma during adolescence into still more devastating experiences and hence into cancer triggers. But it's quite possible that they *did* experience such turbulent emotions while young. Larry, for instance, may have missed having a father or may have unduly grieved over the death of his substitute parents, his grandparents, and these losses might have compounded his later distresses over his twin outdoing him and deserting him and over not having a son. John may have missed having a father, and this deprivation might have aggravated his bereavement over the loss of his land. Peter may have suffered a major setback when his alcoholic father separated from his mother, and this grief may have enhanced his distress when his parents finally divorced.

On the other hand, the psychological stresses that these cancer victims experienced as adolescents might have been sufficiently devastating in themselves at that age to spark cancer.

Obviously, vastly more needs to be learned about the influence of personality, behavior, and life events on cancer susceptibility. For instance, how many of the traits, behaviors, and experiences that frequently characterize the lives of cancer victims actually contribute to disease formation? All or only some of them? How does someone who possesses most of the characteristics of the cancer biotype end up escaping cancer or perhaps getting another disease instead?

And then there's the formidable challenge of determining whether personality traits, behaviors, and life events are alone sufficient to cause cancer or whether they must interact with other causative factors, such as radiation, chemicals, and viruses. "No responsible researcher," Dr. Lawrence LeShan wrote in 1976, "has ever suggested that . . . emotions cause cancer. The evidence has been that a combination of factors, including genes, environment and life history experiences, result in a suppression of the cancer defense mechanisms."

A good example of personality and the body's immune system conspiring together to cause cancer occurred in the case of Trish P. of Nashville, Tennessee. As a young child Trish had mumps. At age twenty-five she married and soon had several children. When she was thirty-five her father died, leaving her terribly depressed, and several months later her children had mumps. Three weeks later she developed swelling of the glands under her jaws, which she thought was mumps again. But it was cancer of the lymph glands. So it appears that her psychological distress over her father's death, coupled with her immune system's response to mumps virus either early in life, later in life, or both, helped set the stage for her disease.

2
THE
HEART ATTACK
BIOTYPES

JUST AS A PERSON'S primary life experiences seem to shape his susceptibility (or resistance) to cancer later in life, the same is true for the heart attack biotype. But the early life events that pave the way for cancer—such as loss of a parent at an early age or parental rejection—are not those that predispose a person for heart trouble. On the contrary, the critical issue appears to be excessive closeness to one's parents.

Take the long-term, prospective study of Dr. Caroline Thomas of the Johns Hopkins Medical Institutions discussed in Chapter 1, where psychological characteristics of youth have been found to have predictive potential regarding the later occurrence of specific diseases. Dr. Thomas reported in 1973–74, as part of her ongoing findings, that medical students who in later life had heart attacks had been much closer to their parents than had medical students who later came down with cancer or mental illness, or who committed suicide. In fact, those students who experienced heart attacks had been even a bit closer to their parents than had students who remained healthy in later years, especially rating their parents as "warm, understanding and companionable" and feeling "warm, confiding and admiring" in their parents' presence. What's more, only a few healthy subjects, and *not one* heart attack victim, gave one of the rare responses checked by cancer victims and several other disease personalities, such as "is detached from mother," "was hurt by father," or "dislike father."

What might there be about being excessively close to one's parents that might predispose a person to a heart attack later in life? Is it domination by one's mother? Dr. Thomas's study suggests not. Heart attack patients in her study were found to have experienced even less maternal domination than healthy subjects had. However, her study does give us another possible lead. Although her numbers were small, 50 *percent* of all her heart attack victims had been only children, compared to only 21.3 percent of healthy subjects, 38 percent of mentally ill subjects, and zero percent of cancer subjects. A 1966 study also concurred that heart attack victims are more often only children than are control subjects.

Now, parents usually expect more of an only child (and of a first child) than of subsequent offspring. They want him to meet their own ideals, fulfill their own unrealized dreams. It's no accident that only children (and firstborns) identify with parental attitudes, including persistence and determination in reaching goals; are generally superior in schoolwork and dominate the rolls of colleges and universities; and later in life conform to their parents' values. Might excessive parental emphasis on achievement and competition be one of the factors that predispose people to heart attacks in life? It seems so.

In 1945 a clinical assessment of nine heart attack patients led a physician to conclude that heart attack victims are running a race with their father's image. The same year, another doctor visualized the heart attack patient as "a stubborn, self-willed child, who early entered a competitive relationship with a much-feared and envied parent." In 1970 a study by Dr. Rayman W. Bortner of Penn State University and Ray H. Rosenman and Meyer Friedman of the Mount Zion Hospital and Medical Center reported that hardworking, competitive boys in the San Francisco area had fathers with the same traits. Then in 1976 Karen Matthews of the University of Texas and Dr. David Krantz of the University of Southern California attempted to see whether the tendency to achieve and compete is more learned than inherited, and if so, whether one acquires such traits from one's parents.

They compared thirty-five sets of identical twins and twenty-one sets of nonidentical twins on characteristics such as job involvement and hard-driving competitiveness. They used identical and nonidentical twins since the former are the same genetically, and the latter are only half alike genetically. Thus, if identical twins were found to be more alike on a particular characteristic than fraternal twins, and the environments of the twin pairs were comparable, then one could conclude that the characteristic is inherited. On the other hand, if identical twins were found to be no more alike than fraternal twins on the characteristic, then one could conclude that the trait is acquired from the environment, not genes.

Identical twins, the researchers found, were somewhat more alike, but not all that much more alike, on achievement-oriented characteristics, suggesting that such traits have a strong environmental input as well as an inherited one. What's more, those twins in the study who were especially achievement-oriented also tended to have mothers who were too, reinforcing the hypothesis that parents teach their children to achieve and compete early in life.

But the strongest evidence to date that parents alchemize their children into achievers and competitors early in life comes from a 1977 study. Fifty-eight boys, four to ten years old, were evaluated by two classroom teachers on items that would indicate whether they were achievement- and competition-oriented, such as, "Does this child work very hard on his school work?" "When this child has to wait for others before beginning a task, does he become impatient?" "Does this child like to argue and debate?" and so forth. These boys and their mothers were then greeted by a researcher who explained that the sons would be working on several tasks designed to measure "personality characteristics which may influence whether people have heart attacks later in life." Each mother was told that she would assist in giving the tests. An observer, present to record the mother-son interactions, was introduced as an assistant who would be making notes about the child's behavior. Both experimenter and observer were ignorant as to the classification of the children as achievers or nonachievers.

In the first test, each boy was required, while blindfolded and with one arm behind his back, to stack wooden blocks one on top of the other. A trial was completed when he either stacked all the blocks successfully or more than one block fell off the stack. Mothers of older boys were told that the average child her son's age could stack nine blocks; mothers of younger boys were told that the typical child her son's age could stack four blocks. During the block-stacking trials, the researchers expected mothers of achievers to be less satisfied than the mothers of lesser achievers with their children's performances and to reveal their dissatisfaction with such comments as "You're doing very well" or "You're doing it wrong." This expectation was strongly confirmed.

While each child was given a series of geometric designs to duplicate with a set of nine blocks, the scientists explored the notion that mothers of achievers are supportive during success and withdraw support during failure. The child was allowed a maximum of sixty seconds to complete each design. The mother was told to time the child in this task and to call out at the end of thirty seconds that half his allotted time for the trial remained. The results were not exactly what the researchers had expected, but close. Mothers of achievers gave both more support *and* more rejection during failure than during success than did mothers of lesser achievers. In other words, achievement-oriented mothers were more likely to tell their sons to keep trying when they failed, yet also to berate them for their unsuccessful efforts, than were the mothers of lesser achievers. So if children try hard to accomplish things in life, it may be because their parents reinforced their successes and discouraged their failures.

Not only parents may be responsible for turning young people into achievers and competitors, however. Society at large probably helps mold them along those lines as well. Back in the early 1960s, for instance, a Harvard University clinical psychologist named David McClelland wrote a fascinating book called *The Achieving Society,* in which he presented his own research as well as other people's historical and sociological findings in order to demonstrate that those societies most advanced economically are also the most achievement-oriented. Some of the most intriguing data he presented showed that those countries advancing the fastest economically are also those whose children's stories have strong achievement themes.

A country's children's stories, McClelland explained, describe a variety of situations, sometimes from the world of fairies, giants, and dwarfs and sometimes from real life, but the intent of every country is the same, to provide something interesting and instructive for the child to read. In this sense, the stories tend to reflect the nation's values. Also, children's stories are considered appropriate for all children in a country, regardless of social class, and so are less biased than novels, which often reflect the values of only a segment of a society. And as the late anthropologist Margaret Mead has wryly noted, when a culture transmits its values to children, as through stories, it does so so simply that even the most obtuse social scientists can understand them!

Convinced, then, that children's stories reflect a country's emphasis, or lack of emphasis, on achievement, McClelland and his co-workers attempted to collect twenty-one children's stories from two time periods—1925 and 1950—from nations all over the world except in the tropics, whose tendencies toward achievement are apt to be limited because of the hot weather. When a set of books arrived from a particular country, McClelland and his colleagues chose twenty-one stories at random without reading any of them. These stories were sent out to be translated literally, not in a literary fashion. The stories were then typed, using standard names for all characters and places, so that the identity of each country was not apparent. For instance, the girls were all called Mary, Jane, and Judy, the boys Peter, Bob, and John, and towns Big Town, Little Town, and so on. The national source was in-scribed on the back of the story with a code number. In the final edit-ing and translating, the stories of a few countries got lost; one translator disappeared with all the stories he had been asked to trans-late, and no translator could be found for one language, so that the final sample to be analyzed for achievement themes was somewhat reduced. Even so, there were still thirteen hundred stories ready for analysis.

These were then turned over to two judges to see whether they had achievement themes or not. The number of achievement stories for each country for the 1925 period was then totaled, the totals compared, and each country's achievement-story rating in respect to other coun-tries was matched to its economic growth for the period. The same was then done for the 1950 sample. And indeed, as McClelland had expected, those countries with the greatest number of achievement stories of a particular period tended to be those with the greatest eco-nomic growth for the same period. Such a correlation existed whether a country was democratic, communist, or developing.

Turkey, for instance, was found to have more achievement stories in 1950 than any other country besides the United States, and her eco-nomic growth at this time was well above average. In one of the achievement stories that Turkish youngsters were reading at that pe-riod, a young man appeared before the head of a company and asked for a job. The boss liked the young man's speech and manners and said that he wanted to give the young man a job. But first the young man had to work for the company on a trial basis. The young man agreed and went off to negotiate with the company bursar about wages. A bit later the bursar commented to the boss that the young man was mod-est indeed in his pay request—that he wanted only one cent for his first day of work, two cents for the second day of work, four cents for the third day, and so on, doubling his salary each day for the trial month. The boss agreed with the bursar, but thought, if we can get help for such puny wages, why not? What seemed even more unusual, though, is that throughout his trial month, the young man was exceed-ingly sharp, neat, and conscientious. But then the end of the month came, and the young man went to the bursar to collect the previously-agreed-on wages. When the bursar totalled them, they came to a whopping $10,737,418.23! The bursar then conferred with the boss; what to do? The young man, however, put them both at ease by com-menting that he knew from the start how much money they would owe him at the end of the month, but that he really didn't expect them to pay him all that. What he was trying to prove, he said, was that he was astute about financial matters and a promising employee for them. So that day, he signed a contract with the company, and at a fat salary indeed.

The above observations and studies, obviously, do not prove that individuals who learn from their parents or society to achieve and compete will necessarily have heart attacks later in life. However, there is some indication that such persons will be at special risk. A Dutch psychologist took McClelland's data on the need of countries to achieve, as reflected in their children's stories, and compared them to the incidence of heart attack deaths in the same countries. He reported in 1972 that those countries with strong achievement needs also had the most deaths from heart attacks. And what *is* certain is that persons who reach early adulthood as achievers and competitors are far more likely to have a heart attack than those who are less achievement- and competition-directed.

Back in 1910 a physician named William Osler reported in the highly respected British medical journal *Lancet* that "It is not the delicate neurotic person who is prone to angina (chest pains that often precede heart attacks) but the robust, the vigorous in mind and body, the ambitious man, the indicator of whose engine is always 'full speed ahead.' There is indeed a frame and facies at once suggestive of angina—the well-set man of from 45 to 55 years of age, with military bearing, iron-grey hair and florid complexion." In 1943 Flanders Dunbar, a twentieth-century pioneer in psychosomatic medicine, interviewed several hundred hospital patients and found that heart attack patients shared certain personality characteristics, notably a compulsion to work long hours and not to take vacations. Then, in the early 1950s, two San Francisco cardiologists—Meyer Friedman and Ray H. Rosenman—began to suspect that the known risk factors for heart disease, such as high cholesterol in the bloodstream, cigarette smoking, inheritance, lack of exercise, and overweight, could not always explain heart disease developing in their patients. Might there be some other yet-to-be-discovered coronary risk factors? It seemed so, and the heart specialists got tips as to what they were from two most unexpected sources.

One was an upholsterer who came to fix the seats of chairs in their reception room. After looking the chairs over, he asked, "What sort of a practice do you have?"

"We're cardiologists, but why do you ask?" was Friedman and Rosenman's reply.

"Well, I was just wondering, because it's so peculiar that only the front edges of your chair seats are worn out."

What was it about heart disease patients that might make them fray only the front edges of chairs? Nervousness? Irritation? An impatience to get their appointments over with and to get back to work? Friedman and Rosenman stored that possibility away in their minds.

Then, some time later, the San Francisco doctors studied the diets of volunteers from the San Francisco Junior League and their husbands. Because American white females develop heart disease much less frequently than do American white males, the cardiologists had expected to find that the wives in their study ate less cholesterol than their spouses. But this was not the case. So what was protecting the women from heart attacks yet opening their husbands to them? Differences in sex hormones? Friedman and Rosenman had reason to doubt this. The president of the Junior League then expressed her opinion on the subject: "I told you right from the first that you would find that we are eating exactly as our husbands do. If you really want to know what is giving our husbands heart attacks, I'll tell you."

"And what's that?" Friedman and Rosenman asked, with both curiosity and a touch of arrogance that physicians reserve for laymen's medical theories.

"It's stress, the stress they receive in their work, that's what's doing it!"

And that is when Friedman and Rosenman decided to seriously evaluate the behavior of persons who succumb to heart attacks, to see if indeed excessive work or related characteristics might have precipitated their condition. First they sent a questionnaire to one hundred and fifty businessmen immersed in the industrial and commercial milieu of San Francisco, asking them to check on a list those habits that they believed had preceded a heart attack in a friend of theirs. More than *70 percent* of the men who responded believed that indulgence in "excessive competitive drive and meeting deadlines" was the outstanding characteristic exhibited by heart-stricken friends. Less than 5 percent of the responders thought that their friends' heart attacks had been precipitated by foods high in cholesterol, cigarette smoking, failure to exercise, or other well-documented heart disease risk factors.

Friedman and Rosenman then chose eighty men from the business and professional community and compared them to eighty men who exhibited no competitive drive. (Needless to say, locating such uncompetitive men for comparison was hard in modern-day America, but the researchers finally found some from the embalmers' union and the municipal clerks' union.) Twenty-eight percent of the competitive subjects already had had heart trouble, the investigators learned. Indeed, *seven* times more heart disease could be found among the competitive subjects than among the noncompetitive ones, yet the diets and exercise habits of both groups were similar, ruling out these factors as causes of the competitive men's heart trouble.

This study, however, did not convince many cardiologists that competitive, achievement-oriented men are more liable to have heart attacks than less-competitive, less-achievement-directed ones. The most flattering comments they made about the study was that it was "interesting," "provocative," or "controversial." "If you really want to prove that competition and hard work trigger heart attacks," Friedman and Rosenman's colleagues challenged them, "then you'll have to perform a prospective study, that is, analyze a group of men's personalities while they are still healthy, and then correctly predict which ones will succumb to a heart attack in the future."

Rosenman and Friedman rose to the challenge in the early 1960s. They invited healthy men to join such a study. Thanks to help from the Bank of America, Standard Oil of California, Kaiser Industries, Safeway Stores, United Air Lines, The Bechtel Corp., and Lockheed Aircraft and Missiles Co., they enlisted over thirty-five hundred men and analyzed each subject for driving, competitive behavior. By 1969, more than two hundred and fifty of the subjects had suffered heart attacks, and *the majority* were competer-achievers. Those who were not were high in other heart attack risk factors. In contrast, *not one* of the non-competitive, less-achieving subjects experienced a heart attack, even if he ate a high-cholesterol diet, smoked a lot, was overweight, or came from a family with heart disease. These results dramatically documented that achievement-centered, strongly competitive behavior is indeed a harbinger of a heart attack and may well be as crucial if not more so than other, better-accepted risk factors.

Rosenman and Friedman's retrospective and prospective findings that strong competitive and achievement behaviors help set the stage for a heart attack have meanwhile been confirmed and extended by thirty retrospective studies and two prospective studies performed throughout the world. One of the more fascinating was reported in a 1969 issue of the *Journal of Chronic Diseases*. Benedictine priests, who head up parishes and run schools, were found to have experienced considerably more heart attacks than less-worldly Benedictine monks, although both ate a high-cholesterol diet, a major heart attack risk factor. The more worldly priests, rather than the reclusive monks, also tended to possess the following characteristics: outgoing, assertive, bold, enthusiastic, imaginative, shrewd, disciplined, and conscientious. Concludes the investigator who conducted the study: "The characteristics of the Benedictine priests seem to fit the description of the 'modern coronary-prone man.' "

The heart attack biotype thus possesses a number of traits that are prized by Western society. He sounds like an individual who is going to do great things in life, and he may well do so. Persons with these traits alone are usually deeply committed to their jobs or professions and often have achieved success in them. But the heart attack biotype also often tends, in his keen need to live up to his parents' and his own high expectations, to become a workaholic, to take on as many projects as possible in the shortest amount of time. Such behavior is bound to overload his mental and physical circuits and open him to disease.

One investigation, for example, revealed that heart attack victims tend, in contrast to healthy subjects, to work incredibly long hours, up to fifty or even seventy hours a week, and not only for a few months but even years on end. The heart-attack-prone individual also often holds down two jobs at once and strives to do two or more things simultaneously. "This is one of the commonest traits in [the heart attack prone] man," assert Friedman and Rosenman. "Nor is he always satisfied with doing just two things at one time. We have known subjects who not only shaved and ate simultaneously but also managed to read a business or professional journal at the same time."

The heart attack biotype also has an obsession with numbers—to sell twenty ads, get ten accounts, build sixty buildings, win five sets of tennis, make five holes in one, and so on. In between he is constantly glancing at his watch, furrowing his brow, giving loud orders to his underlings, and swearing at drivers who keep him down to seventy miles per hour.

Still further proof that the heart attack biotype is pushing his mind and body too hard and hence opening himself to disease can be found in the draw-a-person test that Dr. Thomas gave to the medical students participating in her study. Whereas many of those students who drew a figure with one arm outstretched and the other tucked close to the body (an ambivalent stance toward life) came down with cancer, a number of those students who drew a figure with both arms outstretched (as if inviting too many stimuli into their lives) succumbed later in life to heart attacks.

So far, then, the heart attack biotype appears to be someone who is not only an achiever and competitor but anxious to strike as many coups in life as possible and in the shortest amount of time—a modern Hermes, if you will, who was off to find Apollo's cattle after he jumped out of the cradle and who wore many hats—thief, trickster, shepherd, athlete, winged-foot messenger of the gods, and patron of travelers. Several case histories illustrate these qualities.

Dr. Robert G. is one of Chicago's busiest gynecologists. Before he gets out of bed at five in the morning, he dictates patient histories and correspondence. He works fifteen hours a day and boasts to both colleagues and friends that he has the largest gynecology caseload in the Midwest. Much of his limited nonprofessional time is also taken up with professional matters—running the county medical society, building a new medical arts building, and so forth.

Then there is Staunton W., an international steel magnate. He takes delight in talking over the phone to two or three clients at once, much as a ringmaster synchronates a three-ring circus. And when he isn't speeding home in his Mercedes 450 at eight in the evening, he is usually en route via a Boeing 747 for Singapore or Rio de Janeiro.

As if the potential heart attack victim isn't asking for enough trouble physiologically, he also insists on being a perfectionist in everything he does. So by trying to accomplish far too much in far too little time, and to do a good job in all he undertakes, he often fails to accomplish all he sets out to do and, as a result, is frustrated rather than satisfied with his efforts. There is a discrepancy between his self-concept and his ideal self-image. What's more, he feels controlled by external forces, is insecure, and constantly dreads that his efforts will lead to failure rather than to success. Which is often the case. The result: he acquires a Sisyphus complex, which the cancer biotype also suffers from, but for different reasons, as discussed in the last chapter.

A prime example of a person with these character traits is Dan S. of Los Angeles. At the age of thirty-eight Dan is still attempting to make a success of his life—to compete, in a way, with his father, who was a highly successful movie producer, and to rise to the expectations of his mother, whom he tends to worship. Yet Dan gets so bogged down with the details of trying to set up a movie company—finding the right partner and office, having company stationery made—that the company never even gets off the ground. Meanwhile, he needs money to live on and decides to become a car salesman. And when the market goes bad, he turns to another challenge. That too goes sour for him. Needless to say, Dan is an unhappy, even bitter individual, who considers himself a failure in life. No matter how hard he shoves a boulder up the hill, it seems to tumble back down on him.

The unfulfilled needs of the heart attack biotype can in turn make him all the more desperate to achieve, to rise to his ideal self-image. They make him all that much more aggressive, competitive, and in need of dominating others. He resents superiors and fellow workers who seem to stand in his way to success and advancement. Yet he tends to cover his hostility and resentment with a calm, polished, friendly, extroverted front. In fact, he tends to repress most of his negative emotions and to deny those thoughts, feelings, and experiences that do not dovetail with his ideal self-image.

His self-destructive habits can spill over into his private life, too, or at least into what is left of his private hours. His excessive behaviors aren't discarded at the front door but only assume new forms—a tendency to eat rapidly and to overeat, to smoke and drink too much (not only alcohol but coffee, milk, and other liquids), to fail to get enough sleep and to wake up tired, to plan his weekends hour by hour, to engage in no physical activity whatsoever or in too much (the former is more typical), to depress fantasies and to stick to pragmatic thoughts (what French scientists call operational thinking). With his obsessive habits and the attitude that "life is deadly serious business," it's not surprising that he has few friends, sex problems, an unhappy wife, or is divorced and lonely.

The heart attack biotype is also given to frequent anxiety, especially over money matters, is sometimes depressed, and is preoccupied, at least unconsciously, with thoughts about growing old and dying. Potential heart attack victims give many more morbid interpretations to inkblots—such as "human dying and death," "torn, jagged or fragmented human limbs," "dental surgery," and "medical symptoms"— than do healthy subjects. Whirling responses (symbolic of one's dizziness over life quickly passing?) are also twice as common among future heart attack victims than among ongoing healthy subjects.

On the basis of these traits, one can't help wondering whether the following subjects might not be courting a heart attack. Take the case of a forty-year-old businessman who works, eats, drinks, and smokes excessively and who stays up until all hours of the night. "I sometimes wonder if Bob puts off going to bed," his wife speculates, "because he is afraid that he won't wake up in the morning." Or take the case of a thirty-two-year-old executive with a national food-and-hotel chain who fears he will "burn out" by age forty. Or the case of a young man fresh out of college who was upset when he turned twenty-one!

All the heart attack biotype's hard work, coupled with lack of professional satisfaction and a less-than-fulfilling personal life, are bound to weaken his body and open it to illness, especially when his life becomes particularly stressful and he is unable to cope with the excessive demands placed upon him. A 1974 Finnish study noted a greater number of major life changes in heart attack victims six months previous to their attacks than in the same six-month period of twelve months earlier. In 1975 a scientist found that twins who died from heart attacks had sustained more demanding life changes previous to their attacks than had their co-twins, who had likewise had heart attacks but had survived. In 1976 the lives of heart attack subjects and healthy subjects of the same sex, age, and occupational level were compared. The former experienced more challenging life events anywhere from up to three months down to three weeks before their attacks.

But is it only the *number* or *severity* of stressful life events that fuses a heart attack? How about the *desirability* versus the *undesirability* of these events? Some research suggests that it is not important whether the events are traumatic—such as the loss of a loved one or of a position—or happy—such as the birth of a child or a promotion—but rather how many stressful events were incurred within a short period of time. Other findings imply that distressing events tend to take their toll more than do joyful ones. Many widowers, for instance, suffer heart attacks a few months after their wive's deaths. And even back in 1806, Corvissant, a famous French physician of Napoleonic times, wrote that "repeated depressing emotions, the sorrow and vexation that follow great emotional disturbance, may be the origin of refractory disorders of the heart."

A third batch of studies argues that it is not so much the number of life events experienced, or their *desirability* or *undesirability* but *how a person reacts to them* which determines whether or not he will have a heart attack. More specifically, heart attack victims may experience no more stressful events preceding their attacks than healthy subjects do; in fact, they may even experience somewhat fewer such events. However, they may be more likely than healthy persons to translate emotional reactions to stressful events into bodily symptoms—for example, to find that their work upsets their digestion and ability to sleep, to perspire easily even on cool days, to find that their hands shake when they try to do something, and so forth. As one psychosomatic-medicine researcher puts it, "The heart attack personality feels that he is under greater stress than other people are, even when this isn't true. The cancer personality, in contrast, may be under greater stress than other people are, but he will say, 'Everything is fine.' "

Finally, even one recent traumatic life event, coupled with other heart attack biotype traits such as achievement, competition, and repression of negative emotions, may be enough to do in the heart, as the following case history illustrates.

A thirty-nine-year-old educator, Al T., was admitted to a hospital for fibrillation of the ventricles of his heart, which is a kind of heart arrhythmia that can lead to cardiac arrest and death, in contrast to a heart attack, which consists of damage to the heart muscle and which then may be followed by heart arrhythmias and death. The day Al T.'s heart fibrillated was not unusual. However, for some reason he decided to come home early. Shortly after roughhousing with his two teen-age daughters, he collapsed unconscious. His wife, a registered nurse, initiated cardiopulmonary resuscitation. On arrival at a community hospital, he was found to be in ventricular fibrillation. Although defibrillation of his heart was difficult, it was finally achieved, and he became fully conscious again.

Clinical tests revealed no sign of organic heart disease. What's more, Al was an athletic, robust man who looked even younger than his thirty-nine years. So what triggered his heart arrhythmias? Psychiatric interviews over the next few days gave the clue.

Control of aggression was a pervasive theme in Al's life. He grew up in a tough mining town, was intensely competitive with his only brother, overcame great obstacles to achieve higher education, and fiercely devoted himself to every enterprise he undertook. He often found himself surging with anger, which he tried to counter with vigorous, solitary exercise, and avoided violent television programs. Violence often appeared in his dreams, yet he insisted it was not part of his true self. His strong moral prohibition against aggression was matched by his sexual restraint. He insisted that he had no sexual thoughts about women other than his wife, although his work as a teacher brought him into close contact with numerous other women, and he was often around his daughters, who had matured considerably of late. In the six months preceding his heart fibrillation, Al suffered his first career setback, when a faltering economy frustrated his promotion. In addition, his wife was depressed over the recent death of her father and unresponsive to his need for sympathy and support at this time. So were his daughters, who were increasingly active outside the family.

The roughhousing with his daughters, then, appeared to have aroused both aggressive and erotic impulses in Al, urges he was ashamed of and tried to repress. This emotional strain, coupled with the stress of a recent professional disappointment and a lack of support from his wife and daughters, was too much for his heart to take. Even as Al slumped to the floor, he gasped to his daughters, "I'm sorry."

So far we've looked mostly at the male heart attack biotype. Are women who have a strong need to achieve, compete, and be time-urgent, who repress negative emotions, and who neglect their private lives for their work also subject to heart attacks in the wake of excessive or particularly negative life changes? It appears so, and several personality sketches aptly illustrate the modern coronary-prone woman.

Joan C. is a troubleshooter for an international machinery firm, and she flies almost continuously from New York to Copenhagen to Cape-town and other cities throughout the world in order to bail out clients whose machines are giving them trouble. Although Joan adores her work and dealing with people in different countries, being constantly on the go and having to shift her biological rhythms frequently is bound to take its toll on her health.

Carole R. is a petite but tough forty-year-old woman who has been rising the managerial ladder of a national lingerie firm for eighteen years. Carole's work is her world. She puts in long hours night after night and even on weekends, and the few leisure hours she pursues are usually with colleagues from her company, talking shop. Carole does everything with an executive's sleight-of-hand, whether it is sending memos to her mother or mimeographed newsletters to her friends. If you want a lunch date with Carole, you had better book it a few weeks in advance.

Sarah G., in contrast to Joan and Carole, is married and the mother of a three-year-old, but she shares many of their heart attack personality traits. She juggles her duties as wife and mother while holding down a full-time job as a department store buyer and draws up lists of what must be done for her husband, child, and household as well as for her profession. Sometimes she even makes master lists to coordinate the other lists, truly an excessive, compulsive behavior so typical of the heart attack personality. Sarah also books her professional and private life so tightly that there is no room left for such emergencies as sickness or inclement weather. Unlike Carole, however, Sarah allows herself some fantasized thinking and emotional expression, and unlike Carole and Joan, she is beginning to realize that professional fulfillment and status aren't everything.

Now that increasing numbers of women are entering the work force and occupying more and more positions traditionally held by men, it will be interesting to see whether women's susceptibility to heart attacks increases commensurately. In fact, there are already indications of such a trend. Deaths from heart attacks have risen dramatically among young American women during the past few years, and since Japanese women were "liberated" from domestic isolation twenty-five years ago, their incidence of heart disease has quadrupled.

So far you probably have the impression that it is only white-collar workers, and particularly executives, who are prone to heart attacks.

Not so! Blue-collar workers are just as vulnerable if they engage in similar thoughts, emotions, and behaviors. Many heart attack victims put in long hours of physical, rather than mental, labor before they succumb, and whereas many bank and corporation presidents are decidedly not heart attack personalities, many truck drivers and janitors are.

Nor are heart attacks limited to persons with higher socioeconomic or educational backgrounds. In fact, the opposite may be true. In a large, industrial population, persons with less than a college education were found to have significantly more heart disease than those at identical job levels with a college education. What's more, those individuals who are at variance socioeconomically with their parents or a spouse appear to be particularly vulnerable to a heart attack, perhaps because the discrepancy puts excessive stress on them.

Are persons from certain religious backgrounds more likely to suffer heart attacks than others? Protestants and Jews may be more susceptible than Catholics. A 1964 study, for instance, found that American Protestants had the greatest incidence of heart disease, American Jews ranked next, and American Catholics had the least.

Protestants and Jews are more vulnerable than Catholics to heart attacks probably because of certain differences in values and behaviors among the three groups. For instance, the Protestant Reformation of the sixteenth century introduced an unprecedented emphasis on personal autonomy (a person had to find his own way to heaven), in contrast to the prevailing Catholic emphasis on dependence (if a person did what the Church said, he would get to heaven). The Reformation also introduced a new emphasis on the here and now as well as on the hereafter; a person was expected to do the best he could in his station in life and to remember that "God helps those who help themselves." The Protestant Reformation thus turned many Europeans into independent achievers, and achievement—remember—is a major heart attack risk factor. A number of historians have attributed the rise of capitalism and the Industrial Revolution in Europe to the rise of Protestantism.

The greater Protestant emphasis on independence and achievement has endured to modern times. In the 1950s more German Protestant than German Catholic boys sought higher education (presumably to succeed in life), and more American Protestant than American Catholic parents expected their sons to do well in school at an early age (presumably such an expectation would constitute parents pushing their child toward achievement). And in 1960 more German Catholic than German Protestant parents bought playpens and walking harnesses (presumably because the former were more interested in having their children submit to authority than in having them strive toward autonomy and achievement).

As for Judaism, it stresses the importance of education—a religious value that probably encourages achievement. Jews may also strive to achieve as a compensation for persecution by Gentiles, since many of the Jews who survived concentration camps have gone on to become financially successful. What is certain, however, is that Jews have been superachievers throughout the centuries, especially in business and the professions, that Jewish mothers have high levels of aspiration for their children, and that Jews had a greater need for achievement by the middle of the twentieth century than did Catholics.

Studies from the 1950s, for instance, revealed that more American Jewish boys were interested in becoming physicians, executives, or professionals of some kind than were American Catholic boys and that the former more strongly disagreed with the following statement than the latter did: "A good son would try to live near his parents even if it means giving up a good job in another part of the country." American Jewish parents of that era also placed greater emphasis on early independence and mastery of different tasks than did Catholic parents.

Now that we're into the last lap of the twentieth century, however, more Catholics may be subscribing to the Protestant-Jewish work ethic. A 1973 study showed that while American Jews had the highest heart attack rates, Catholics had outpaced Protestants in that respect.

Whether or not one religious group or another is more prone to heart attacks, heart attacks do seem to be rare among those persons who are deeply religious, that is, more interested in the life hereafter than in scoring in this world. For as Friedman and Rosenman have written: "We cannot say positively that the increase in [the heart attack] behavior pattern has been directly influenced by the continuing loss of religious faith and other sustaining rituals. We can declare, however, with considerable certainty, that we have rarely encountered [the heart attack] behavior pattern in any person whose religious and patriotic beliefs take precedence over his preoccupation with the accumulation of 'numbers' or acquisition of personal power."

And how about heart attack risk factors other than personality? Are they more, less, or just as crucial as personality? It's pretty hard to say at this point. There is some reason to believe that personality factors are more important. For example, Somali camel herdsmen appear to be relatively free from hardening of the arteries, a heart attack risk factor, although they eat a high cholesterol diet derived from five liters of camel's milk a day. The reason they don't get hardening of the arteries may be because they pursue a pastoral life-style that has been unchanged for centuries, freeing them from serious psychological stress. Other evidence, though, suggests that a high level of cholesterol in the blood, not personality, is the best heart attack predictor, or that personality is not all that strong a risk factor when present by itself but that it is crucial if combined with other risk factors, such as a genetic predisposition toward heart disease, high-cholesterol levels, heavy cigarette smoking, high blood pressure, and so on.

Some interesting insights into the personality of persons with high blood pressure, in fact, have also emerged in recent years. Because a number of individuals with high blood pressure (hypertension) eventually have heart attacks, one would expect them to share many of the characteristics of the explicit heart attack personality. Many persons with high blood pressure, for instance, were just as close to their parents as were heart attack victims. Many are also only children or at least firstborns. These traits suggest that they, like heart attack patients, were probably pushed by their parents to achieve and compete.

But are hypertensives as keen on achieving and competing as the full-blown heart attack biotype? Very possibly. Hypertensives tend to be extremely tense people and, like heart-attack-prone persons, insecure about life. Unlike the heart-attack-prone individual, however, the hypertensive-prone person tends to latch onto a stronger person, an umbilical-cord arrangement of sorts, and to engage in deferential and self-effacing behaviors. "Deferential" includes getting suggestions from others, finding out what others think, following instructions and doing what's expected, praising others, accepting the leadership of others, reading about great men and women, and conforming to custom and the conventional. "Self-effacing" includes accepting the blame when things don't go right, feeling the need to be punished if one does something wrong, preferring to give in rather than fight, feeling the need to confess one's mistakes, and becoming depressed by the inability to handle a situation.

The hypertensive biotype also represses negative emotions, perhaps even more than the heart attack personality per se does, and has learned such suppression early in life. A dramatic correlation between early emotional repression and later susceptibility to high blood pressure was noted in a study of twins. Those twins who were more submissive, quiet, withdrawn, and obedient as children tended to have higher blood pressure later in life than did their more aggressive, rebellious co-twins. And like the heart attack biotype, the hypertensive person tends to be anxious. One fascinating case history, in fact, suggests that this trait alone may be sufficient to bring on high blood pressure.

Matthew C. came from a family with normal blood pressure. He didn't have any trouble with it while young. Then, at age nineteen, upon facing the prospect of being drafted into the army, he learned from some of his friends that he could induce high blood pressure by thinking anxious thoughts. So when he appeared before the army induction center's examining physician, he concentrated on things that upset him. Sure enough, the physician found that he had a high blood pressure reading. "Come back in several days for another test," the doctor ordered. During the next few days Matt kept himself as anxious as possible, and when he returned for reexamination, he was once again found to have high blood pressure. "Go to your private physician and see what reading he gets," the army physician then commanded. Off Matt went, thinking anxious thoughts; once again his blood pressure was found to be high. So Matt escaped being drafted into the army and was pretty proud of himself.

After Matt had finished college and entered medical school, he learned that high blood pressure is a severe heart attack risk factor. So he started taking his own blood pressure readings regularly, and each time, unless he was very calm, his readings were high. Matt is now convinced that he is a victim of chronic high blood pressure and that he brought it all on himself by anxious thinking.

Whether Matt is right or not, what is sure is that *unintentional* anxiety brought on by stressful events can launch high blood pressure. Men who lost their jobs through a plant shutdown found their blood pressure soaring, but as they found new positions, their pressure tapered off. The continual threat of shock, separation from a mate, threats from a predator, or territorial conflict gave monkeys and mice hypertension.

Several other traits appear to be peculiar to the hypertensive biotype—introversion, emotional excitability, and an extreme sensitivity to stress. Is personality more likely to trigger high blood pressure than some other factors? Although inheritance accounts for excessively high blood pressure, personality can explain most of the less-severe cases.

And how about the angina personality, since individuals with angina (chest pains) often suffer heart attacks? They too share a number of characteristics with the total heart attack biotype.

Whereas the heart attack and hypertensive biotypes tend to be insecure and fear failure, angina-prone persons have dependency needs that they cover with aggressive bravado. Like the heart attack and hypertension biotypes, angina-prone persons also suppress negative emotions. In fact, rather than express their rage against someone, they may shout, "You'll be sorry if I die," or "I'll show that you are killing me," and then proceed to produce anginal pain, in a sort of self-fulfilling prophecy. And, like the other two biotypes, angina sufferers are prone to anxiety and have their conditions triggered by recent stressful events in their lives.

Take the case of fifty-five-year-old Sid G., who started complaining about a slight tightness in his chest, left shoulder, and left arm six months after a traffic accident. Medical diagnosis revealed that his angina pains were not due to a heart problem but rather to his dissatisfaction over the financial settlement for the accident. And then there was Henry K., whose anginal pain began after he had a leg amputated. As Henry came to realize that emotions sparked his angina, his attacks lessened and finally disappeared.

Angina victims, however, have several other traits peculiarly their own—they dream dreams with intense emotional conflicts and often convert their emotional conflicts into physical symptoms. Such translation requires a lot of fantasy, something which the blatant heart attack biotype is not likely to bring off.

Take the case of Gladys P., a sixty-five-year-old housewife suffering from anginal pain so intense that once, while she was reading a newspaper, the pages turned blank. The cardiologist was not able to find any heart abnormalities to explain Gladys's chest pains, but he did find some psychiatric ones. Eight years earlier, when her daughter was tragically dying of leukemia, Gladys had suffered temporary blindness, as if to say, "I don't want to see this situation." And when her cousin had a brain tumor, Gladys started experiencing excruciating headaches, in fear that she too might have a brain tumor. And as for Gladys's angina attacks, they commenced the day after her husband was rushed to the hospital for heart trouble. Gladys was obviously identifying with her husband's problem and was especially distressed by it because she had depended on her husband for many years. After the cardiologist clarified the cause of Gladys's angina attacks, they promptly disappeared.

More insights into the heart attack, hypertension, and angina biotypes will undoubtedly emerge during the next few years, because heart attacks continue to be a leading cause of death in many countries throughout the world.

3

THE
GASTROINTESTINAL
BIOTYPES

UNLIKE CANCER AND HEART attacks, which constitute single diseases, gastrointestinal-tract disorders are much more varied and include ulcerative colitis (chronic inflammation of the lining of the large intestine), ulcers (erosion of the lining of the small intestine or stomach), anorexia nervosa (self-starvation), vomiting, obesity, constipation, bad breath, diarrhea, gas, and so on. There are significant psychological inputs into all these diseases. As Dr. Vernon M. Smith of the University of Maryland School of Medicine has written: "The gastrointestinal system is unparalleled among the systems of the human body in its susceptibility to disorders arising from, or aggravated by, emotional disturbances." And in the view of Dr. Charles W. Heck of Augusta, Georgia: "In the field of gastroenterology, perhaps the only time, or nearly the only time, that the psyche does not enter is in the laxative habituate who, following surgery, was instructed to keep the bowels open with regular use of laxatives." The enormous role that emotions play in GI disorders is also revealed in everyday expressions such as "What's eating you?" "It's enough to make you vomit," "I felt my stomach churning," "I'm fed up," "It left a bitter taste in my mouth," and so on.

But there are specific GI-disorder biotypes, and they tend to share a number of traits. Notably these include a traumatic childhood leading to excessive dependency needs and living for others rather than self, repression of negative emotions, an obsession with perfection and neatness, sexual problems, emotional sensitivity, and its triggering by one or numerous stressful events, especially the loss of a person on whom the victim has been especially dependent. Each GI-disorder personality, however, is unique, and some are better researched than others. So let's take a look at them one by one.

The Ulcerative Colitis Biotype

Ulcerative colitis is one of the most serious and perplexing of all gastroenterologic conditions. It afflicts hundreds of thousands with complications that may be crippling or even fatal. Yet no physical cause for the disease has ever been found. This fact, plus numerous insights that have been obtained into the personalities of ulcerative colitis victims, suggests that the psyche alone can trigger the condition.

Ulcerative colitis victims have usually had a less-than-ideal childhood. This may have been a dominating mother and passive father and/or having grown up in an emotionally repressed atmosphere. A British investigator noted that ulcerative colitis in London was especially prevalent among Jews, and he hypothesized that one reason Jews were particularly susceptible to the disease is because Jewish mothers often dominate their children. The British researcher then noted that in Suffolk, England, where there are few Jews, members of strict Gentile sects called the Plymouth Brethren and Salvationists had the most ulcerative colitis. Members of these sects have tightly knit families, as do Jews, but they are patriarchal rather than matriarchal. Individuals belonging to these sects also insist on "never an angry word." Dr. Don D. Jackson and Dr. Irvin Yalom of Palo Alto, California, who interviewed the families of young ulcerative colitis victims, noted striking similarities among the eight families they interviewed. One was that the mothers tend to dominate their children, especially the ulcerative colitis child. One mother and patient, for instance, claimed an ESP type of communication. Another patient talked like her mother. One mother devoted so much of her time to her ulcerative colitis child that she ignored her husband and other children. The fathers of ulcerative colitis victims, in contrast, are often passive, remote, and even jealous of their children. Another striking similarity among families with an ulcerative colitis patient, the California researchers noted, was that they repressed emotional expression, especially any comments that suggest that their lives are less than perfect.

A typical family in this regard—we'll call them the Blakes—are decidedly embarrassed about being interviewed by a psychotherapist and insist that all is well within their family. Such insistence comes not only from Mr. and Mrs. Blake but from twenty-one-year-old daughter Linda, seventeen-year-old daughter Kelly (the ulcerative colitis patient), and fifteen-year-old Chris. One time, however, Linda lets slip that "I raised sheep when I was a teen-ager. Dad approved of it, but Mom was against it." Linda then senses her parents bristling, so hastily adds, "This, of course, was the only time they ever disagreed."

Another time the psychotherapist learns that Chris, who until now has been polite and expressionless, once expected to be picked up by two other boys. Three hours later he was still waiting; his father suggested he call one of the boys' homes. Sure enough, the boys had stood Chris up. "Of course Chris was not upset by this incident," Mr. Blake insists. The therapist probes for more details. Chris finally shows emotion and is even close to tears. "Really, there is no use making a big deal out of it!" Mr. Blake snaps, and the episode is closed.

The therapist pushes further: "Why are you all so reluctant to talk?"

"We have nothing to say," the family concurs.

"Are you sure you have nothing to say, or is it that you don't allow things to be said in your family?"

At this charge, Linda blurts out, "When I was young, I wanted to talk and would come into the living room, but everybody said 'Be quiet! We're watching T.V.' "

"Oh, she's making that up!" Mr. and Mrs. Blake object.

And a few minutes later Linda herself denies ever having mentioned such a thing.

There is a reason why the families of ulcerative colitis patients often conspire to such silence, of course. As the California study revealed, such families tend to be unhappy and to deny their problems rather than face up to them. The fathers of ulcerative colitis patients, for instance, are often self-deprecating and underachieving and spend long hours at work with little job satisfaction. The mothers of such patients are often depressed and have phobias, nervous breakdowns, back pain, sleeping sickness, gynecologic disorders, thyroid abnormalities, breathing trouble, acne, and other health problems. In addition, the parents of ulcerative colitis patients are seldom affectionate with each other, and even *their* parents often had a history of unhappiness and poor health, such as alcoholism, suicide, dying in a psychiatric hospital, being killed in an auto accident, and so on. In other words, ulcerative colitis may be the end product of several generations of psychological turbulence and numerous health problems of one sort or another.

With a demanding mother and passive father and/or growing up in an unhappy, emotionally repressed atmosphere, it is little wonder that the ulcerative colitis personality tends to be passive, compliant, timid, and reluctant, just as a dependent, immature child would be. A 1970 study of twenty-three ulcerative colitis patients and their respective healthy siblings, conducted by Dr. Arthur W. McMahon and colleagues at the Tufts–New England Medical Center, revealed that the former were more indecisive, immature, ingratiating, and apt to deny conflicts, whereas the latter were more independent, rebellious, and adventurous. The patients tended to describe their families in glowing terms, whereas their siblings painted less-rosy pictures. The siblings were also much more open to being interviewed than were the patients.

An example of an ulcerative colitis patient with these qualities and of a sibling without them are twenty-eight-year-old Charles K. and his fraternal twin, Robert. Even as a youngster, Robert had always been more outgoing, aggressive, and capable of resolving conflicts than Charles. During his first semester in college, at age eighteen, Charles developed ulcerative colitis. After college, Robert struck out on his own, whereas Charles returned home to live with his parents and to work for the same company his father did. Such a move was hardly logical, since his father despised his work, putting in long, irregular shift hours. Today Charles is still living with his parents. Sometimes he gets caught in conflicts between his parents, and when that happens his ulcerative colitis is exacerbated.

Still another example of an ulcerative colitis patient with dependent, immature qualities and of a sibling without them are forty-one-year-old Vera P. and her sister Maxine. Unlike many ulcerative colitis patients, Vera did not have a dominating mother but a father who adored and overprotected her. Maxine did not get such preferential treatment. So today Vera is a dependent type of person, whereas Maxine is not. And since their father is dead, Vera is bent on always obtaining her mother's approval, something Maxine gave up as an adolescent. "Vera has always been more idealistic and perfectionistic than I have," Maxine claims. "She is unable to accept situations as they are and wants to make them better, but in an unrealistic way." A tendency to be a perfectionist is likewise common among ulcerative colitis patients.

The ulcerative colitis biotype likewise tends to be emotional, sensitive, and intellectually bright. Take the case of Lisa M., an outstanding high school senior. Lisa was all set to leave her home in McLean, Virginia to take competitive exams for entering one of New England's "Seven Sister" colleges. The day she was to fly to Boston, her plane was grounded by bad weather. A harrowing night train ride, intense anxiety, and a relatively poor showing the next day on the stiff exam caused Lisa to experience, within days, an explosive case of ulcerative colitis. The disease was so severe that even drastic intestinal surgery could not save Lisa's life.

Ulcerative colitis patients also often have sexual problems. They tend to date late in adolescence or early adulthood, to rarely court more than one or two persons before marriage, and to have minimal sexual intercourse both before and after marriage. A good example of an ulcerative colitis patient with these qualities is Charles K., discussed above. Although Charles's twin, Robert, is married at age twenty-eight, Charles hardly dates, using his ulcerative colitis as an excuse. The ulcerative colitis personality has sexual problems possibly because he is a dependent, immature person and thus of immature sexuality.

What is certain, however, is that ulcerative colitis is triggered by events that are particularly stressful in the lives of the victims. For example, a 1970 study of ulcerative colitis patients by Dr. F. Patrick McKegney of the Yale University School of Medicine indicated a high incidence of emotional disturbances and life crisis within six months preceding the disease, and the more devastating the emotional disturbance, generally the more severe the disease. What types of situations trigger ulcerative colitis? Quite a gamut—rape, birth of a deformed child, an ear operation, moving to a new home, divorce, hysterectomy, a business crisis, job change, boyfriend's death, school exams (which sparked Lisa's ulcerative colitis), a shotgun marriage, son arrested, birth of a sibling accompanied by father's molestation of a schoolgirl, and not surprisingly, disappointment in love, as the two following cases from the Middle East demonstrate.

A twenty-eight-year-old man was referred to a Middle Eastern hospital for bloody diarrhea, alternating with constipation, and lower abdominal pains—symptoms of ulcerative colitis. The doctors couldn't find any pathogens in his stools, showing that he did not have a gastrointestinal infection, but they did learn that the patient had been upset by the loss of his girlfriend a few months previously—enough, in fact, to put him in a mental hospital for a month.

A twenty-year-old girl was admitted to the same hospital for diarrhea and passage of blood and mucus from the rectum—symptoms of ulcerative colitis. The doctors kept her in the hospital for five months, but she failed to respond to treatment. After she left the hospital and took two months vacation in Lebanon, however, her condition improved considerably, apparently because she was removed from her beautiful younger sister, of whom she was jealous. Now she is doing well without any treatment because she is happily preparing for her own wedding.

But the most frequent trigger of ulcerative colitis is the death of a parent, which makes sense, since the loss of a loved one is traumatic for most people and would be especially so for a person who tended to be overly dependent on his parents, which is frequently the case with ulcerative colitis victims.

Usually, a person's psychological distress manifests itself as either physical or mental disease, not both. Columbia University researchers, however, have found that this is not the case with schizophrenics who have ulcerative colitis. When their psychological symptoms increase, those of their ulcerative colitis do too. The investigators aren't sure why, but this certainly demonstrates the powerful input of the mind into ulcerative colitis.

The Ulcer Biotype

Ulcers of the small intestine and stomach are another gastrointestinal condition that have long been recognized as having a strong psychological component, and, like ulcerative colitis, they seem to have their origin in childhood experiences. But these conditions have not been explored to the degree that those of ulcerative colitis have. Nonetheless, one study suggests that ulcer victims often had an unhappy childhood and another that they lost a parent at an early age more frequently than the normal population had. And what *has* been well documented is that the prospective ulcer victim, whether child or adult, often has a conflict between the desire to be dependent and the desire to be independent. Back in the 1930s and 1940s, for instance, psychosomatic-medicine pioneer Franz Alexander used psychoanalytic principles to study the personalities of ulcer patients. He found that they often had a conflict betwen the infantile wish to be loved and cared for and a yearning to be independent.

Alexander's findings were confirmed to a remarkable degree in a 1957 prospective study. Herbert Weiner of the Albert Einstein College of Medicine in New York City, and his colleagues, evaluated some two thousand army inductees for personality traits and whether they secreted a lot of stomach acid or not, because ulcers only occur in the presence of acid. Weiner predicted that those men with high levels of acid plus strong oral needs—wanting to be fed, lean on others, seek close bodily contact, and so forth—would eventually get an ulcer. Sixteen weeks later, nine out of the two thousand men came down with an ulcer, and Weiner had correctly predicted seven out of the nine.

The same characteristics have also been noted in a 1974 study of ulcer patients in India. Fifty-six percent of them were found to have a marked dependency on their mothers, 80 percent an excessive craving for love, and 72 percent a role conflict, in contrast to control subjects, of whom only 12 percent showed a dependency on their mothers, 24 percent an excessive craving for love, and 32 percent a role conflict.

The ulcer biotype, then, appears to be someone who is not sure whether he wants to be dependent or independent and who also secretes a lot of stomach acid. Is the acid secretion genetically determined, or does a conflict over whether to be dependent or independent create the acid? There are opposing views here. Some persons secrete a great deal of acid at birth, which suggests that acid secretion is inherited. That more than half the ulcer patients in one study came from families with ulcers likewise suggests that excess stomach acid is inherited. Alexander, on the other hand, believed that it is the prospective ulcer victim's excessive oral cravings that increase his acid secretion, much as the anticipation of food does. Still further support for the notion that dependency needs trigger acid can be found in a fascinating yet rather pathetic observation of a little girl being studied for acid secretion. When the child whined and reached out for passing nurses, her stomach secreted a lot of acid. But because the nurses had been instructed to ignore her during the study, she became depressed, lay down, and went to sleep. And during this period she secreted no stomach acid whatsoever.

Aside from strong dependency needs, ulcer biotypes share some other traits. They tend to be hardworking, meticulous, and ambitious (possibly to obtain the approval they found hard to win in childhood); to be somewhat self-centered; to internalize hostility rather than confront someone who upset them; to fantasize their bodies as weak, vulnerable, and susceptible to outside influences (which fits in with being a dependent individual); to be extremely sensitive to stress; and to have sexual problems (probably because of their extreme need for dependency and affection).

A prime example of an ulcer victim with several of these characteristics is Ned G., of Chicago. Ned is an attractive bachelor accountant with a well-paying government position and a tasteful apartment—a fellow who looks, at first glance, like a good marital catch for some young woman. But Ned can't make much headway with the four bachelorettes living next to him, because he is always dropping in on them for chitchats, backrubs, and sympathy for his ulcer, and when he invites them to his pad, everything has to be kept just so, thank you.

Like ulcerative colitis (and cancer and heart attacks for that matter), ulcers usually strike after a person has been through one or numerous traumatic life stresses, and in the case of ulcers, they especially occur in the wake of events that threaten to take away the person on whom the victim is dependent. Consider the case of a pair of identical twins who each got ulcers when their dependency needs were jeopardized. Both Al and Bob K. are passive and dependent, traits typical of ulcer victims. Al developed an ulcer during a conflict with his dominating wife. Bob didn't get an ulcer at that time because he was married to a motherly woman who satisfied his dependency needs. Ten years later, however, Bob's wife lost her job and thought herself pregnant, events that would deprive Bob of the usual financial and emotional support he received from her. That is when Bob came down with an ulcer.

That stress can trigger ulcers has also been documented by animal experiments. In one, "executive" monkeys had to learn to press a paddle whenever a red light came on in order to avoid an uncomfortable body shock. The periods of performance were six hours on and six hours off, meaning that for six hours the red light was on, with danger of body shock present unless the animal pressed the paddle rapidly enough to reset the shocking mechanisms. After three weeks of this schedule, the monkeys got ulcers.

Other interesting personality aspects of ulcers have also emerged in recent years. Ulcers strike men five times more often than women (because of some sex hormone difference or because men have more trouble than women admitting to dependency needs?). Ulcers have been known to afflict unborn children (because of a genetic predisposition or because of some traumatic event incurred by the unborn child?). Ulcers rarely occur in children between the ages of two and seven (because children before and after these ages are more prone to conflicts over dependence versus independence?). And, most intriguingly, an epidemic of ulcers struck Western countries between 1900 and 1950 and since then seem to have been replaced by an epidemic of heart disease.

Why is this? One reason ulcers may have been so rampant during the first half of the twentieth century is that people living at that time had been exposed to Victorian-type childrearing, often lost their parents in World Wars I and II, or had parents devastated psychologically and financially by the Great Depression. Such childhood experiences could have deprived them of needed affection and moral support, thus predisposing them later in life to ulcers. During the latter half of the twentieth century, in contrast, Western children have encountered more relaxed childrearing, no world wars, and ample material prosperity. As a result of such conditions, they have undoubtedly received more affection and moral support than did children during the first half of this century. With their affection-dependency needs met during childhood, they would not then be prone to ulcers later in life. On the other hand, the lavish affection and support they have received may now be exposing them to another health risk—heart attacks—as we saw in the last chapter. A 1950s study, in fact, may have documented the transition from an ulcer to a heart attack society, because it found a high incidence of heart disease among ulcer patients.

Even today, however, some 10 percent of all Americans can expect to get an ulcer at some point in their lives. Hence, psychological factors that help set the stage for this gastrointestinal disorder are still of keen interest to psychosomatic-medicine researchers.

The Anorexia Nervosa Biotype

Anorexia nervosa consists of the pursuit of excessive thinness through self-imposed starvation, usually interspersed with savage attacks on food without discrimination as to their quality. The patient then feels grave remorse and induces self-vomiting and once again continues to starve himself. In brief, anorexia consists of an obsessive-compulsive preoccupation with, yet horror of, food. One anorexic, for instance, takes each little morsel of food, wraps it in toilet paper, and twists the ends like a candy kiss. These she presents to other people like presents. Claims another anorexic, "I crave something all the time, want to keep sucking on something, and when I finally let go, I attack food with my hands, like a child or animal." Says another, " I won't even lick a postage stamp—you never know about calories." Anorexia usually starts in adolescence and can lead to death unless medical intervention is provided. Its cause appears to be entirely psychological.

Like ulcerative colitis, anorexia often has its origin in a dominating mother, usually one bent on making her child fill her own unmet ambitions. Take the case of Rita F., a fifteen-year-old anorexic. Rita's mother sacrificed her dream of a theatrical career to be a conscientious, devoted mother. Yet in return for this sacrifice, she expects Rita to excel not only in school but in sports and the arts. Rita tried to do so, but finally she felt so overwhelmed by her mother's demands that she revolted—by starving herself.

On other occasions, anorexia is like ulcers in that it has its origins in unmet dependency needs stemming from childhood. Take the case of Kristine H., whose mother gave all her attention to Kristine's brother. From the ages of seven to twelve, Kristine experienced frequent abdominal cramps and involuntary vomiting whenever she saw her mother lavishing her brother with hugs and kisses. By adolescence, Kristine was overeating in compensation for the love she so desperately craved. And by age eighteen, Kristine was starving herself, satisfied that this desperate act was at least directing some of her mother's attention toward herself. Then Kristine got married and had a daughter named Lydia, to whom she gave little love and whom she left alone frequently in order to lock herself in the bathroom for orgy-vomiting sessions. Lydia felt so deprived of love that she often put herself to sleep with fantasies of being sick and cared for by her mother. At age fifteen Lydia started starving herself. "Not eating made me feel close to my mother," she claims. "I couldn't do it any other way."

Anorexics also share another trait with ulcerative colitis victims: they tend to come from homes where emotions are repressed and where parents often pretend that everything is perfect. For instance, Hilde Bruch, a Baylor College of Medicine psychiatrist who has worked with the families of numerous anorexics, says that when the family of an anorexic is seen today, "it is rare that any one member speaks in direct terms about his or her own ideas and feelings. Each one seems to know what the other feels and truly means, at the same time disqualifying what the others said. . . . Such features are of various intensity in different families, but add up to a complete denial of illness or of any need of change."

As a result of their parents' emphasis on repressed emotional expression and the insistence that all is perfect within the family, it is little wonder that the anorexic often tends to be a perfect child—never to get angry, never to talk back, to be extremly neat, and so on—until he starts to intentionally starve himself. In this respect, too, he resembles the ulcerative colitis victim.

Anorexics, however, often experience something during childhood that ulcerative colitis and ulcer victims usually do not—mothers who are preoccupied with food. The mothers of anorexics, for instance, frequently use food as a means of communicating with their children, nag their children to eat everything put on their plates, or even smear their faces with food if they refuse. One mother of a child who later became anorexic forced food down him which he had regurgitated. Another mother often mixed spaghetti, meatballs, applesauce, milk, cake, or a mishmash of other incongruous foods together in a blender and forced them down her infant. Little wonder that by seventeen months of age the little girl was already displaying anorexic symptoms—putting her hand in her mouth and gagging whenever she heard the blender turned on. Still other mothers of anorexics insist that their children eat well and that they don't understand why they weigh so little. Invariably, these women are obsessed with watching their own weight and deeply envy their children the willpower of existing on so little food.

Another trait unique to anorexics is that they suffer from a distorted body image. Even though they often resemble concentration camp victims, with hollow eye sockets and shoulder blades that stick up like little wings, anorexics insist that they like the way they look and would hate themselves if they gained an ounce. Anorexics also tend to overestimate the size of their own mirror images. In fact, the bigger the anorexic perceives his body to be, generally the more severe is his illness. Yet another peculiar trait of anorexics is their compulsion to exercise vigorously, even when they are so thin and weak, as if to demonstrate that they can indeed live by mind over body. One patient, for instance, spent hours each day swimming, fencing, and playing tennis and at the same time maintaining an A average in school. Deep inside, however, anorexics usually suffer from a profound sense of helplessness and worthlessness, and their pathetic ego strength is reflected in inkblot interpretations, such as "It looks like a face that's been bombed" or "like somebody totally disabled who can't fight for her life."

Like ulcerative colitis and ulcer patients, anorexics tend to have sexual problems. For some, their preoccupation with eating usurps their sexual needs. Says one patient, "Eating is carnal, eating is whoring; to eat is sin." Most anorexics, however, have no interest in sex (the stories they tell lack sexual fantasies), and female anorexics tend to despise their sex, probably because they resent their dominating or unaffectionate mothers and don't want to identify with them. Lydia, for instance, fought against pubertal changes by shaving her axillary and pubic hair.

And like ulcerative colitis and ulcer patients, anorexics tend to have their conditions triggered by stress in their lives, events with which they feel they cannot cope. Rita, for example, started starving herself when she could no longer meet her mother's excessive demands. Still other anorexics begin dieting when they are sent away from home to school or camp, move to a new neighborhood, experience pubertal changes, or are otherwise confronted with growing up. For many of them, dieting seems to be a means of declaring their independence against a too-dominating mother or a means of gaining the respect and admiration of a mother who has ignored them. Whatever the anorexic's secret intent, though, thinness becomes his pride and joy, his raison d'être.

There are still other thought-provoking aspects of the anorexic personality. Three-fourths of anorexics are female; patients are often the oldest or youngest member of the family and usually from middle- or upper-middle-class backgrounds (anorexia is virtually unheard of among poor people or persons in developing countries); anorexia strikes more Catholics and Jews than Protestants (which may be due to the traditional Catholic and Jewish rituals connected with food, because some anorexics incorporate these into their pathological eating patterns). Finally, whereas anorexia used to be rare, it is rapidly increasing in incidence in countries as diverse as the United States and the Soviet Union and becoming a widespread problem in secondary schools and universities. This is undoubtedly because of the enormous emphasis that television, magazines, movies, and the fashion world today place on being skinny. "We might even speculate," Bruch declares, "that if anorexia nervosa becomes common enough, it will lose one of its characteristic features, the representing of a very special achievement. If that happens, we might expect its incidence to decrease again."

The Obese Biotype

You would think that with obesity being such a massive health problem in developed countries—there are 15 million obese Americans, and 30 million are overweight—that medical researchers would have gotten the causes down pat. Not so. Weight gain is an incredibly complex medical-research challenge, perhaps because it is tied up so much with such other "oral" behavioral problems as smoking, drinking, and drug addiction and because the physiological defect underlying obesity has still not been pinpointed beyond the fact that the appetite-control mechanism in the hypothalamus of the brain has gone awry. Nonetheless, the best evidence to date suggests that while genes, socioeconomic factors, or cultural factors are the culprits in many cases, psychological factors are the culprit in others, and where psychological factors are involved, they are similar to those that trigger other gastrointestinal disturbances.

There seem to be three kinds of obesity—that which is acquired early in life, that which results as a reaction to a life crisis, and that which sets in with maturity. Researchers disagree over what proportion of obese people fall into each category. Nevertheless, genes may well be the culprit in cases where the obese victim has other family members who are obese as well (although the genetic mechanisms of obesity are not well understood). Socioeconomic factors and cultural attitudes toward eating undoubtedly contribute to many cases of obesity, because obesity is more common among lower socioeconomic groups and cultures such as Italians, Jews, Irish, and West Indians, who eat a lot of carbohydrates. But psychological factors appear to be the culprit in other obesity cases, notably those that fall into the first two categories—obesity from an early age or obesity acquired in reaction to a life crisis.

A study reported in a 1967 issue of *Psychosomatic Medicine,* for instance, on twenty-one superobese persons (all but four of whom had been huge since adolescence) revealed that most had had a traumatic childhood of some sort. Nine of the twenty-one had had a parent die before their sixteenth birthday (a 1962 study also found that a lot of obese individuals had lost a parent during childhood); fourteen out of twenty-one had parents who were divorced, separated, or not happy together; and eleven out of twenty-one had had a domineering or overprotective parent, and were still pathologically dependent on their parents as adults. One girl, for example, eloped at age nineteen but moved back home when her mother tracked her down and demanded that she do so. She stayed at home for five years, seeing her husband on the sly, until her first pregnancy. At that time she secretly left home again with her husband and didn't return. A young man lived with his parents until age twenty-four, then married a girl because his father advised it. Still a third patient married a man she had never met, after her mother arranged the match with the groom's family.

Obese patients are often only or youngest children, this study (as has another) likewise revealed. Such birth positions are understandable, because those in them are in a favored position for overprotection or domination by parents; and obese victims, as we have seen, often have overprotecting and dominating parents. Obese patients likewise tend to have distorted body images, to make somewhat greater than average use of fantasy, and to overeat in reaction to a wide variety of emotional stimuli, such as worry, distress, boredom, excitement, amusement, or even sexual arousal. In one test, obese people ate significantly more food after viewing an arousing film dealing with humor, sex, or violence than they did after watching a travelogue. In fact, persons prone to obesity may be more emotional in general than nonobese persons. Obese students were found to react far more emotionally than nonobese students to tape recordings of detailed accounts of the Hiroshima bombing and leukemia cases.

The Psyche and Other Gastrointestinal Problems

Gastroenterologists have long observed that constant bad breath is a common physical manifestation of depression, that teeth grinding may be the result of repressed anger, that trench mouth may occur in periods of emotional disturbance and life stress, and that constipation may result from depression or obsessive-compulsive thoughts and behaviors. More research is needed to explain why the stomach is the target organ in some emotional conditions, the large intestine in others, the esophagus or gallbladder in still others, and so on, and how the psyche conspires with genes, various foods, drink or drugs, food poisoning, allergies, or other physical factors to produce various GI disorders.

4

THE ASTHMA
AND OTHER
ALLERGY BIOTYPES

THERE IS NO DOUBT that people's lungs, noses, and skin react dramatically to thoughts and emotions. We await revelations with "bated breath," astonishment "takes away our breath," and we "hold our breath" in trepidation. When we experience envy and hostility, our "noses are out of joint." We describe painful experiences as "paying through the nose," and noses also "sniff out trouble." If you squeak through a tough situation, it's by the "skin of your teeth." Sensitive persons are admonished: "Don't be so thin-skinned!" "No sweat!" means that there is nothing to worry about.

But can thoughts, emotions, behaviors, and specific life experiences cause so-called allergic conditions of the lungs, nose, or skin—conditions like asthma, hay fever, perennial rhinitis, eczema, or hives, which are generally believed to be due to somatic reactions to pollen, animal hairs, dust, or other physical allergens? Yes, in many instances. A classic example can be found in the case of a lady who, in 1886, was convinced that she had an allergy to roses. Her physician, however, suspected that her allergy was of psychological origin. So on her next office visit, he exposed her to an artificial rose. She immediately started tearing and sneezing.

In a 1968 study, subjects with asthma, emphysema, or other kinds of lung disease, as well as healthy subjects, were led to believe that they were inhaling allergens that cause constriction of the lungs, whereas they were only inhaling spray from a salt solution. Out of the forty asthmatics, nineteen reacted to the bogus allergens with lung constriction, and twelve developed full-blown asthma attacks. One subject developed hay fever as well as asthma when she was told that she was inhaling pollen. On another occasion, when she was informed that the allergen was dust, she developed asthma only. The forty healthy control subjects, in contrast, did not react to the artificial allergens.

Further evidence that the psyche can trigger so-called allergic conditions comes from clinical observations of psychiatric patients. Such patients rarely suffer from asthma, but when they do, their asthma usually alternates with their psychological symptoms rather than occurring simultaneously, strongly suggesting that the same psychological conditions are triggering either asthma or psychosis. Two men, for example, suffered asthma for years, but once psychotic depression set in, their asthma disappeared. A young boy alternated between bouts of schizophrenia and asthmatic wheezing. A woman who was successfully treated for asthma promptly succumbed to paranoid delusions and hallucinations; when her psychosis cleared, her asthma crisis returned.

Other factors than the psyche can spark apparently allergic conditions too, notably: a genetic predisposition (immune weakness) toward pollens, molds, dust, animal hairs, or other allergens in the environment; weather conditions, especially changes in temperature or barometric pressure; respiratory infections; menopause or other hormonal changes; fatigue; and noxious fumes. And in still other allergy cases—perhaps the majority—both psychological and physical factors conspire together to create the disorder.

A 1966 study reported in *Psychosomatic Medicine* found both somatic and psychological predisposing factors present in 75 percent of hay fever, perennial rhinitis, asthma, and eczema victims, whereas both factors were absent in 75 percent of a control group of subjects without allergies—a highly significant difference. More specifically, when a person in either the allergic or control group had an intense psychological or a minimal somatic predisposition toward allergies, neurotic disturbance was likely; when neither factor was intense, no overt emotional or somatic complaints were likely; and when both predispositions were intense, allergic symptoms were the rule. A fourth category was also observed in a small number of cases in which an intense somatic predisposition alone resulted in allergies. Most frequently, though, somatic and psychological factors occurred together, strongly suggesting that the combination of the two usually leads to allergic illness.

Granted that the psyche is involved to a greater or lesser degree in most so-called allergy cases, are there also specific thoughts, emotions, behaviors, or life experiences that often set the stage for specific allergic conditions? There seem to be, and they are remarkably similar to those of some other disease personalities discussed so far—notably a dominating mother and ineffective father, leading to excessive dependency needs; repressed hostility and other negative emotions; an attempt to redeem one's self-esteem through neatness, conscientiousness, self-sacrificing works, or other obsessive-compulsive behaviors; an unusually sensitive nature; sexual problems; and a triggering of the disease by stressful life situations. In some cases, the helplessness heightened by an extremely stressful situation is also accompanied by a deeply ingrained sense of hopelessness about life, and a victim may even die. Nonetheless, there are some variations on this personality theme and some unexpected inputs too. So let's examine each individual allergy biotype.

The Asthma Biotype

Bronchial asthma, which consists of periodic attacks of wheezing and breathing difficulties, can be not only extremely frightening and debilitating but even lead to death by suffocation unless medical treatment is promptly initiated. Other attacks, however, are less severe. Asthma also frequently has its debut early in life. Whether asthma starts in childhood or later in life, though, it often has its origin in a less-than-satisfactory childhood setting.

Retrospective studies conducted during the past forty years suggest that many asthma victims have a dominating mother and ineffective father, a situation also often encountered among gastrointestinal sufferers, as we saw in the last chapter. A 1975 investigation started with an editorial letter being placed in three leading newspapers in the Boston area. The letter called for volunteers to participate in a study examining high-risk factors in asthma sufferers ages six to eleven. Some two hundred parents of such children responded to the letter. The researchers then selected twenty-one asthmatic boys from the volunteer families and carefully matched them with nineteen nonasthmatic boys, because childhood asthma is twice as common among boys as girls. Both the subjects and their mothers were then psychologically tested. Attachment patterns between the mothers and their sons and even between the mothers and their own parents were especially probed. As the investigators reported in a 1976 issue of the *Annals of Allergy,* the asthmatic boys were significantly more overprotected and overindulged by their mothers than were the nonasthmatic boys. Also intriguing was that the mothers of the asthmatic boys tended to have been overprotected and overindulged by their own mothers and to have been rejected by their fathers. This finding suggests that the psychologically unhealthy childhood environment that often predisposes one to asthma may go back more than one generation, as we also saw for ulcerative colitis in the last chapter.

Overprotection and indulgence, however, aren't the only forms of maternal domination that can set the stage for asthma. Domination can also consist of excessive stimulation or physical affection; manipulative, intrusive behavior; or even seductive, erotic behavior. Regardless of the forms maternal domination takes, however, it often persists even after the asthma-prone person reaches adulthood. Likewise, asthma victims are frequently only children or the youngest child, which is understandable, because these children are particularly susceptible to maternal attention and domination. Several case histories illustrate how maternal domination and paternal ineffectiveness, especially in only children, often precedes asthma.

Henry C. had a mother who spun a maternal cocoon around him, while other youngsters his age moved step by step out into the world of independence and responsibility. "No dear, you must stay home; it's safer that way," was his mother's frequent admonition. When Henry suffered his first asthma attack at age ten, his mother became even more solicitous. Rough-and-tumble games with his peers were severely limited; sports were out. Henry was not even allowed to go away to college because Mother was sure that he couldn't take care of himself properly. Even now that Henry is grown and married, his mother complains that his wife is not giving him the care he needs.

Then there is William F., the only child of an upper-class family. Although William's father is an Ivy League graduate and a highly successful business entrepreneur, he left William's upbringing to his wife, a handsome, outspoken, and aggressive woman who antagonizes many people she meets. Mrs. F. mapped William's future out from A to Z, more specifically from a fancy prep school to Yale. Then, when William suggested that he would like to become a physician, Mrs. F. pulled strings with a medical school so that her son could enroll. William is now grown and a doctor, yet his mother still orders him about when he comes home. Not surprisingly, William was asthmatic from childhood.

A third asthmatic with a dominating mother is Douglas J., age ten. Because Douglas was born after three miscarriages, his mother smothered him with care. "He was such a weakling as a baby!" she claims. By age four Douglas developed asthma. Today Douglas is only a mild asthmatic, whose breathing is virtually unimpaired. Yet his mother still often keeps him home from school and takes him to the doctor's frequently.

Other asthmatics, however, seem to have mothers who treat them with ambivalence rather than overprotection, as the following case history illustrates.

Joshua H. had a mother, a member of a fundamentalist religious sect, who preached hellfire, frequently beat her children with a belt, and claimed she had toilet-trained Josh by the time he was eight months old. Yet she was also a practical nurse, loving toward Josh when he was ill, rubbing his head and ministering to his physical needs, sometimes even seductively. Meanwhile, Josh's father fluctuated between jovial and volatile moods, taking his children to the circus or terrorizing them with a hot poker. Josh was also deeply anxious that his father was going to leave him, especially one time when he lost his father in a railway station. Josh's father did in fact eventually drift away from the family. So neither Josh's father nor mother gave Josh the childhood love and security he needed. He became asthmatic at age seven.

Still a third group of asthmatics seems to have parents who are outright harsh and rejecting, as the following histories reveal.

Lyle L., age nine, has been asthmatic since infancy. He spends a lot of time in the hospital. Lyle's father was away from home for long periods when the boy was very young, and he is extremely intolerant of illness in himself or others. So he constantly exhorts Lyle to stop taking his asthma medication. Lyle also has a two-year-old sister, who is asthma-free and clearly his father's favorite. Although Lyle's mother gives Lyle affection, she is a weak person and incapable of altering her husband's behavior toward Lyle.

Theodore S. suffered from asthma during childhood. His mother was a driving, ambitious woman, his father a hardworking physician, and, like Teddy, an asthma sufferer, but he took great pride in denying his illness. Neither parent gave Teddy much attention, even during Teddy's asthma attacks. Then, when Teddy was 12, his father died from an asthma attack, and his mother died from kidney disease a year later. Teddy didn't feel much grief over either parent's death. He went to live with his aunt and uncle and, interestingly, his asthma attacks stopped, perhaps because the source of his problem—his parents—had been removed.

Maternal domination and paternal ineffectiveness, or parental ambivalence or rejection, affect the asthma-prone person apparently by filling him with excessive dependency needs—either because he was made too dependent while young or because his dependency needs at that time went unfilled—a situation comparable to that of the gastrointestinal personalities, as we've seen. Such dependency needs can be seen in Teddy, discussed above. After Teddy's parents died and he went to live with his aunt and uncle, they were critical and even disparaging of him. Though his asthma ceased, these attitudes, combined with his own parents' neglect of him, turned Teddy into a timid, fearful person who all his life was nagged by a sense of dissatisfaction and failure, especially in comparison to his successful father.

Excessive dependency needs can also be detected in an asthmatic named Trevor S. Trevor's father died when he was young, and he was raised by his wealthy, sensuous, redheaded mother. Trevor worshiped her, but her affection for him was not that strong, and in fact, when she fell in love with her riding master and married him, Trevor was forced to go live with his aunt and uncle. The aunt and uncle didn't give Trevor much love either. So as Trevor grew up, he became increasingly quiet and passive. He didn't marry until he was thirty-five, and then only to a woman remarkably like his mother, wealthy and strong-willed. But unlike his mother, she loved him. Trevor thus found the mother figure he had craved since childhood and lived happily with her for many years.

Similar to other dependent, helpless biotypes, the asthma biotype likewise tends to be fatalistic. George W., for instance, didn't develop asthma until he was fifty-four years old. Yet he often neglected to take his asthma medication and refused to give up smoking. When his doctor berated him for his behavior, he neither pleaded guilty nor was apologetic. "What will happen will happen," he insisted.

The asthma-prone person frequently learns to repress hostility and other negative emotions early in life. The parents of asthmatics often teach their children that the expression of angry, hateful thoughts toward one's parents, siblings, or other people is unacceptable. The parents of Josh, described above, for instance, insisted that Josh should protect and love, not hate and envy, his six younger brothers and sisters. Their overall command was: Grow up!

Having thus learned to repress negative emotions during childhood, the asthma biotype tends to sublimate them later in life as well. Only when Teddy, described above, saw a psychiatrist because of recurrence of his asthma, did he begin to realize how angry he felt over the lack of love he had received as a child. Similarly, Sylvia R., a fifty-year-old asthmatic, remembers her childhood only in glowing terms—belonging to a popular girls' club, being on the school paper, attending gala parties, and so forth—yet asthma delayed her entry into grade school, and her father committed suicide when she was twelve. Asthma, in fact, is sometimes a substitute for expressed anger, because, when asthmatics learn to express their rage, resentment, or other repressed negative emotions during psychotherapy, their asthma can improve dramatically.

The asthma-prone person often attempts to redeem his low self-esteem through obsessive-compulsive behaviors, such as neatness, conscientiousness, and altruism. A 1956 study compared four hundred asthmatics to a large number of control subjects and found the asthmatics to be significantly more obsessive-compulsive than the controls. A Swedish researcher studied thirty adult asthmatics and found that they were usually punctual, polite, conscientous, self-disciplined, and had a keen sense of duty. Many had been employed at the same place all their lives, worked in spite of severely debilitating asthma attacks, and would even go to work the day after an all-night attack. Like the cancer biotype, in fact, the asthma biotype tends to give more than he receives. Take again the case of Sylvia R. As an adult, Sylvia gave extravagant gifts to people and supported at one time an unemployed husband and at another time an alcoholic boyfriend.

An oversensitive nature is another hallmark of the asthma biotype. Seventy-nine percent of a group of asthmatics were found to be oversensitive, compared to 56 percent of a healthy control group. Sexual problems also crop up rather frequently among asthma victims. Sometimes these difficulties arise from an asthmatic marrying out of dependency needs. After high school, Jackie I. married a twenty-two-year-old bank clerk, "because the other kids were doing it." In two years she was divorced. Her second marriage was to an unemployed lifeguard, whom she supported by working as a department store buyer. The following year she divorced him, too. Then she married an attorney ten years her senior and probably a father figure for her, since her own father had committed suicide when Jackie was an adolescent. After they were married a short time, however, her husband stopped having sexual intercourse with her. Rather than confront him about it, probably for fear of losing him, she put up with it—for ten years. Finally the reason for her husband's behavior became evident: his sole means of sexual gratification during those years had been photographing naked girls. When this activity came to the attention of a grand jury, he committed suicide—ironically, just as Jackie's father had.

Other times, though, the asthmatic's sex problems hark back to toilet training, because those asthmatics with the greatest psychosexual conflicts often had their asthma start right after this period. This period, which extends from ages two to three, is, in Freudian terms, the "anal phase" of psychosexual development. A prime example of an asthmatic whose sexual difficulties started at this phase of his life is Josh, discussed above. Josh's mother toilet trained him at an age much earlier than average—eight months. She also alternated between harsh and indulgent behavior, and Josh's father was largely ineffective, ulti-

mately deserting the family. At three years of age, Josh started dress-
ing up in his sister's clothes. Eventually, he started trying on his
mother's clothes. Even as an adult he indulged in transvestite urges.
The reason? "Part of me wants to be hard, part of me wants to be soft,"
he told his psychotherapist. In other words, his transvestite desires
probably arose from his having a dominating, yet indulgent mother
and an inadequate father. He was not sure which parent to identify
with sexually, and even if he identified with his mother, he was not
sure which aspect of her personality it should be.

Loneliness is another characteristic of the asthma biotype. A 1966
psychological probing of seventeen asthmatics revealed varying de-
grees of dissatisfaction in interpersonal and social relationships. Many
of the patients made comments such as "I feel left out in the cold,
alone," or "I feel shut out." (Other reseach, intriguingly, has shown
that the physiological changes in the lungs that accompany such emotions are similar to lung changes that actually occur when people are
exposed to the cold.) A prime example of an asthmatic suffering from
loneliness is Josh, whose parents had not given him the love and security he needed. In later years Josh sublimated these negative experiences with happy, nostalgic recollections of his childhood, particularly
as his parents died and his siblings moved away. Such nostalgia might
not have been particularly harmful to Josh, but he was so wrapped up
in it and in his unfulfilled childish needs that he failed to make friends
with colleagues at work or with his neighbors.

Josh's life also underscores one of the major psychological triggers of
asthma—loss of a mother or mother figure. Josh suffered his first
asthma attack at age seven, when his grandmother died. His grandmother represented the only real love and security he had ever known.
Josh also experienced asthma later in life under similar circumstances.
His asthma recurred when his wife became pregnant with their first
child, probably because pregnancy deprived him of the support and
attention his wife had previously given him. Then, when his wife became pregnant with their second child, his asthma became virtually
continuous and crippling.

Another example of a person whose asthma flared up when he was
threatened with loss of a mother figure was Oscar W. Oscar was hospitalized with severe asthma at age seventy-six. His doctor found him to
be sensitive to cat and dog hairs and told him to get rid of his cats.
"Nonsense!" he replied. "I've been around cats, dogs, and horses for
more than sixty years, yet I haven't had an attack of asthma since I
was fourteen." Oscar then went to see a psychiatrist on his own initia-

tive, suspecting that his asthma might have a psychological basis. And sure enough, that was the problem. Oscar had developed asthma after his wife had become an alcoholic. His wife was loving when sober but verbally and physically abusive when drunk. Oscar couldn't tolerate the latter behavior and was furious with her. Yet because he was excessively dependent on his wife both emotionally and financially, he didn't dare to confront her about her drinking. The result: attacks of asthma.

Other kinds of adverse life events can spark asthma, too, such as marital or family problems, divorce, threat to the security of a loved one, sexual conflicts or temptations, one's children leaving home, or even fears about sex. Mabel K., for instance, had had asthma since childhood, but it required only occasional treatment. Yet when Mabel's two daughters left home, one to marry and the other to go to college, Mabel's asthma attacks became more frequent and severe. Then there was Martha P. Although Martha had suffered from asthma as an adolescent, she was free from attacks until right before she married. Wheezing then began to occur, mainly in the evening, when she would see her fiancé. Her doctor gave her medication and advised her to marry as quickly as possible. During the wedding ceremony she felt well, but then she became so breathless that the honeymoon had to be canceled, and her mother took care of her. Eventually, as she was getting no better, her physician probed into her life and discovered that she had some deep fears about sex. He reassured her on this subject and urged her to return to her husband. After that, Martha's asthma began to improve.

Asthma can also be set into motion by repressed negative emotions or by adverse life events combined with repressed emotions. Take Bill B., an accountant who was continually reprimanded by his boss in front of junior staff members. Bill made no attempt to defend himself. Instead, the reprimands gave him asthma attacks, and as the recriminations became more frequent and severe, so did Bill's asthma. Finally he was forced to see a psychiatrist about his health, and after the psychiatrist helped him stand up to his superior, his asthma gradually went away. Or take the case of Ralph J., who enjoyed a happy, healthy childhood until age sixteen, when the family business, which he was to eventually inherit, went bankrupt. The bankruptcy devastated Ralph's parents, yet they refused to discuss it among themselves or with Ralph. Ralph became tired and listless and withdrew from his friends. His school grades plummeted. Summer came; his nose stuffed up. Autumn arrived; he developed a cough. Then asthma struck him so forcibly that he had to be hospitalized. When a physician probed into

Ralph's life, Ralph was reluctant to discuss the family bankruptcy. Finally he mentioned it but hastily added, "We never think any more about it."

When adverse life events are combined with an allergy or with a respiratory infection, they sometimes trigger asthma too. In the nineteenth century a French physician and asthma sufferer named Armand Trousseau returned home unexpectedly early and heard a noise in the loft of his stables. He climbed to the loft and caught his coachman stuffing oats into a sack, ready to steal them. Because Trousseau had trusted this man, he was especially angry. But just as he prepared himself to confront the coachman, Trousseau was seized with the most severe asthma attack he had ever experienced. When writing about the attack later, Trousseau decided that it had been triggered by dust in the loft plus his anger, because he had been exposed to loft dust many times before and had suffered only mild asthmatic attacks. Then there is Nancy P., a teen-age victim of frequent attacks of bronchitis. One night, while Nancy was home alone and in bed with bronchitis, a burglar broke into the house. She was so terrified that she developed an asthma attack. After that, whenever she had bronchitis and was emotionally distressed, she experienced asthma. Yet neither bronchitis alone nor emotional upset by itself was sufficient to bring on asthma.

When stressful life events are combined with entrenched hopelessness about life, they can spark not only asthma but death. Take the case of Josh, whose life we've followed above. Because Josh suffered increasingly severe attacks of asthma after his children were born, and because he became increasingly depressed about life, he decided to undergo psychoanalysis. His despair was revealed in one of the comments he made to his analyst: "Everybody takes away everything I've got, or so it seems—one by one. Everything that I've got has to go; and what do I have left? Nothing but an empty bag. [Pauses, breathes heavily, sighs, then sobs.] First it was my teddy bear, then my blanket, then my crib. I don't know. I'm always losing something. Pretty soon I'll have nothing." Then Josh took a break from work and analysis to visit his brother. The trip lifted his spirits and improved his asthma considerably. On September 1, however, as Josh and his wife returned home, Josh admitted to her that he dreaded having to go back to work and analysis. On September 6 Josh experienced a severe asthma attack. Then on September 10, the day he was to resume work and analysis, he left home in apparent good health. But while driving to work he suddenly pulled his automobile over to the side of the road and slumped over the steering wheel. Two men working nearby saw what had happened and rushed over to the car. But it was too late: Josh was dead from an asthma attack—and smiling, perhaps because he had fulfilled his own prophecy, "Pretty soon I'll have nothing," or perhaps because he had finally obtained what he wanted most, to be united with the mother he had never really had. Indeed, during his analysis, he had made frequent references to "wanting a loving, caring, touching mother," and once said that he created his mother inside himself in the "feeling of asthma."

The Hay Fever and Associated Biotypes

Hay fever, which consists of an itchy nose and eyes, nasal discharge, sneezing, and some other symptoms, generally occurs in the fall and spring. Of all the so-called allergic disorders, it appears to be most clearly due to a bodily response to allergens—specifically to pollens that are wind-borne in the spring and fall.

Nonetheless, hay fever can have personality inputs as well. A longing for mother love or a rejection by one's mother has been linked with hay fever. One study found that hay fever sufferers, when compared to healthy controls, tended to be somewhat more unstable, timid, anxious, and sensitive and considerably more obsessive-compulsive and hypochondriacal. Adverse life situations, such as bereavement, marital or work problems, or sex conflicts have also been known to trigger hay fever.

Personality, however, appears to play a greater role in perennial rhinitis, which is characterized by a chronically stuffy, runny, or itchy nose, particularly when no allergic basis can be found for it, when it is not caused by a deviation of the septum of the nose—thus obstructing breathing on one side of the nose—and when it is not caused by polyps, an unfavorable climate, abuse of nose drops, or chronic sinusitis. The chronic-rhinitis biotype, some anecdotal evidence suggests, tends to be a dependent individual of low confidence, similar to the asthma personality. And like hay fever sufferers, when chronic stuffy or runny nose victims were compared to healthy subjects, they too were found to be somewhat more unstable, timid, anxious, and sensitive and considerably more obsessive-compulsive and hypochondriacal. Chronic stuffy or runny nose has also been known to be sparked by a number of situations—emotional stress, emotional stress combined with an allergy, emotional stress combined with a perfectionist trait, and, interestingly, boredom, which is a sort of inverse emotional stress. Several case histories illustrate these situations.

A year ago, Alex N. was a remarkably successful landscape artist. She made a lot of money, and her services were in great demand. Then she fell in love, got married, and gave up her career because her husband didn't want his wife to earn more money than he did. Besides, he looked forward to Alex cooking delicious meals for him, as his mother used to. Now Alex is so bored she could climb the walls, and she dreams at night of planting huge bushes and trees on rolling, green lawns. She has also succumbed for the first time in her life to a chronically stuffed-up nose, postnasal drip, and weepy eyes.

Marsha C. of Canada, in contrast, is a longtime chronic-rhinitis sufferer. Marsha has also been long aware that her condition is triggered both by her allergy to mold, dust, and cigarette smoke and by emotionally stressful situations. For instance, if she is apprehensive about a social affair, the smoke in the room bothers her a lot more than usual, so that her nose and eyes run. And when she is under a lot of pressure at work, she is also more likely to have a runny nose than otherwise.

Then there is JoAnn T., who admits to being a perfectionist and who notices that her nose stuffs up and her eyes water when she gets involved in church work. "I get so keyed up," she exclaims, "and I want everything to turn out just so."

Another perennial rhinitis victim, Sam E., says that at any first sign of a stuffy nose or eyes watering, he knows what the problem is—boredom. When he does something exciting, like racing his sports car or playing rock music, his symptoms vanish instantly.

Skin Allergy Biotypes

So-called skin allergies, such as eczema—which can irritate a person so badly that he scratches himself bloody—and hives—which causes itchy, inflamed welts on the skin—can indeed be caused by allergies to pollen, poison ivy, foods, drugs, insect stings, and other physical irritants. However, they can also be triggered by psychological factors. Personality, in fact, plays a considerable role in hives, probably more so than in hay fever and perennial rhinitis.

Eczema sufferers, for instance, often have, or had, parents who stroked and patted their skin a lot, slept with them when they had eczema to keep them from scratching, gave them everything they wanted when they were sick, yet treated them strictly when they were well. Such parental behavior tended to encourage dependency and sickness in these individuals, rather than independence and health. And throughout their lives they have an excessive need for physical contact.

Like many asthma sufferers, numerous eczema patients tend to repress negative emotions, and like many asthma, hay fever, and rhinitis sufferers, they tend to be exceptionally sensitive by nature, especially to situations where they lose love, approval, or status. Their exqui-sitely sensitive nature, in fact, is yet another reason why they repress negative emotions. That way they can avoid confronting people and getting hurt.

As might be expected, many of the personality traits found in other allergy victims can also be detected in hives patients. Chronic hives sufferers are often timid and dependent, anxious about the loss of a mother figure, extremely sensitive by nature, and obsessive-compul-sive in their habits. They tend to turn negative emotions in on them-selves; such repression alone, in fact, is sometimes sufficient to spark hives. Yet hives can also be set into motion by a variety of stressful life events. Eighteen-year-old Patty F., for instance, developed hives fif-teen minutes after hearing of her father's death by a horrible accident. He worked in a factory, and one day his clothes got caught in the ma-chinery. He was pulled into the machine and suffered a mutilating, painful death. Similarly, Jack F., a longtime hives sufferer, was relax-ing in an armchair, free from hives, when the phone rang. Because his wife was seriously ill in the hospital, he feared that she might have died. By the time he picked up the receiver, he was covered with hives.

On still other occasions, though, hives can be sparked by a stressful life event combined with a physical vulnerability toward a particular allergen. Rose M. developed hives when exposed to sunlight while her husband had a long and serious illness. But as soon as he recovered, sunlight no longer gave her hives. Then, several years later, family members accused Rose of influencing the drafting of a will in her favor. Rose was so upset by the accusation that sunlight once again gave her hives. After the will was settled, however, Rose no longer in-curred hives from sunlight.

One aspect of hives, however, differs from other so-called allergic conditions discussed in this chapter. It usually doesn't strike people until they reach their late twenties and usually stops afflicting them by the time they reach their senior years. Why should hives be so selec-tive about a victim's age? Is it due to some difference in the body's sus-ceptibility to allergens during these years? This is unlikely, because the body's immune system tends to be at its peak during adolescence and to decline progressively from then on. It's hard to imagine what would be so different about a person's personality between ages thirty and sixty-five that would trigger hives only at this time of his life. More stressful life events? Possibly. A number of challenging factors con-verge in middle life—physical prowess declines, youthful beauty fades, goals may not have been achieved, childbearing becomes more difficult if not impossible to achieve, grown children leave home, and so forth. But even if one's middle years are characterized by exceptionally stressful events, why don't asthma, hay fever, chronic rhinitis, and eczema also selectively strike victims during those years, since they too are often triggered by traumatic life events?

The hard truth is that much more needs to be learned about the role of personality in various allergic disorders. For instance, while asthma has long been linked with an unhappy childhood, the scientific basis for such a connection is not as strong as that which has been made between an unfavorable childhood and some other diseases. There is probably stronger evidence that specific personality constellations influence the severity and chronicity of asthma. What is really needed to convince skeptics that a traumatic childhood, specifically a dominating or rejecting mother, can help set the stage for asthma is a prospective study, and none has been conducted to date.

How might such a study be set up? Dr. Caroline Thomas of Johns Hopkins Medical Institutions, who exhaustively analyzed the personalities, physical health, and family health histories of medical students some years ago, and who has since found that certain childhood conditions helped set the stage for cancer and heart disease in some of her subjects later in life, might use her extensive data bank to learn more about the role of an unhappy childhood in asthma. How many of her subjects, who are now in their forties and fifties, have succumbed to asthma later in life? How many of those subjects had dominating or rejecting mothers? If Dr. Thomas could find that asthma sufferers in later life tended to have dominating or rejecting mothers as children, it would certainly strengthen retrospective evidence of such a link. It would also strongly suggest that even individuals who suffer asthma as children may well have incurred the condition because they have dominating or rejecting mothers rather than that their mothers became dominating or rejecting because of their children's precarious health.

Dr. Thomas might also be able to use her extensive prospective data base to learn more about when allergy triggers asthma and when personality does or when both factors conspire together. For instance, how many of her subjects who later in life suffer from asthma had dominating or rejecting mothers as children? How many were found to be allergic to allergens when younger and how many come from a family with a history of allergies, suggesting a genetic predisposition toward allergens? Such information could go a long way toward clarifying the role of early-childhood conditions in precipitating asthma.

More studies, too, are needed to confirm and further elucidate the childhood experiences as well as other personality traits common to allergy sufferers. If these studies cannot be prospective investigations, then they should at least be retrospective ones that use carefully matched health subjects as controls. Such controls have frequently been lacking in the past. As W. Linford Rees, a leading researcher into the psychosomatic aspect of allergies, wrote in a 1976 issue of *The British Journal of Psychiatry*, "The success of future research in this field will depend on the precise definition of hypotheses which are capable of being subjected to rigorous scientific testing."

5

THE
RHEUMATOID ARTHRITIS
BIOTYPE

HER NAME WAS Charlotte T. She grew up with many privileges that young girls of her era and even today would envy—frequent trips to the opera and theater, ice skating and skiing, summer vacations on an indigo blue lake, the best in books and clothes. Yet Charlotte's well-to-do, swashbuckling father, complete with moustache, vested suit, and gold pocket watch, was also arrogant, emotionally cold, excessively strict with Charlotte and her brother (sometimes strapping them with a belt), and a Victorian male chauvinist as well. Scorning women's inferior mentality, he expended generous funds to send Charlotte's brother to college but refused to put out a dime for Charlotte's higher education. Yet it was Charlotte, not her brother, who loved to learn. In fact, the brother eventually flunked out of college.

Many years later, at age fifty-six, Charlotte came down with rheumatoid arthritis, the most serious, painful, and crippling of all kinds of arthritis. It not only assailed Charlotte's joints and crippled her limbs, wrists, and fingers but eventually wore down and corroded the rest of her body. Charlotte died from RA at age seventy—a tragically gnarled and scrawny caricature of her formerly elegant, youthful self.

Might there be a connection between Charlotte's unfavorable confrontations with a strict, cold, and unfair father and her later devastation by rheumatoid arthritis? Very possibly, because a personality basis for RA has been increasingly well identified, and particularly because numerous rheumatoid patients recall having had one parent who was harsh, punitive, arbitrary, outright rejecting, or interested in his or her children only for enhancing his or her own ego.

Another RA patient who experienced a rejecting and dominant parent (this time a mother) was Fern D. Fern's childhood seemed to be that of a Cinderella without benefit of a prince charming. She was the youngest of several sisters. Her very attractive sisters had been sent to private schools at great financial sacrifices to the parents. But the parents did not give Fern the same luxuries. Fern recalls shopping with her mother for evening dresses for her sisters and understanding well that Mother would fix up one of her sister's old dresses for Fern's own school dance.

Yet another RA victim who had a harsh mother was Wilhelmina G. Willie recalls her mother tying her hands to her crib so that she wouldn't masturbate. Once Willie's mother got so angry with Willie while bathing her that Willie was afraid her mother might actually drown her.

Rheumatoid arthritis patients often remember their other parent as gentle and compliant but essentially ineffective next to his or her more flagrant spouse. (Charlotte recalled her mother in warm, glowing terms, yet it was clear that her father overshadowed her childhood). In other instances, though, the other parent is inconsistent rather than milquetoast. As one rheumatoid patient said about her father, "He was quiet, but watch out!" And in still other cases, the other parent was physically absent from home beginning early in the patient's life. In all cases, however, it was the dominating parent who left her (or his) imprint on the future rheumatoid victim.

That many RA patients are firstborns or only children also fits in with many of them having had an excessively dominating, strict parent, because more is generally expected of firstborns and only children than of youngsters in other birth positions. On the other hand, a number of rheumatoid patients, like Charlotte and Fern, cited above, tend to be the youngest children. Might such a birth position also predispose a person to RA? Possibly. Although the baby of the family often gets the lion's share of the parents' love, this is not always the case, as Charlotte and Fern illustrate. They actually got less love than their older siblings. Such unfair treatment left them feeling embittered and probably helped prepare them for arthritis later in life. So it's quite likely that other RA patients who were the babies of the family might have incurred similar abuse from their parents.

Other unfavorable childhood experiences can precede RA, too, however, and may likewise set the stage for the disease. A 1969 Finnish study of one hundred adult RA patients found that over a third had come from broken homes—thirty-two had lost a parent through death before age sixteen, two had parents who divorced or separated, two were born out of wedlock, and one was rejected by his parents and left to outside care. Moreover, sixteen of the one hundred patients had lost a sibling through death by age sixteen. Then in 1978, eighty-eight children with rheumatoid arthritis in the Rochester, New York, area were compared to some three thousand nonarthritic youngsters in the same area. Twenty-nine percent of the youngsters with RA were found to have lost a parent through death, divorce, or separation, compared to only 11 percent of the controls. Furthermore, three times more arthritis patients than controls were adopted, implying that adoption might sometimes serve as a psychological stressor that can help prep a person for RA.

A prime example of an adult rheumatoid victim who experienced not only one but a number of these psychological stresses as a child is Ann P. Eight months before Ann was born, an older brother got diphtheria and died. So Ann arrived in an atmosphere of grief, and at her birth her mother had an accident that resulted in hemiplegia and speech impairment. Ann was then cared for by an aunt, who died when Ann was eighteen months old. After that, Ann was raised by her grandmother, who restricted her thumbsucking and pushed her into toilet training. Finally, Ann was given back to her natural parents when she was age seven, and her memories of them both are profoundly tragic—her mother "just a stick on a head in bed," and her father "a pair of legs going down stairs."

However distressing one's childhood, however, it does not seem to be sufficient in itself to pave the way for RA. Susceptibility also seems to depend on how a person reacts to such a childhood, because siblings of rheumatoid patients often remember their parents being as strict as the patients do, but such harshness didn't upset them nearly as much. Still other evidence suggests that rheumatoid victims are overly sensitive by nature. So possibly it's hypersensitivity combined with a traumatic childhood experience that helps prepare a person for RA. (Hypersensitivity, in any event, can definitely exacerbate RA once it sets in. One rheumatoid patient, Linda G., received a mildly critical letter from her mother; within a few hours her finger joints swelled up so badly that she couldn't remove her rings. Another patient, Polly R., experienced a painful swelling of her joints hours after she felt that her mother had snubbed her.)

How can the distressing childhood experiences so often incurred by the rheumatoid biotype actually affect them? Usually by shattering their egos, by leaving them feeling worthless and rejected. Such psychological castration, in fact, seems to persist for life, because many adult rheumatoid patients have been found to be timid, submissive, conforming, and helpless. These qualities are often translated into their leading quiet lives; being shy and introverted; having trouble making friends; being reluctant to change jobs, residences, political or religious views; feeling inferior and being unduly concerned about their looks, clothes, and the impression they are making on other people. Charlotte T., for instance, often complained to her husband and children, "I would so much like to go out and get a job, but who would hire me?" Charlotte, in fact, had secretarial and bookkeeping skills that she could have readily marketed, yet she never did pluck up the courage to sell herself. Before Fern D. actually came down with RA, she saw a psychoanalyst because she had a phobia about becoming pregnant. "During Fern's first year of therapy," the analyst recalls, "Fern cried incessantly and presented herself as a helpless little girl who could not cope with sexuality, let alone maternity."

Rather than act like clinging vines, court the favor of others, or allow themselves to be used, rheumatoid biotypes often try to mask their weak, dependent natures with brash, bossy, or even tyrannical behavior. In many instances, in fact, they seem to deeply resent leaning on others and want to be more independent. Such a desire is revealed in their often dominating their own children, just as their parents often dominated them. In other words, while rheumatoid persons tend to worry and do a great deal for their children, at the same time they tend to "lord it" over their children.

Regardless of the form that the rheumatoid biotype's weak ego takes, it probably helps prepare him for the disease. One reason to believe that this is the case is that relatives of rheumatoid patients who have rheumatoid factor in their blood—an antibody complex often found in the blood of rheumatoid patients and which may be a sign of a biological predisposition toward the disease—have been found to show greater ego strength than do relatives without the factor. By ego strength we mean a more positive, self-confident outlook on life. The former more often answered "true" to statements such as "I am inclined to go out of my way to win a point with someone who has opposed me," whereas the latter more often answered "true" to comments such as, "I worry quite a bit over possible misfortunes," and "People often disappoint me." So, just as ego strength might save persons with rheumatoid factor from coming down with rheumatoid arthritis, a weak ego combined with the factor might well open individuals to it.

Even with a stressful childhood, hypersensitivity, a weak ego, and rheumatoid factor, however, a person might still not get RA if he didn't also bottle up his negative emotions and assume a Pollyanna stance that "Everything is fine." In 1957 thirteen rheumatoid patients and their siblings were compared psychologically. The former were found to show pronounced signs of introversion and repression of emotions, while the latter manifested extroversion and less emotional repression. In 1958 Seymour Fisher and S. E. Cleveland, two psychosomatic researchers, wrote in their book, *Body Image and Personality:* "We were struck by how much difficulty arthritics had in expressing anger. They rarely lost their tempers and even in situations of considerable frustration maintained an affable attitude. It seemed as if they were afraid to express anger and felt it necessary to contain it inwardly in a tightly controlled fashion." In a 1963 study, male rheumatoid patients admitted to angry feelings to a lesser extent than did a control group of their male relatives. And in 1969, a California psychologist compared thirty rheumatoid patients with other disease patients and found that the former were particularly prone to checking their hostility.

Charlotte T., for instance, illustrates the rheumatoid biotype's tendency to rein in negative emotions. In all the years they were growing up, Charlotte's children saw her become outraged only two or three times. Otherwise, she tended to express her anger in an indirect, rather childish manner. Once Charlotte was so tired of her husband being away from home on business that she collected her children together and quietly stole off with them for a weekend in another city. When her husband came home, he was frantic that something had happened to his family—precisely the effect Charlotte wanted to achieve. This, then, was her way of telling her husband she didn't like him traveling so much rather than directly confronting him on the issue.

Another rheumatoid patient who has always repressed negative emotions is Fern D. During Fern's psychoanalysis, her therapist noted that "hostility and aggression appear to be unknown to her." A third rheumatoid patient who tends to check his hostility is Abe J. At one time in his life, Abe was pretty good about "blowing his top" when he was mad at somebody. But during the past several years, he has taken to restraining his irritation more and more and to "stew" about problems rather than try to solve them. It was during this period that Abe got his first symptoms of arthritis. A fourth rheumatoid victim, Kevin O., goes so far as to boast that he never fights or gets upset with anyone, and a fifth rheumatoid patient, Frank J., says, "If I get mad, I just swallow it and keep the fire inside."

But why should rheumatoid victims withhold their negative emotions? One reason is that they probably were not allowed to express such emotions as children, particularly by their domineering, strict parents. Another reason, it seems, is that they are afraid that expression of rage, anger, or resentment might deprive them of the emotional support they so desperately crave from their parents, spouses, children, or friends. If Charlotte had told her husband off for traveling so much, for instance, she might have alienated him, and he might have ended up spending even more time on the road than he was already doing. Abe is afraid that if he doesn't always play "Mr. Nice Guy," fellows down at the plant won't continue to include him in their after-work visits to Teddy's Pool Hall. In still other instances, however, the rheumatoid-prone person appears to repress negative emotions because the expression would reveal not only his helplessness but his profound sense of despair about life. A prime example is Ann P. After Ann's aunt (substitute mother) died, Ann changed from being an irritable child, who was a feeding problem, to one who was silent and rarely cried. When Ann went to live with her real parents again at age seven, she was overwhelmed by her mother's sad mental and physical condition. She felt her mother was "different" from other children's mothers, in the sense of "mutilated and insane." She wept bitterly but soon regained control and never showed her feelings again until years later, in psychotherapy.

That repression of negative emotions can so often be found among rheumatoid victims, of course, does not prove that such repression is one of the factors that triggers the disease. A number of studies, however, suggest that this is the case. One researcher, in fact, claims that persons who keep a tight rein on their hostility are *five* times more likely to develop RA than are persons who "let it all hang out." What's more, when rheumatoid patients express repressed rage in psychotherapy sessions, or as a result of psychotherapy, their disease often goes into remission, strongly implying that repressed anger got the disease underway in the first place.

Carla N. showed no emotional response to psychotherapy over a year. She finally broke down during an interview and wept because her husband had forgotten her birthday, then became furious for the first time in her life. This outrage was followed by total disappearance of her symptoms—pain, joint swelling, fatigue, and morning stiffness. And as a result of her psychotherapy, another rheumatoid patient, Mabel S., finally vented years of pent-up resentment against her husband by hitting him over the head with a chair. Although the encounter didn't enchant her husband—he had to be rushed to the hospital emergency room for a head-suturing job—it made Mabel feel fantastic. Her rheumatoid symptoms subsided dramatically after the encounter and remained quiescent for many weeks.

Still another reason to believe that the withholding of negative emotions can help set the stage for rheumatoid arthritis is that the disease is common among New Englanders. Aha, you say, New Englanders are especially prone to this disease because of the harsh New England winters! Yet cold has never been shown to cause RA, although it is known to aggravate the disease once it sets in. On the other hand, New Englanders are famous for their emotional reserve. Might the fact that they tend to check their emotions make them particularly susceptible to rheumatoid arthritis? It certainly is a possibility.

Rheumatoid biotypes don't *always* suppress negative emotions, however. And when female rheumatoid patients let such emotions out, they usually direct them against their husbands, even if their spouses weren't the immediate cause of their charged feelings. That the husband is often the target of the rheumatoid wife's pent-up rage might in fact explain why the husbands of rheumatoid wives often get stomach ulcers. If these husbands are typical ulcer personalities, they probably have a strong need for emotional support but get a cold shower instead. As a result, an ulcer may ensue. The reason why female rheumatoid patients, who often have strong dependency needs, got together in the first place with men with strong dependency needs is not altogether clear. Even with clashing dependency needs, though, rheumatoid wives and ulcer husbands are apt to report that their marriages are satisfactory. Why is this? Because both rheumatoid wives and ulcer husbands tend to be Pollyannas? Because the wives have some sadistic tendencies and the husbands some masochistic ones? (The husbands of rheumatoid wives are known for waiting on their incapacitated wives.) Or perhaps because they complement each other in areas other than emotional support?

Male rheumatoid patients, on the other hand, are not often married to women with stomach ulcers, probably because they don't direct anger toward their wives as much as female rheumatoid patients do toward their husbands. In fact, male rheumatoid victims have been found to channel even less anger toward their spouses than do healthy men. Possibly, rheumatoid husbands don't feel as mad as rheumatoid wives do. Or maybe their anger is so submerged that it never surfaces toward their wives or anybody.

What both male and female rheumatoid patients do tend to share, however, is sexual difficulties. The men often abstain from sexual intercourse or have trouble satisfying their wives sexually. The women often have little sex drive or obtain little sexual satisfaction from intercourse. And most crucially, such problems existed long before their rheumatoid set in, so the problems cannot be blamed on the physical disability and pain that comes with the disease.

Why should rheumatoid patients have sex difficulties? For one thing, as discussed above, they tend to be shy, inhibited, and conforming, and persons with such traits often have trouble expressing themselves sexually. A good indication that the rheumatoid personality withholds his sexual urges can be found in the fact that he draws figures, tells stories, and interprets Rorschach inkblots with voyeuristic, exhibitionistic, sexual connotations—such as "a figure in transparent dresses," "a man with something on under his suit," or "a woman undressing, but spied on by a peeping Tom." Yet when researchers confront the rheumatoid personality with the sexual implications of his fantasies, he flatly denies them and complains of his shyness and sexual inadequacy. Still another indication that the rheumatoid person would like to express himself sexually but is afraid to do so is that show-offs, loudmouths, braggers, and eager beavers tend to incense him. A matter of jealousy perhaps?

As far as female rheumatoid victims are concerned, however, there may be yet another reason why they have sex problems. They often despise being women, probably because they dislike being dependent and submissive ("feminine") and yearn to be tough and independent. Rejecting their sex role, they undoubtedly find it hard to submit to a man during intercourse. Some female rheumatoid patients, in fact, admit that they prefer to assume the topside male position during intercourse.

There is another trait that probably also keeps rheumatoid patients from expressing themselves freely in the sexual arena—a mental rigidity that also transforms itself into a physical one. Rheumatoid patients are apt to be righteous and moral. They tend to perceive their bodies as firm, enclosed, and well delineated, in contrast to ulcer patients who are likely to visualize their bodies as open, diffuse, vulnerable, and mushy. Rheumatoid patients interpret Rorschach inkblots as "a man in armor," "a cement-covered post," "a sea crab with a hard shell," or "a hollow container filled with uncontrolled fluid material and surrounded by a hard, inpenetrable surface," whereas ulcer patients interpret inkblots as "a body cut open" or "a bullet piercing flesh." Rheumatoid patients seem to be physically rigid even before they get arthritis. For instance, Fern D.'s therapist writes about her: "Her hands were not only immobile but lifeless and inert. This was an interesting phenomenon, since it occurred at a time when she had no arthritic involvement whatever."

The rheumatoid biotype's mental and physical rigidity, in fact, probably translates itself literally into disease because RA is a disease of the body's "hardware," particularly one that makes the body stiff and rigid. As the authors of *Body Image and Personality* write: "One could conceive of the arthritic as a person who has certain unacceptable impulses over which he is so fearful of losing control that he has found it necessary to convert his body into a containing vessel whose walls would prevent the outbreak of those impulses . . . selectively utilizing a particular layer of his body (striate musculature) to achieve a protective wall about him. . . ." A psychoanalyst noticed that when one of his patients suppressed anger, she tensed up certain areas of her body. It was precisely those areas of her anatomy that were eventually afflicted with rheumatoid arthritis. Another patient, accused of infidelity by her husband, developed RA in her wedding ring finger that ultimately spread to all her fingers.

In spite of their physical rigidity, though, rheumatoid patients—at least before rheumatoid sets in and often even afterward—tend to be very active physically. They hunt, fish, engage in other sports, garden, vigorously houseclean, or serve others. In the 1940s some researchers collected extensive psychological information about patients with seven different diseases—rheumatoid arthritis, asthma, ulcer, ulcerative colitis, high blood pressure, neurodermatitis, and thyrotoxicosis. On the basis of this material they formulated personality profiles for the seven diseases; one of the outstanding characteristics of the rheumatoid personality was excessive physical activity coupled with a strong need to serve others. The material was then altered so that the disease of each patient was not mentioned, and turned over to nine independent psychoanalyst judges. The judges scrutinized the material and solely on the basis of the disease personalities drawn by the researchers guessed what disease each patient had. The judges were more successful at picking out the rheumatoid patients than any of the others, and one of the characteristics that particularly tripped them off was the rheumatoid personality's excessive activity and need to serve.

Why should the rheumatoid biotype be so active? One reason might be that the suppression of negative emotions and sexual urges, combined with a mental and physical rigidity, probably fill him with lots of energy that need an outlet of some kind. Another explanation is appealing, too, though: because the rheumatoid personality's mother (or father) punished him by depriving him of physical freedom, whenever he had a chance as a youngster he found release by climbing trees and fences and engaging in sports. Indeed, many rheumatoid patients were exceptionally active as children, and many female rheumatoid patients were tomboys. Fern D., for instance, not only swam but hunted and fished. In fact, it's extremely interesting that rheumatoid-prone persons often prefer hunting and fishing to other kinds of physical activity. Perhaps these two sports gave them an exceptional opportunity to get away from a dominating parent—that is, to escape to the fields and lakes—and they continue to prefer such sports as they get older because they help make them feel free and independent.

The physical involvement of the rheumatoid biotype is in fact so blatant that in many instances it can be considered obsessive-compulsive. Rheumatoid patients were often outstanding varsity players or even professional sportsmen when younger or before their disease struck. And if given a choice, they would "fish Lake Ochechobee for six weeks straight." What's more, they tend to be neat, clean, and punctual and to work so hard for others that it borders on masochism. Charlotte T., for instance, would have preferred holding down a paying job after her children grew older, but because she didn't have the courage to seek a job, she threw herself into housework and cooking— which she despised. In the evenings, after dinner, Charlotte's husband and children would urge her to quit the kitchen and watch television with them. Yet Charlotte rarely did, preferring to fuss around in the kitchen and to fume "poor me." Even as an adolescent, Fern D. assumed a great deal of responsibility for the care of her baby brother. For many years she was nursemaid and practically a second mother to him. Another rheumatoid patient, Dale C., helped support her family for sixteen years after her father died, and during these years she was incredibly active physically. On some days she would walk several miles home from work, then after dinner take the bus across town in order to rollerskate. She also helped maintain and repair her family's house.

Why should the rheumatoid biotype carry his physical activity to such extremes? It doesn't seem to be due entirely to his sublimination of negative emotions, sexual urges, aggression, and other impulses. Such activity also helps the rheumatoid individual achieve the praise and other ego reinforcements he so desperately needs. Fern D., for instance, admitted to her therapist that she had taken care of her brother to court her father's praise, since her mother had never cared much about her. Physical activity probably also helps the rheumatoid personality mask his dependency needs. And by serving others, he can sometimes even dominate and control them, thus fulfilling his yearnings for independence. Charlotte T. would often make her husband and children feel so guilty while fussing around the kitchen in the evenings that they would leave their favorite television shows to help her clean up. Such a move gratified Charlotte's need for attention and praise. Yet another reason why rheumatoid patients are hardworking, self-sacrificing, and perfectionist is that they often had mothers who were the same way. One patient recalls: "Mother was an excellent organizer and a hard worker in the home. She could do more work than all the kids." Says another: "Our home was open to anyone, even strangers. You were always welcome. Mother would give anyone anything and go without herself." That many rheumatoid patients are particularly interested in cooking may be because they unconsciously identify with their dominating, obsessive-compulsive mothers.

Do the rheumatoid biotype's obsessive-compulsive behaviors help set the stage for his disease? Scientists aren't sure. Some believe that such activities are an outlet for self-destructive impulses that cause RA. Others believe that such behaviors help trigger RA because they reinforce the rheumatoid personality's weak ego, dependency needs, and lack of personal and sexual fulfillment. What is certain, however, is that such behaviors can wear down the body and aggravate rheumatoid after it has already set in (see Chapter 8).

And what is also a certainty is that stressful life situations ultimately set the stage for rheumatoid arthritis to strike, just as they do with so many other diseases. In fact, evidence for such a link is ancient. According to Proverbs (17:22): "A merry heart doeth good like medicine, but a broken spirit drieth the bone." In the seventh century A.D. rheumatoid arthritis was attributed to emotional shock. In 1909 R. I. Jones wrote in his book *Arthritis Deformans*: "That mental shocks, continuous anxiety and worry may determine the onset of rheumatoid arthritis is, I think, beyond question. In one of my own series, the patient, a woman, developed rheumatoid arthritis within a few days of seeing her husband killed by an accident. In another, the disease set in rapidly in a female who, whilst skating, fell through the ice and received an acute fright as well as a severe chill."

Many other kinds of psychological trauma have also been known to trigger rheumatoid—death of a loved one; loss of a loved one after nursing him through a long illness (Charlotte's arthritis set in after she nursed her best friend through terminal cancer; a lady named Bessie E. developed rheumatoid after the death of an aunt whom she had nursed for three years and who ultimately turned against her); witnessing one's husband being convicted of a crime; sex problems (Harry M. got rheumatoid after a homosexual encounter; Eleanor O. after a hysterectomy that left her feeling "like a neuter"); pregnancy; nightmares; fears of bodily harm; strange surroundings; being inducted into the U.S. Army. (The incidence of rheumatoid arthritis, incidentally, shoots up during wartime.)

Children who get RA are also often struck with it in the wake of a psychological trauma, such as parental separation, divorce, or death or even sibling rivalry. Although personality inputs into other kinds of arthritis than rheumatoid have scarcely been documented, emotional stress has also been noted to trigger muscle rheumatism on occasion. And while animals do not get rheumatoid arthritis, the stress of over-crowding can intensify arthritis artificially induced in rats and also slow their recovery from it. What is the time span between a psycho-logically upsetting event and the time that rheumatoid strikes? Gen-erally, anywhere between two months and two years.

It's not only the events themselves that finally trigger rheumatoid arthritis, however, but also the rheumatoid biotype's tendency to feel helpless or even hopeless about them. And when a rheumatoid victim feels hopeless, as is the case with numerous other disease personali-ties, the emotion seems to be even potent enough to kill him. Take the case of Charlotte T., whose life we've been following. At age sixty-five, Charlotte found the professional outlet she had always wanted when her husband bought a boutique and let her run it. Even though Char-lotte had had arthritis for a few years, and she put in long, arduous hours at the store, her disease became remarkably quiescent, and Charlotte would come home in the evenings effervescing with stories about her customers and boasts about her sales. After several years, however, Charlotte's husband pressed her to sell the boutique so that they could retire in Arizona. Many wives would have been overjoyed by such an opportunity, but Charlotte was devastated by it. She would have to give up what she had always dreamed of—professional self-fulfillment and social status—to become again a hausfrau, a nothing. Nonetheless, she finally gave in to her husband, and six months after they sold the boutique her arthritis flared up more severely than it had ever done before. In spite of moving to Arizona and receiving the best medical care, Charlotte's health plummeted distressingly over the next three years. Charlotte died from RA at age seventy, showing that rheumatoid can kill, at least when combined with helplessness and despair.

Several other traits can also often be found among rheumatoid vic-tims and deserve some mention. For one, the victims often come from lower-class backgrounds, which may explain why they are particu-larly prone to having dominating, strict parents who end up shattering their egos. In addition, the limited education, unfulfilling jobs, and fi-nancial problems that often haunt individuals from lower-class back-grounds might serve as psychosocial stressors that help predispose select persons to rheumatoid arthritis. Another characteristic found among female patients is that they often had parents who were status incongruent—that is, the husband had more social standing or educa-tion than the wife, or vice versa—or that they themselves have more or less status and education than their own husbands. Social discrepancy would undoubtedly put a person under some stress, even in a socially loose society like the United States. Further, there are indications that persons who come from families that are socially incongruent tend to have less self-esteem than those who come from families that aren't. So if a person is already a rheumatoid personality—has a weak ego, repressed negative emotions, obsessive-compulsive habits, and so forth—then the mental stress and lower self-esteem that comes from social inconsistency might be just the extra emotional strain needed to tip the scales in favor of rheumatoid arthritis.

Male rheumatoid patients, however, are less likely than female rheumatoid patients to come from homes with status inconsistency. Female rheumatoid victims also especially recall a parent being unduly strict with them and are particularly incensed by such treatment. That both parental domination and parental social incongruency are especially common among women may help explain why rheumatoid arthritis is more prevalent among women than men, particularly as it does not seem to be due in any way to female sex hormones. In fact, just the opposite seems to be true. Female sex hormones may actually protect against RA, because female rheumatoid patients generally feel much better during pregnancy, a time when sex hormones are at exceedingly high levels in the female body.

Yet another reason why more women today have RA than men do may be because they had Victorian parents who downgraded the female sex and who, as a result, nurtured unfulfilled, frustrated, and hence disease-prone adult women. As we've seen, many rheumatoid females despise their sex. One rheumatoid patient, Jessica I., gets extremely anxious and angry at men during menstruation, although she keeps her feelings tightly in check. Charlotte T. never recovered from her father's conviction that women are inferior to men. Throughout her life she proclaimed, "Men have it easier, men get all the breaks," etc. Charlotte also hated her broad, womanly hips and large female breasts, envying women with "Twiggy" figures. Fern D. once told her therapist about a dream she had in which she ripped her husband's penis out of his body. "But the dream is directed at you and my father as well as at my husband," she insisted. "You men are all so cocky!" Another rheumatoid-prone woman who hates her sex is Florence E. Flo, who had a conscientious, cold mother and a father who deserted the family when she was two years old, feels that even today the position of women is unbearable. She once said, "I would rather die than tell my husband I love him. Then I could never be on top." Still another rheumatoid victim who despises being a woman is Janet A. Although Janet has never had an orgasm during intercourse, she takes on one lover after another to control them psychologically. She often dreams of destroying and castrating her lovers. "I feel like grabbing what they have," she declares.

Now that most Victorian parents have passed on, and younger generations of women with more enlightened parents are achieving social status and professional fulfillment comparable to that of men, it will be interesting to see whether the incidence of rheumatoid arthritis among women declines. If so, it would provide ammunition for the position that rheumatoid arthritis is a disease that especially strikes frustrated women.

Meanwhile, though, rheumatoid arthritis is vastly more common than most people realize—8 million Americans and 350 million people throughout the world have it. Consequently, more insights into the rheumatoid biotype are urgently needed. For instance, a prospective study should be undertaken to convince the skeptics that personality traits identified in rheumatoid patients via clinical impressions or retrospective studies precede the disease and are not the result of it or of the powerful drugs that rheumatoid patients often take. More information is also needed about how personality causes RA. For example, RA appears to have an autoimmune basis; that is, the body's immune system mistakenly attacks the body rather than bacteria, viruses, or other foreign invaders. How might thoughts, emotions, and behaviors interact with an autoimmune phenomenon? Might personality actually translate itself into an autoimmune disease? (More about this in Chapter 8). Another pressing question is what percent of rheumatoid cases are caused by autoimmunity, what percentage by personality, and what percentage by other possible causes, such as genes or viruses? (Evidence for a genetic basis is not very strong, however, even though RA can sometimes be found in more than one member of a family, and evidence for a viral cause for rheumatoid is presently more speculation than established fact.) And in what cases does personality interact with one or more of these other triggers?

Even while these questions are pending, though, evidence for personality contributions to rheumatoid arthritis is strong and consists not only of the above but of some other provocative aspects that simply cannot be ignored. For instance, you would think that rheumatoid patients would be particularly depressed while suffering from the symptoms of their disease. Yet many of them seem to feel *less* depressed while suffering than when they are not. Their depression and physical disease may have a common psychological origin that expresses itself in either psychological or physical terms, not both. Similarly, rheumatoid arthritis, like asthma, is rare in psychotics, but when it does occur, it tends to alternate with the psychotic symptoms, suggesting that both have a common psychological basis that expresses itself in either a mental or physical disorder. What's more, the appearance of certain patients severely crippled with RA resembles that seen in catatonia—both conditions display rigid, expressionless faces and mutism. The catatonic patient cannot move because of psychological inhibition; the arthritic patient because of physiologic restriction. It is conceivable that rheumatoid arthritis, when accompanied by such severe disability, may represent a physiological counterpart of the psychological stage of catatonia. Take, for instance, Fern D., whose life we've been following. Even before Fern got RA, you may recall, her hands tended to be immobile and lifeless. And when she got angry at her mother during psychoanalysis, the anger awakened such a deep terror in her of being killed by her mother that she became temporarily paralyzed. Fern's later RA, then, might also have stemmed from a similar terror.

In fact, rheumatoid arthritis may even defend some patients against a psychotic breakdown. Certainly this is the belief of one rheumatoid patient, Elmira W. Elmira recalls occasions in her childhood when she was extremely frightened by her mother's sudden attacks of vomiting. At such times, Elmira indulged in a sympathy protest of sorts—intense abdominal pains of her own. Later she reacted to her mother's vomiting attacks with overeating, and then with some of the psychological traits of the rheumatoid biotype, such as obsessive Hausfrauing. Then she came down with RA. Today she claims, "My stomach pains, overeating and arthritis are my reality, security and sanity. Without them I can't live. If I were to ever really relax, feel and weep, I fear I would disintegrate."

Yet another intriguing item that substantiates the rheumatoid biotype is that husbands of rheumatoid patients may be at risk of getting the disease themselves. And finally, the fact that remissions among rheumatoid patients are very common and can last weeks, months, or even years suggests that personality factors can not only spark the disease but reverse it as well.

6

THE
HEADACHE
BIOTYPES

BACK IN THE SIXTEENTH century a young woman, the first child of King Henry VIII of England, was disowned by her father when he divorced her mother to remarry one woman after another. In fact, the young woman even had to fear being poisoned because she represented a threat to his other heirs. Finally, however, the political climate in England was such that she became its ruler. And once she was queen, she launched a persecution against Protestants that earned her the name of "Bloody Mary."

Unknown to many people, Mary Tudor was subject to migraines. This is one of the most common and severe kinds of chronic headaches—usually on one side of the head, terribly painful, and often accompanied by nausea, vomiting, visual and other neurological disturbances. In fact, Mary even got a migraine during her coronation. As one of her biographers writes: "Mary rode in an open litter, clad in splendid blue velvet, with a jeweled diadem so heavy that its weight on the usual headache—she was having one of her bad days—was sheer agony, so that for part of the way she tried to ease the blind pain by resting her head on her hand." Intriguingly, Mary also possessed a trait that is considered to be the hallmark of the twentieth-century migraine personality—an extremely strong conscience: a compulsion to do what's right, to achieve perfection, to do one's duty. Or, what Freudians call a tough "superego."

Early in life Mary became a carbon copy of her Spanish mother, Katherine—pure, pious, rigid, a staunch believer in doctrinaire Catholicism, with a spirit that brooked no compromise in matters of faith. Mary's major guide throughout her life was her "conscience." For instance, her father once urged her to turn her living quarters over to the brother of her Protestant stepmother, Anne Boleyn. Mary refused. "If I agreed," she wrote her father, "I should offend God." Later in life Anne courted Mary's friendship. Mary gave her the cold shoulder, explaining that it was a matter of honor and "conscience." And even though Mary was in love with Philip of Spain, the reason she married him was because he too was a Catholic and thus able to help her reinstate the Church in England. She spoke to God of her husband as "a man who, more than all other . . . reproduces Thy image. . . ."

A conscience fills a valuable function in society. It keeps people within the bounds of what is considered acceptable behavior, and it often even earns them the highest praise—"a fine, upright man or woman." Because conscience is closely allied with idealism—after all, both traits boil down to striving for perfect results—it also helps people produce great works of art, science, and technology. However, excessive scrupulosity can hurt society, because the individual with such a trait tends to be rigid and intolerant of imperfection in others as well as in himself. In her effort to purge England of Protestants, for example, Mary exhibited such intolerance. But also crucial is that the excessive pursuit of "one's duty" can hurt the person possessing the trait—by setting the stage for a migraine.

Take today's prospective migraine sufferer. He learns early in life to do his duty, whether it is excessive work, striving toward perfection, or both, thanks to the influence of a dominating parent, grandparent, babysitter, or even the military service. As one adult migraine sufferer, Monica S., recalls, "Dad was irritated as hell whenever he caught us reading a book instead of working." Says migraine victim Fred K., "Mother considered sitting down such a waste of time that we boys weren't even allowed to sit down for meals." And a third migrainer, Maribelle G., comments, "Mother would beat me every time I made a fuss about working."

However, it doesn't seem to be only exposure to a duty-oriented figure that turns a child into an excessively scrupulous person. Such molding is more apt to take place in an extremely sensitive and impressionable child, because siblings exposed to the same model don't necessarily end up becoming duty-bound. Migrainer Charlie D., for instance, was considered by his mother to have been the most obedient of her three children. In recalling his childhood, Charlie says: "If mother told me to be there or do something, I would do it. My necktie had to be just right and my scarf pin in the correct place. My trousers had to be the proper size and length, and I was always polishing shoes. I took time about bathing and getting dressed. I was the last one to appear at table at every meal because I was so concerned about washing my hands properly. That was quite the opposite of one of my brothers, who always arrived with dirty hands."

Migraine biotypes also tend to take exceptionally good care of their toys, protecting them from destruction and from other children. Says migrainer Dolly Q., "I was extremely careful with my dolls. In fact I still have all of them, carefully preserved and clean."

In other words, the strong attention to duty acquired by migraine biotypes as children carries over into their adulthood as well. Even back in 1937, psychosomatic-medicine pioneer Harold G. Wolff pointed out that most migraine victims are unusually ambitious and preoccupied with achievement and success in one or more areas of their lives, conscientious, perfectionistic, persisting and exacting, bestowing order wherever possible. They love lists, headings, titles, subtitles, card indexes, arranging, classifying, enumerating, and statistically manipulating.

Such traits are benign or even commendable, of course, in that they bring people considerable productivity, personal satisfaction, and praise from others. They are detrimental, however, in that persons with these traits often fail to meet their own high standards, cannot delegate responsibility, tend to reduce their lives to cold mechanics, and even turn recreation into a chore. Migrainer Frances O. is so obsessed with housework that she calls herself a "Dutch cleanser." "When I wash," she says, "I change the water for each dish and rinse it thoroughly until I know that it's clean." Migrainer Linda B. admits: "If I tell the housemaid to do something, I like to follow her up to see that it is properly done." Lilly M., a migrainous schoolteacher with two teen-age children, says, "I realize now [after psychotherapy] that I was trying to make everything right in the *machine of my life*—my religion, my marriage, motherhood and social appearance for the sake of my children." Lillian P., a gardening migrainer, comments, "If there is one weed in 50 flowers, I'll see it." Otto W., a migrainous fisherman, observes, "I never take my eye off the end of the rod all night."

Sometimes the migrainer is so driven to "do his duty" that he is consciously haunted by the person who imbued him with such a harsh superego. Says migrainer Ian M., "Mother has been dead for 20 years, but I feel her ghost is looking over my shoulder." (Or as they say in a rural area of England, "Mother never be dead!")

The results of excessive duty, then, are often exhaustion, frustration, unfulfillment, or guilt. Comments Linda B., above, "I fuss and bother and worry about matters that I have turned over to someone else." A migrainous hairdresser, Jenny E., says, "If I give a wave, and it doesn't come out just right, it annoys me frightfully." Migrainer Larry

Q. admits, "Whenever I send a letter I feel compelled to place a postage stamp an exact number of millimeters from each edge of the envelope. I can't tell you what a chore that is for me." Migraine sufferer Bob B. asserts, "If somebody interrupts my tight schedule at work, boy, does that upset me." Then there is the case of two migrainous American missionaries taken prisoner by the Japanese during World War II. After they were freed, did they rejoice? No! They felt guilty because they hadn't been able to do any work during their capture. Said one: "The major tragedy of prison life is that one gets to like it."

The emotional and physical states described above place quite a strain on the migrainer's body. Then along comes an exceptionally stressful event. It is more than the migrainer's body can take. A migraine strikes.

Yet a second trait often characterizes the migraine biotype and helps set the stage for his attacks. This is the repression of negative emotions, revealed in such comments as "I am critical of other people but don't express it," "I can blow my stack at something but not someone," "I am very uncomfortable showing my anger," and "When I am tense, I don't show it." This trait, like excess duty, is also learned in childhood, tends to persist throughout life, and places a strain on the body, particularly when combined with excess duty. Then along comes an especially stressful situation, and a migraine strikes.

Mary Tudor possessed not only a grave attention to duty but also a tendency to repress negative emotions. At age seventeen she heard that her father had remarried Anne Boleyn—news that to her was both disgusting and a harbinger of danger. Yet rather than rant about it, Mary received it in silence and even tried to act cheerful. On another occasion, while queen, Mary was enraged by a French diplomat. Instead of telling him off, she swept by him without a word. As the diplomat later wrote: "She did this with such a wrathful countenance that there was no womanly gentleness in it."

A modern migraine patient who represses negative emotions is Carrie H. Carrie married a man who resembled the father she despised. She often got furious at him, yet all the time she was married to him she didn't suffer any migraines. A few years later, however, she married another man, who also occasionally angered her. Yet she was afraid to show anger because he filled important social needs for her, and she was afraid of alienating him. The result? Frequent migraines.

A third characteristic found among quite a few migraine biotypes can also help prep them for a migraine. This is an immaturity and insecurity that results from having a dominating parent and that leads to violent immature emotions, notably jealousy and rage, in the face of frustration—just as a small child would act. In other words, a migraine sufferer with such a trait is stuck at a very early narcissistic level of psychological development, and the slightest injury to his ego can provoke an intense emotional response. If a migrainer with such a trait is likewise prone to excessive duty and repression of negative emotions, then his body is a real powder keg of nerves. Along comes an especially stressful event, and poof, a migraine!

One migraine patient who is given to violent childish emotions is Melissa N. As a little girl, Melissa was exceptionally attached to her mother, both because her mother encouraged it and because her father didn't love her. Melissa remembers that traumatic day when she was four years old and her mother brought her baby sister home from the hospital. "I felt as if Mother dropped me in favor of Ellen," Melissa recalls. "Some weeks after that, Mother literally dropped Ellen, and I hoped that Ellen would die from the fall. But she didn't." Sibling rivalry is common among children, of course, but what is unusual in the case of Melissa and some other migrainers is that it persists well into adulthood. Melissa, at age thirty-six, is still extremely jealous of her sister. What's more, she sometimes transfers this jealousy onto other people, whether it's her husband, her own son, or herself.

Angela C. is given to both excess duty and explosive childish emotions. Angela was the youngest of seven children, timid, bashful, and obedient. "I was always a fussy person," she recalls. "I wanted things done just right." However, Angela was also extremely prone to temper tantrums and even throws them now that she is an adult. One time, for instance, Angela flew into a murderous rage against her daughter. "I started to undress her," she admits. "I wanted to murder her in the nude. It ended by my having a hysterical crying attack."

Interestingly, migraine patients who are subject to violent immature emotions are often prone to accidents as well. The reason? If a patient does not actually express his rage against others, he may turn it on himself, either as a migraine or in the form of an accident.

Fifteen-year-old Edna F. has suffered from severe migraine attacks since age ten. At that time, she fought with her brother, hitting his head against the stairs and almost killing him. She was terrified by her loss of control and shortly thereafter started having migraines, which were obviously a redirecting of her rage against her brother onto herself. Edna is also prone to accidents, particularly falling accidents, which also seem to be a redirecting of hatred toward her brother onto herself. In fact, even when she was four, Edna felt such intense jealousy after her brother was born that she "accidentally" set herself on fire and nearly burned to death.

Melissa N., cited above, is also highly accident-prone. Twice she almost burned to death—once, falling against the stove, so that her clothes caught fire, and another time when she cooked over the stove in a housecoat with long sleeves that caught fire. Melissa has also had numerous tripping and falling accidents and a near-fatal car accident, although she is an excellent driver. Psychoanalysis has revealed that both her migraines and her accidents are really suicidal equivalents, or the rechanneling of murderous rages against her sister Ellen onto herself.

Still another accident-prone migrainer is forty-four-year-old Rick E. Rick, who suffers from incapacitating migraines, also has frequent dizzy spells and lapses of consciousness. He claims he has "walking dreams" and often feels as if his head is "clouded." No wonder he often succumbs to automobile accidents and on several occasions was nearly run over while crossing the street. Interestingly, his father was also killed in a auto accident, and Rick has likewise witnessed a fatal car accident, which may have heightened his psychological vulnerability toward accidents.

Why are migraine patients particularly liable to fire and falling accidents? There is no ready answer. However, it may well be because "falling" signifies "falling from a parent's favor alongside a hated sibling," and fire represents "the total immolation of oneself alongside a vastly superior sibling against whom one cannot begin to compete." Some evidence for the former can be found in the case of Melissa N., who felt that her mother had "dropped her" in favor of her younger sister, and some evidence for the latter can be found in the case of Helen G.

Helen experiences a migraine whenever she smells something burning, because it reminds her of her dead brother, whom she envied and hated. Helen is also prone to fire accidents. Once she left the gas on on the stove and almost caused an explosion. Further, after her despised brother died, Helen developed a peculiar habit of masturbation. She would pull out her pubic hair, burn it, and experience an orgasm as it burned. The reason for this behavior? Apparently migraines and fires represented for her the opportunity to obliterate herself beside her hated, superior brother, and the burning of her pubic hair afforded her the opportunity to destroy that aspect of herself that she felt was most inferior alongside her brother—her female sex.

Not all migraine sufferers engage in such pathological sexual behavior, of course. Nonetheless, sex problems are rather common among migraine patients. One reason, it appears, is that migrainers are often rigid and intolerant of others. Hence they find it hard to adapt to the sex standards and techniques of their sexual partners. Another reason may be that migrainers are often so involved in hard work and perfectionist endeavors that they have little energy left over for sex. A third explanation is that migraine-prone persons, often scrupulous in general, frequently tend to be squeamish about the morality of sex as well. Such discomfort could understandably interfere with sexual spontaneity and fulfillment. Sometimes, in fact, migrainers' sex difficulties contribute to their migraines.

Rhoda P. loved her husband when she married him. After a year of marriage, however, she saw some serious defects in his character, and after two years she had lost total respect for him. At that time, she became sexually frigid and also started having severe migraines, which only relented when her husband was out of town on business.

Rich K., a medical student, not only strove to be an "A" student but held a part-time job as a night clerk in a hospital—pressures sufficient to set the stage for frequent migraines. Another crucial factor was also contributing to Rich's headaches. He was having an affair with a girl he could not afford to marry and, because of his staunch Irish-American Catholic upbringing, felt extremely guilty about it.

Sex problems, in fact, can even be implicated in some cases in directly launching a migraine. Mildred W., for instance, despises sex yet feels that it is her "marital duty." She often gets a migraine after intercourse with her husband. Jesse C. also despises sex but does not feel that it is her marital duty. She often gets a migraine when her husband wants sex and thus has an excuse to turn him down. Tina C., on the other hand, fears pregnancy. Several times lately she has had a nightmare in which she dreamed she was having a baby. Each time she woke up with a painful migraine.

Social problems, too, are frequent among migrainers, and the reasons are rather apparent. If a migrainer is sensitive and not able to take criticism, people are not going to feel very comfortable with him. If a migrainer is self-righteous and critical of others, he doesn't make very pleasant company either. What's more, those migrainers who are tense and worried and who turn play into work also usually lack a sense of humor and are incapable of fantasizing. But those migrainers to whom people are particularly liable to give a wide berth are those with explosive immature emotions—not because such migrainers necessarily express their emotions (they often take them out in their headaches) but rather because they tend to be dramatic, vain, selfish, and demanding—or what psychiatrists call hysterical personalities.

The migrainer's difficulty in getting on with other people can sometimes even directly spark his migraine. Jill S. has migraines whenever she has to spend an evening in the company of men beside whom she feels inferior and whom she deeply envies. Kistern P., being sensitive to criticism, gets a migraine whenever she has to meet someone who, she fears, will cut her down.

More often than any other disease or disorder, migraines can be set into motion by a great diversity of stressful events. What type of event will trigger a particular migrainer's headaches is largely determined by the particular character traits he possesses—whether he is sensitive, hardworking, and perfectionistic, represses negative emotions, is given to violent immature emotions, has sex problems, social problems, and so forth. Regardless of the kinds of events that trigger the migraine, however, the events all have something in common: migrainers feel helpless to cope with them—a situation comparable to what sparks many other kinds of diseases. And when a migrainer's sense of helplessness is combined with a sense of hopelessness as well, exceptionally frequent and excruciatingly painful migraines usually result.

While much is known about the personality characteristics of the migraine biotype, vastly more still needs to be learned, since the psyche plays an enormous role in this kind of headache (and in most kinds of chronic headaches for that matter). For instance, why do migraine sufferers whose headaches have a psychological basis select the head as a target organ for their distress? Researchers aren't sure. Some think it's because migrainers try to run their lives by "their wits," to the exclusion of their emotions, thus making the head a target for their pain. Others think that the head is a substitute for a sexual organ in those migraine sufferers who are always trying to "give birth" to a creation—in Greek mythology, Athena sprang from the head of Zeus; and "brainchild" and "laboring over problems" are common terms in today's vocabulary. Still other researchers suspect that the head represents a sexual organ for migrainers with sexual difficulties, and that for them, a headache, with its splitting, bursting, explosive pain, represents an orgasm. Migraine sufferer Emma G., for instance, had a traumatic relationship with her father and a homosexual relationship with a girlfriend and now has a frigid sex life with her husband. Because nearly all of Emma's migraines are followed by sexual orgasm and a feeling of "delicious relaxation," they appear to be Emma's sole means of deriving sexual pleasure.

How many migraines are genetic and how many are psychological? Because migraines can often be found in more than one family member, it is quite likely that they have some genetic basis. This might express itself as an extreme sensitivity of the blood vessels of the scalp to various influences, because abnormal reactions of these blood vessels underlie migraines. At the same time, it is possible that migraines are learned early in life from another family member suffering from them.

Can migraines be triggered by alcohol, chocolate, cheese, fried foods, weather, hunger, or sleep? Study results are conflicting. Also, might psychological inputs into a migraine conspire with such physical factors to trigger a migraine far more often than most people realize? Some seasonal migraines, for instance, which were attributed to allergies, have since turned out to be due to psychological stresses that occur seasonally. Geraldine H. is an ambitious, perfectionistic school teacher who has had migraines in the early fall for ten years. Although allergies might at first glance appear to be the cause of her migraines, this is really not so. Rather, her migraines are due to her great anxiety at the start of each school year over whether she will do a good job or not. Cindy W., on the other hand, is subject to migraines from June through October—months when her county welfare activities are at a lag and when she is bored and has no outlet for her sexual tensions (her husband is practically impotent). The result: migraines twice weekly until October rolls around again.

Psychological factors may conspire with sleep to trigger a migraine, according to a report in a 1977 issue of the British medical journal *Lancet.* A perfectionistic migrainer might have an especially tough day. While he is going through the rapid-eye-movement phase of sleep, his brain is desperately trying to integrate all the stresses he incurred during the previous day. But it doesn't manage to do so. The migrainer wakes up with an explosive migraine.

Why are migraines much more common among women than men? Is it due to some sex hormone differences, since female migraine sufferers often get migraines at the time of a menstruation and are often free of migraines during pregnancy? This is a strong possibility because sex hormones are known to influence blood vessels, and blood vessel abnormalities are known to underlie migraines. On the other hand, millions of women go through menstruation without migraines. So it's quite possible that women are more likely to get migraines than men not only because of their sex hormones but also because they are more prone to those psychological characteristics that predispose a person to migraines. The possibility of such a double jeopardy, however, has not yet been tested experimentally.

Finally, how about the fascinating psychological states experienced by migrainers before, during, and after migraine attacks? Are they the result of psychological changes that come with a headache? Or are they determined by the psychological predisposition of the migraine sufferer?

Although virtually no research has been conducted on these questions to date, it's plausible that the psychological sensations that often accompany a migraine—time-image distortions (everything around a patient seems to be moving fast), hallucinations and body-image distortions (one part of the body grows way out of proportion to the rest of the body or actually separates from it)—are the result of the headache altering the visual nervous pathways of the brain. Body-image distortions that come from migraines, in fact, gave author and migraine sufferer Lewis Carroll some ideas for his classic fantasy, *Alice in Wonderland.*

Alice, you may recall, entered a rabbit hole and saw a tiny passageway that led to a lovely garden. But she couldn't even get her head through, as the hole was so small. Then Alice saw on a table a bottle that said, "Drink me," proceeded to down all of its contents, and found her body "shutting up like a telescope." Indeed, she was only ten inches high. But then she remembered that she had forgotten the key on the table that unlocked the door in the tiny passageway. Now she was so small that she couldn't possibly reach the tabletop. Then her eye fell on a tiny box lying under the table, which contained a little cake that said, "Eat me." Alice ate it, in hopes of growing larger. And indeed, she opened "out like the largest telescope that ever was!" When "she looked down at her feet, they seemed to be almost out of sight, they were getting so far off." Then her head struck the roof of the hall. She was nine feet tall! and so on.

The depression that often precedes a migraine and occurs during it, however, as well as the exhilaration that often follows a migraine, could very well be due to the psychological state of the migraine sufferer rather than to the physiological changes brought about by the headache. In other words, a person comes down with a migraine when his mind and body are overtaxed; that is why he's depressed. The migraine purges him of whatever psychological and physical demons assail him. The headache then goes away and he feels like a new individual. Sound preposterous? Maybe. But consider these comments and reactions from migrainers after a migraine:

Watson H.: "That is one time when I feel like the person I really want to be, refreshed and renewed." Larissa R.: "I feel like a newborn baby." Ivy F.: "I begin to plan and dream; life seems full of freshness and glow." Then there is Eileen E., a middle-class, generally prudish spinster who dresses up "fit to kill" after a migraine and then parades down the street. At such times, she admits, "I have to be careful that nothing happens." But would Eileen be really upset if something did? In brief, it looks as if there is far more psychology to migraines than headache scientists have even begun to contemplate.

The Tension Headache Biotype

Along with migraines, tension headaches are the most common kind of chronic headache. However, whereas a migraine usually strikes one side of the head and inflicts sharp pain, a tension headache tends to encompass both sides of the head and create pressure or tightness on the head rather than pain per se. And whereas a migraine comes from abnormal expansion of blood vessels in the scalp, a tension headache derives from overcontraction of scalp, neck, jaw, and face muscles, accompanied by constriction of scalp blood vessels. Chronic tension headaches can be caused by physical factors such as defective vision, poor neck posture, sinus infection, or jaw clenching. However, they are also often triggered by the psyche. Several personality characteristics, in fact, have been noted among numerous tension headache sufferers and might be considered to constitute a tension headache personality.

A 1971 study reported in the journal *Headache* compared the personalities of chronic tension headache victims, migraine sufferers, and headache-free subjects and found some marked differences among the three groups. Whereas the headache-free subjects tended to be happy, carefree, and easygoing, and migrainers worrying perfectionists, tension headache sufferers were more apt to be chronically despondent and angry. But what particularly separated the migrainers from the tension headache sufferers was not so much a difference in the negative emotions experienced (after all, a number of migrainers are subject to jealousy and rage, as we've seen) as that the latter translated such emotions into muscular tautness and thus into tension headaches rather than into migraines.

What kinds of problems can trigger tension headaches? Quite a diversity, it seems. Take the case of sixteen-year-old Richard I. Richard had been suffering from severe tension headaches for a few months. Richard's physician first checked him out for any organic cause for his headaches. None could be found. However the doctor did unearth some probable psychological causes. Richard was not very happy, for a lot of reasons. He was a tall, gangly youngster with a tic in his left eyebrow, didn't have many friends, wasn't doing well in school, was uncomfortable about his family background (one sister died mysteriously, and two cousins had handicaps), and his domineering father would not let him get his driver's license. What's more, Richard's grandfather, whom he loved very much, died three months before.

It's generally not only despondency or anger that triggers chronic tension headaches, though, but also the repression of these negative emotions. The 1971 study comparing tension headache victims with migrainers and headache-free subjects revealed that both migrainers and tension headache sufferers tend to supress negative emotions more than healthy subjects do. For instance, control subjects, more than migraine or tension headache patients, strongly agreed that anger is the cause of much unhappiness and believed that if more people expressed their anger, they would feel better. In contrast, migraine and tension headache sufferers reported, much more than control subjects, that after they get angry at someone, they cannot stop thinking about what they wish they had said or done. Similarly, a 1972 study showed that both migrainers and tension headache victims tend to repress hostility.

A prime example of a chronic tension headache patient whose headaches appear to derive from repressed negative emotions is Amanda H. For months Amanda had a tension headache almost daily. No physical cause could be found. However, Amanda had a mother who insisted on intruding into Amanda's life, telling her and her husband how to spend their money and how to raise their children. Amanda would not tell her mother to back off, however, because she didn't want to hurt her mother's feelings. The result? Tension headaches.

Chronic tension headache sufferers don't always repress their negative emotions as much as migrainers do. But when they do let such emotions out, it tends to be in a sarcastic, bitchy, or otherwise unsatisfying manner, compared to the way the headache-free subjects express such emotions. Inadequate expression of negative emotions, as well as their total repression, might well contribute to muscular tautness and thus to tension headaches in many instances. Another difference between tension headache sufferers and migrainers is that whereas migrainers are apt to be superorganized, tension hadache patients tend to be disorganized and forgetful. Along with depression, anger, and the repression or inadequate expression of negative emotions, these traits might also lead to muscular tautness and tension headaches.

Still another trait often colors the lives of chronic tension headache patients and probably also contributes to their headaches. Their unhappiness or anger is often long-standing. Forty-six-year-old Rufus D. was a chronic tension headache victim. Although Rufus's physician couldn't find any organic explanation for his headaches, he did come up with a psychological one. For years Rufus had had a complex about his penis. He thought that it was undersized because he had masturbated as an adolescent. When his doctor reassured him that masturbation was almost universal among adolescent boys, that the size of his penis was well within normal range, and that there couldn't possibly be a connection between the two, Rufus exclaimed, "Why didn't somebody tell me that twenty-five years ago?" Rufus was so overjoyed with the news that he now has no more tension headaches.

In fact, the long-standing despondency or anger of the chronic tension headache sufferer may even hark back to his childhood. The 1971 study comparing tension headache sufferers to migrainers and headache-free subjects revealed that the former had been particularly prone to anger and temper tantrums as children.

Interestingly, though, the parents of the tension headache sufferers had been more likely to encourage the expression of anger than had the parents of headache-free subjects, and certainly far more so than the parents of migrainers. If this is the case, then why do tension headache victims often withhold negative emotions later in life or find that they are not able to express them in a satisfying manner? There's no ready answer. Lots more research needs to be conducted on the personality traits of chronic tension headache victims, because considerably less is known about these traits than about those of migrainers.

The Cluster Headache Biotype

Visualize a tall, husky American male with lionlike features and weathered skin reining in a sleek stallion at the foot of the Rockies. He shoves his cowboy hat back on a crop of thick hair, reaches into his leather vest pocket for a cigarette, and lights up. Lusty pleasure, then deep relaxation emanate from him. Sound like your typical cigarette-ad man? You bet!

But the cigarette companies might not be so proud of flaunting this male stereotype on bulletin boards and magazine covers if they realized that he has been known, on occasion, to burst into tears, jump off his horse and run in circles, or even stick his head into an oven or toilet bowl. The reason? The "macho" American male is particularly prone to cluster headaches—a rare kind of headache that can even outscoop migraines for excruciating pain and send a victim into a disoriented frenzy in order to seek relief.

A cluster headache, even more than a migraine, tends to inflict one side of the head. It is often felt deeply behind one eye but may radiate to the forehead, temple, cheek, and upper gum on the same side of the face. The nostril on the same side of the face can also ache and burn and run with fluid. The pain of a cluster headache has been described by victims as "burning, boring, piercing, tearing and screwing." The pain usually lasts anywhere from ten minutes to two hours. It may strike a victim for one day only or recur at the same time every day or night for a few weeks. Months or even years may go by between attacks. The physiological basis of the cluster headache appears to be an abnormality in the blood vessels of the forehead and particularly in the internal carotid artery as it enters the skull. A cluster headache is thus more closely related to a migraine than to a tension headache.

So why, you ask, should the macho American male be particularly prone to cluster headaches? A study reported in a 1974 issue of *Headache* may give us some answers. Men (and a few women) who were victims of cluster headaches were compared to outdoorsy nonheadache subjects and to migraine and tension headache subjects on a number of physical and personality factors. One of the first significant differences that emerged between cluster victims and other subjects was height. The former were considerably taller. Another highly significant difference was that 38 percent of the cluster headache group had hazel eyes versus 10 percent and 9 percent for nonheadache and noncluster headache subjects respectively.

Now, why should a tall person with hazel eyes be particularly prone to cluster headaches? It's unlikely that tallness or hazel eyes per se have anything to do with it. However, it is quite possible that some genetic predisposition toward cluster headaches is inherited along with genes for tallness and hazel eyes.

The 1974 study also revealed that cluster headache subjects tended to have faces that were a lot more weathered and wrinkled than did other headache or nonheadache subjects. This is an observation that had been made before about cluster headache sufferers. However, the study also came up with a reason for such complexion: cluster headachers smoke and drink alcohol much more than do nonheadache and noncluster headache subjects, and excessive smoking and drinking are known to weather the face. In fact, excessive drinking is probably one of the reasons why cluster headache sufferers get cluster headaches, because alcohol is known to be capable of triggering cluster attacks by dilating blood vessels.

But why should cluster headache victims smoke and drink excessively? The reason, the 1974 study revealed, is that they tend to possess certain personality characteristics that would make them particularly keyed up and anxious to let off steam through smoking and drinking. Most of these characteristics are not all that different from those possessed by migrainers or tension headache sufferers—conscientiousness, perseverance, responsibility, staidness, morality, criticalness, frustration, drivenness, overwroughtness, tenseness. However, several of the characteristics—a tendency to be extremely reserved, detached, resourceful, and self-sufficient—are peculiar to cluster headachers.

A good example of a man with cluster headache traits is forty-year-old Jason D. Jason is a well-trained electrical engineer, diligently and successfully building up his own business, which he started three years ago. When Jason visited a doctor about his cluster headaches, he quietly saluted the doctor, then lit up a cigarette. During their conversation, Jason revealed himself as serious and skeptical. He answered the first general questions directed to him in a curt, objective, and precise manner. When questions became more personal and pressing, however, Jason became irritable, anxious, and tense, although he tried to hide these emotions behind a casual mask.

The personality traits of the cluster headacher, in fact, probably not only cause cluster headaches by making him smoke and drink excessively, but quite likely also set a cluster headache into motion directly, at least in the wake of an especially stressful event.

The Psychogenic Regional Pain Headache Biotype

There is yet another kind of headache that can give migraine and cluster headaches competition for excruciating pain. The pain resulting from this headache has been described as "searing, burning, squeezing," like "a nail being driven into the head," "the head being squeezed in a vise," or like "a skewer piercing the eye." This kind of headache is called a psychogenic regional pain headache, both because its cause is exclusively psychological and because it inflicts pain in any number of regions of the head. What's more, skin over the area of the head inflicted by pain is usually tender, and the headache may be accompanied by pain in other areas of the body as well.

Is there a biotype specifically associated with this kind of headache? Perhaps, although the possibility has never been explored through scientific studies. However, the headache is known to be triggered exclusively by distressing emotions, particularly when those emotions are repressed. What's more, the region of the head that is inflicted with pain often has some psychological significance for the victim. Several case histories illustrate these points.

Fifty-year-old Paula C. had been in a car accident fifteen months previously, suffering lacerations and contusions in various areas of her body. Now she had pain on the left side of her head, skin tenderness in the same area, and pain in her neck, both shoulders, and left leg. At the same time, however, she had sensory loss in her right leg and the right side of her head. These discrepancies led her physician to suspect that the sensory losses came from the physical accident, and the pain from psychological distress. When he probed into Paula's life, he found out that he was right. Right before her accident, Paula had been psychologically devastated when her son was arrested for a robbery and sent to jail. This distress, combined with the psychological stress from her accident, had obviously been sufficient to give Paula her head pain and other pain symptoms. In fact, once Paula's son was cleared of the robbery and freed from jail, her pains promptly vanished.

Anita A., a conscientious forty-year-old secretary, became depressed and exhausted after five years of an overload of work in the office. One night she reached the breaking point. She felt as if "bullet-like pains" flashed through the left side of her head and also through her left chest. "I've had a heart attack like Dad!" she gasped and collapsed on the floor. Later, however, her physician discovered that she hadn't had a heart attack at all but was suffering from overwork and exhaustion but feared that she was dying from the same thing her father had. Once Anita realized that excessive stress had precipitated her pains, and she devised a program for dealing with her problems, her pains went away.

Derrick G. suffered left facial pains for a year. A doctor finally discovered the reason. Derrick's drinking had lost him his first wife. Then he remarried, but finally his second wife as well threatened to leave him because of his drinking. And the night she did this, she slapped his left cheek. Although Derrick had stayed off the bottle for the subsequent year, he had never recovered psychologically from that blow to his cheek. It signified for him a sense of failure and rejection. He thus developed pain in his left face—a physiological manifestation of the physical and psychological blow he had received. Once Derrick's physician got Derrick's wife to cooperate in helping Derrick with his drinking problem, however, Derrick's facial pains vanished.

Claudia H. experiences sharp stabs of pain in whatever area of her head has been particularly affected by an emotional upset, and especially when Claudia represses the upset. For instance, she was once harshly criticized over the phone and, rather than fight for her reputation, experienced a sharp pain in her head right behind her phone ear. Another time she was at a garden party and saw a hated rival with her left eye (her right eye was covered with the brim of a floppy garden hat). Her left eye, but not her right eye, was immediately stabbed with an "icepick of pain."

Psychogenic regional headache, then, is essentially a signal to a person that there is some danger, hurt, harm, or injury in his life and that he had better deal effectively with the difficulty if he wants to get rid of the head pain.

7

THE
MENTAL DISORDER
BIOTYPES

EVEN MORE THAN BODILY diseases, mental disorders—abnormal thoughts, emotions, and behaviors—would be expected to have strong personality inputs. And indeed they do. But what is especially fascinating about the personalities of people who succumb to these conditions is that they strikingly resemble the personalities of persons who fall prey to various bodily diseases.

For instance, suicides, schizophrenics, some criminals, persons subject to severe depressions, and child abusers often had a traumatic childhood, leading to loneliness and unhappiness, and perhaps to helplessness and hopelessness. Mental disorder biotypes, with the exception of criminals, tend to suppress their distress with obsessive-compulsive behaviors, to the point that they are often too good for their own advantage. Their inner turmoil, like that of victims of various bodily diseases, often surfaces in their marriages and sex lives, and they usually become disordered in the wake of one or more especially traumatic events.

Mental disorder biotypes even more than physical disease personalities tend toward nervousness and tension—especially in the face of stress—and toward anxiety and depression. Several traits differentiate mental disorder personalities from those with physical disease—coming from a family in especially poor psychological shape; being a juvenile delinquent or otherwise engaging in abnormal behavior while young; feeling, as a result of childhood trauma, especially hostile, suspicious, and alienated from others; and being of either above- or below-average intelligence. Each mental disorder personality is nonetheless unique.

The Suicide Biotype

On a soft spring evening in 1977, at the foot of the Blue Ridge Mountains of Virginia, a thirty-four-year-old woman placed a .38-caliber pistol against her right temple and pulled the trigger. Leah G. was found dead, in a puddle of blood.

The suicide, at first glance, was both shocking and inexplicable to people who knew Leah. Why should an attractive, well-educated lawyer, the second woman ever to be elected commonwealth's attorney in a Virginia county, and the mother of a charming blond, blue-eyed six-year-old boy, shoot herself, and especially on one of those glorious spring evenings, wafting with apple blossoms, that only the Blue Ridge can serve up? Anyone probing into Leah's past, however, might have discerned some warning signs that Leah would one day take her life, because they were characteristics of a number of persons who eventually commit suicide.

To begin with, Leah had been an extremely nervous, tense person and heavy smoker. In her long-term prospective study of early-life experiences and traits that predispose people to various diseases and disorders in later life, Dr. Caroline Thomas of Johns Hopkins Medical Institutions has found that subjects who have eventually committed suicide had been much more nervous and tense as young adults than were subjects who remained healthy in later life. Suicide victims-to-be, in fact, had been two to three times more prone, when under stress, to have trouble sleeping, to lose their appetites, to experience urinary frequency, and to feel irritable than had subjects who in later years remained healthy or who succumbed to illnesses or diseases other than suicide. Suicide victims had also expressed their nervousness through excessive smoking. Evidence that suicide prone persons are especially high-strung also comes from retrospective studies. Many individuals who attempt suicide, for instance, consulted a physician a few months earlier about "nerves."

In addition, Leah had been a lonely person. A few years before she killed herself, she had lived with some other young career women in Washington, D.C., but she was not close to any of them. Then she married but wasn't happy and separated from her husband. It was at this time that she killed herself. Evidence that suicide biotypes are often lonely can be found in Dr. Thomas's prospective study. Subjects who later in life killed themselves had, as young adults, tended to draw human figures with arms touching or wrapped around the bodies, poses reflecting withdrawal from the world. Many of the suicides had also reacted to stress by withdrawing from other people rather than by confiding their problems to others. In fact, they had been two to three times more likely to behave this way than had other subjects. Other studies reveal that persons are often divorced, separated, or widowed and change jobs and locations frequently before they commit suicide, strongly suggesting extreme loneliness. In fact, many suicide attempters who fail admit that they did not have a close friend with whom they could discuss personal problems and some even said that they felt lonely at all times.

Leah had also been secretive, hostile, and suspicious. When she lived with roommates, she carried a gun and even accused one of her roommates of fixing the gun so that it would explode on firing. Eventually, her roommates couldn't take her paranoia and asked her to move out. After Leah was elected commonwealth's attorney for a Virginia county, she viewed everything as a conspiracy and still carried a pistol. Her view of everything as a conspiracy may, in fact, have prompted her to seek an investigation of the financing of a newly built courthouse some months before her death. She sought indictments against the three builders, upsetting them and their families. Evidence that many suicide biotypes are hostile and suspicious can be found in a 1960s study. One investigator followed up some 13,500 University of Pennsylvania students to see whether any had committed suicide later in life. He then compared questionnaire answers that fifty suicide victims had given before entering the university to answers given by the other students and found that, even as students, the suicides had been much more likely to feel self-conscious, secretive, and seclusive and to believe that people were watching or talking about them.

Leah possessed one more characteristic often found among future suicides. She was given to obsessive-compulsive thoughts and behaviors in that she was exceptionally idealistic, conscientious, scrupulous, overzealous, and unable to compromise. For instance, Leah once said that the day she was elected commonwealth's attorney over a twenty-year male incumbent, "was the happiest day of my life." She was determined to do an outstanding job. She worked late night after night, without an assistant, meticulously preparing each case whether it concerned a felony or a misdemeanor. Probably as a result of her exhaustion, however, she began losing one case after another, and when the grand jury refused to hand down an indictment against the men who had built the courthouse, Leah felt as if she had totally failed as the people's representative in court. She resigned. Her resignation shocked and disappointed a number of people who thought she was a fighter. Yet as her mother recalls, "Leah quit because she cared so much," and as Leah's former law partner commented, "Leah would never compromise, never could accept the idea that she might be wrong."

Still another example of a suicide victim who had been exceptionally idealistic and unable to compromise was thirty-five-year-old Kyle L. Kyle had graduated Phi Beta Kappa from a large eastern university, went to medical school, worked as an intern in a hospital, got married, then applied for a psychiatric residency. Six months later, however, he resigned because of a hostile and bitter divorce from his wife. Faculty evaluations following his resignation stated: "Highly intelligent, idealistic. Has difficulty compromising, however." Two months later Kyle was found dead from a self-inflicted gunshot wound in the head.

Both suicide victims discussed above were intelligent individuals. Is intelligence also common to suicide victims? Yes, in many instances. College graduates are more likely to commit suicide than nongraduates, professionals more than nonprofessionals, and suicide-prone physicians often graduated at or near the top of prestigious medical school classes. Not all suicides have such traits, though. A study reported in a 1976 *British Journal of Psychiatry* compared the personality traits of thirty women and twenty men who had attempted suicide to the traits of women and men carefully matched on age, marital status, and so forth, who had not attempted suicide. One difference that emerged between the two groups was that the suicide attempters were less intelligent. Whether those who attempt suicide are above or below average intelligence, however, those who are higher in intelligence are more likely to *succeed* at killing themselves, probably because they are better acquainted with the effectiveness of various weapons and are more likely to plan a suicide so that it works.

One characteristic often found in persons months or even years before they commit suicide is chronic gloom and depression. Charles T became severely depressed while in medical school and had to be hospitalized for a year. Other future suicides, however, do not seem to feel depressed, at least consciously, in the months and years before their suicide. This surprising finding comes from Dr. Thomas's long-term prospective study. However, Dr. Thomas's study does reveal that potential suicide victims unconsciously felt depressed and even hopeless months or years before they killed themselves. As young adults, many of them had interpreted inkblots in a far more pathological manner than had subjects who have remained healthy later in life. Another researcher found that potential suicides tended to interpret inkblots in various pathological ways—"a decaying tooth," "a rotten tree trunk," "a burned and charred piece of wood," "a pall of black smoke," "something rotten"—but especially with concepts of cancer and drowning.

Moreover, many of them had given the inkblots whirling, rotating, pirouetting, or spinning interpretations far more than other persons, suggesting that their lives were seriously out of control. Rather perplexing, however, is that *not one* future suicide had interpreted inkblots in a blatantly suicidal manner. The only forthright suicidal interpretation—"two people with dunce caps on, either shooting self in neck or playing the violin"—came from a subject who is still healthy to this day.

If suicide biotypes feel gloomy about life months or even years before they kill themselves, why don't they attempt suicide long before they actually do so? The reason, it appears, is that they still have a little hope that life is worth living, that someone will help them. (One of Dr. Thomas's subjects, for instance, who had interpreted an inkblot as "a man with hands upraised, crying for help, drowning," killed himself five years later.) Then along comes one or more especially traumatic events, which trips their gloom into helplessness and hopelessness. The only way out from their anguish, they believe, is self-annihilation.

Evidence that this is in fact what happens comes from a number of sources. According to an investigation reported in a 1975 *British Journal of Psychiatry,* some four hundred unsuccessful suicides had been interviewed to find why they had tried to kill themselves. Sixty-four percent said that it was because of a devastating event in their lives, usually disharmony with a spouse or lover, but sometimes unemployment, financial problems, pain, or physical illness. The distressing event did not necessarily appear to be of major proportions to an outsider. One woman attempted suicide after her husband left home, another after her boyfriend was a couple of hours late for a date. A study reported in a 1976 *Journal of Human Stress,* on the other hand, found that persons who had attempted suicide had experienced significantly more undesirable events in the six months (and especially in the previous month) preceding their suicide attempt than had healthy or even depressed persons. The events that decided them on suicide were usually those over which they felt they had no control, such as loss of a loved one, loss of a job, or illness. In another study, of some four hundred suicide attempters, reported in a 1975 *Journal of the American Medical Association,* it was found that depression has to deteriorate into hopelessness before a person will take his own life. Hopelessness is the view that one can no longer tolerate suffering, that one can no longer see a solution to his problems, even with the help of family, friends, psychiatrist, or minister. In order to become hopeless, psychiatrists believe, a person's reason must first become impaired. In other words, he misconstrues his experiences in a negative way and, without objective basis, anticipates a negative outcome to any attempts to attain his major objectives or goals.

A 1967 Scandinavian study of depressed women who killed or tried to kill their children, then attempted to do away with themselves, showed that they had decided on such drastic actions because they considered them the *only way out* of an impossible situation. The same year, another researcher, in a systematic study of suicide notes, reported that in 81 percent of the notes, there was a theme of "the person's seeing himself as having a desire . . . which could not, cannot or will not be fulfilled." In fact, hopelessness has been the ultimate trigger of suicide since ancient times. The recorded history of suicides among the Jews of antiquity, among the ancient Greeks and Romans, and even among people during the Middle Ages contains many anecdotes about suicides resulting from people feeling trapped in an impossible situation.

But undoubtedly the most pressing question about suicides is why they possess, in the first place, those traits that cause them to react to traumatic events in a helpless and hopeless manner. In other words, why are they nervous, tense, lonely, secretive, hostile, suspicious, idealistic to the point of not compromising, and unconsciously, if not consciously, depressed months or even years before they kill themselves? As you might expect, the answer lies in their early childhood.

Let's assume that the suicide biotype, as a small child, is bright, sensitive, and idealistic. Then something happens that hurts him. The event, or events, might not be particularly devastating for a less intelligent, sensitive, and idealistic youngster, but for the suicide biotype they are. After he experiences these events, he no longer believes that the world is a very desirable, or safe, place to be, and he is no longer sure how to react to the world. Hence his tendency to withdraw, be hostile, suspicious, and depressed. Nonetheless, he still has a little hope that life is worth living, and thanks to this drive and his exceptional talents, he goes on to do well in school and even professionally. Then comes one or more especially distressing events later in his life. Because of his fragile psyche, he feels not only helpless about how to cope with these events but hopeless about life as a result. For him, as for the cancer victim, death appears to be the only escape.

What kinds of traumatic events early in life set the stage for suicide later? Often parental loss or separation, or parental harshness, even to the point of child abuse. A 1965 study showed that 23 percent of successful suicides and 15 percent of unsuccessful suicides had experienced death of one or both parents before their eighteenth birthday, while 9.5 percent of successful suicides and 25 percent of attempted

suicides came from broken homes. As for the four hundred suicide attempters reported in the 1975 *British Journal of Psychiatry*, 37 percent
had been extensively separated from a parent as children, and 20 percent had experienced child abuse. In Dr. Thomas's prospective study,
some 29 percent of subjects who have committed suicide late in life
had not been close to their fathers, compared to only 9.5 percent of
subjects who have remained healthy. In addition, far more of the future suicides had had older fathers and had been the youngest child in
the family than was true for subjects who have remained healthy.
Both these findings suggest that future suicide victims may not have
received enough love and attention from their fathers because their fathers were too old for proper parenting by the time they were born.

The Schizophrenia Biotype

Schizophrenia is a serious mental disorder, or psychosis, characterized by thought disturbances, delusions, hallucinations, and a general
withdrawal from reality. The condition can even deteriorate to the
point where psychological symptoms are accompanied by blatant neurological ones, such as an insensitivity to temperature extremes, loss of
taste, and an infantile urge to put everything in one's mouth.

Because children of schizophrenic parents sometimes become
schizophrenic even if raised by foster parents, the condition appears to
have some genetic basis. However, the offspring of schizophrenics do
not necessarily become schizophrenic, showing that more than genes
is involved. A common genetic defect, or biological abnormality, has
never been demonstrated in all schizophrenics. There is also ample
evidence that certain environmental factors can predispose a person to
schizophrenia.

Stressful experiences at birth, or perhaps even in the womb, may
help set the stage for schizophrenia later in life. When a survey compared identical twins, some of whom suffered from schizophrenia,
while their co-twins did not, those with schizophrenia were twice as
likely to have experienced birth complications; to have been born
weaker, shorter, and lighter; to be less intelligent; and to have suffered
central nervous system illnesses as children. It is possible that such
physiological impairment, especially to the central nervous system,
might somehow then lead to the psychological and neurological symptoms of schizophrenia later in life. Comments from parents of twins
with and without schizophrenia, gathered by Dr. James R. Stabenau
and Dr. William Pollin of the National Institute of Mental Health in
Bethesda, Maryland, point, in fact, to this possibility:

Actually, when I think back, it's been true all Ronny's life, even from the time he was brought home from the hospital, that he hasn't had quite the placid disposition that Johnny has. For a long time Ronny was lighter than Johnny, not much, but seven or eight pounds until they were 13 or 14.

Linda was more a feeding problem than Lucinda was—wouldn't swallow. Linda would hold the food in her mouth, and I had that checked, there was nothing organically wrong. Also I think Lucinda remained the heavier and a little taller, although I now imagine they are about equal.

During that spell where Eddie was a really small baby, he wouldn't eat the way I wanted him to. He would fall asleep all the time, and I had to keep waking him up. Sometimes, in fact, it got so distressing that I would burst into tears, because I was sure that if a baby didn't eat right, he was sick. Freddy, in contrast, has always been a good eater, right from the start.

A neurological-physical disadvantage at birth, however, may not be sufficient in itself to prep a person for schizophrenia later in life. It may be that such a disadvantage disrupts the way parents treat a child, and disturbed parenting in turn is what sets the stage for schizophrenia. In other words, it has been well documented that mothers of neurologically disturbed infants tend to be tenser than the mothers of neurologically healthy infants; that parents of low-birth-weight infants, which are often in peril of death, are apt to overprotect them or to disagree with each other over how to care for them; and that where parents have a healthy twin and a sick twin, they may overprotect the weaker twin or perhaps reject it in favor of the more robust one.

Parental rejection appears to prepare some persons for schizophrenia even if they aren't twins. In her long-term prospective study of early-life experience and traits that predispose people to various diseases, Dr. Caroline Thomas has found that over a half of her subjects who have become mentally ill in later years had been much less close to their parents as children than have subjects who have remained healthy, and over a fourth of those who have become mentally ill had fathers who were not steady, warm, understanding, and companionable, compared to only 10 percent of those subjects who are still well.

In yet other instances, parental loss or separation early in life may be a predisposing factor to schizophrenia. A 1970 study showed that significantly more parental death before age ten had been experienced by psychiatric patients than by healthy subjects. In 1978 a Beverly Hills, California, psychoanalyst reviewed the life histories of patients who had sought his help during the previous several years and found that every one of them had lost a parent by adolescence through death, divorce, illness, or military duty, thus leading to an arrest in emotional development and a splitting of the patient's self-image between reality and the lost parent figure. In a 1975 German investigation of some five hundred schizophrenics, over a fourth were found to have come from psychologically troubled home environments, that is, where a parent had died, been divorced, ill, an alcoholic, or even a criminal while the patient was young.

Regardless of whether a schizophrenic-to-be experiences a disadvantaged birth or parental overprotection, rejection, or loss, however, the experience tends to traumatize him and to impress on him the view that the world is a hostile and threatening place—undoubtedly similar to what many future suicides experience. What's more, such a view can often be observed at a very early age.

One study, for instance, showed that schizophrenics had been more inhibited, shy, dependent, worrying, and unhappy from ages two to five than had their siblings. Later on, they were less affectionate, did less well in school, and had more trouble relating to their peers than did their siblings. Another investigation revealed that preadolescent schizophrenics are often scared, quiet, dependent, and unsociable compared to their more independent and rebellious siblings. A third study of schizophrenic twins compared to their nonschizophrenic co-twins revealed that, as children, the former had been more submissive, sensitive, serious and worrying, obedient, gentle, dependent, quiet, and shy. In a fourth study, child guidance center records for children who later became schizophrenic, and records from matched control children who were nonschizophrenic in adulthood, were compared blindly. The preschizophrenics were found to be preoccupied, self-conscious, embarrassed, insecure, tense, or worried, and more often they related feelings of being vulnerable, defenseless, isolated, unloved, and unable to communicate with others. In yet a fifth investigation, schizophrenics were often remembered by teachers as shy, dreamy, temperamental, and stubborn or even as odd, peculiar, or queer, compared to their classmates. Their teachers also often recalled that they had been awkward at games and had trouble with arithmetic (but not, interestingly, with reading or writing).

Not all children, of course, who are shy, withdrawn, dreamy, tense, or have difficulty with arithmetic become schizophrenic later in life. And some youngsters who go on to become schizophrenic were not "schizoid" at all while young. They may give the appearance of being perfectly well adjusted or perhaps even engage in antisocial behavior—that is, are disobedient, runaways, or have juvenile arrest records.

Even if a schizophrenic did not give evidence to being shy, with-drawn, sensitive, tense, and unhappy as a child, however, chances are that he will do so as he grows older, and certainly as he approaches a psychotic breakdown. For instance, subjects who later in life have succumbed to mental illness were much more likely, as young adults, to react to stress with anxiety, depression, and anger than were sub-jects who have remained healthy, Dr. Thomas reports. The former, in fact, tended to be much more nervous, tense, depressed, anxious, and angry than healthy persons in general, and even more nervous, tense, depressed, and angry than persons who have committed suicide. Fu-ture mental illness victims also drank more coffee and had more in-somnia than suicides or healthy persons. However, they didn't smoke or drink alcohol all that much. Subjects who in later life had mental illness also, as young adults, interpreted inkblots much more patholog-ically than did subjects who had remained well, strongly implying that they were obsessed with morbid thoughts. Their fantasies usually had to do with a literal disruption of body boundaries, such as "a bloody dripping nose," "a split womb," or "part of a bat cut out and bleeding." And even at this early date, they drew human figures with arms touching or hugging the body, pointing toward an attitude of with-drawal from the world, just as future suicide subjects often did.

And like so many other conditions, schizophrenia can be triggered by an especially stressful event or cluster of events with which the victim feels he cannot cope. The event may be the loss of a loved one, a professional conflict, loss of a job. In fact, economic downturns since 1940 have been linked not only with an upsurge in suicides but in mental illnesses. Sometimes traumatic events can conspire with biol-ogy to spark schizophrenia, as the following case histories show.

Rebecca S. gave birth to her first child at age twenty-seven. Two months later she suffered hallucinations, delusions, and hostility—symptoms of schizophrenia—as well as manic-depressive mood swings and was hospitalized. After two months, she was released from the hospital, once again mentally healthy. Then two years later Carole F., Rebecca's identical twin, gave birth to her first child. Three weeks later she became emotionally disturbed, thought people were criticiz-ing the way she handled her baby, believed that her baby was crying when it was asleep, and laughed and cried without reason—symptoms of schizophrenia and manic-depression. Carole was hospitalized, then released a month later, once again mentally sound.

A psychiatrist then examined the life histories of Rebecca and Carole and gave them tests in order to determine what had triggered their temporary psychoses. The major trigger for both women, he decided, was a hormonal disequilibrium following pregnancy that was far more severe than that experienced by most women after childbirth and which usually has no more psychological impact than the "post-partum blues." Because both twins suffered psychoses right after giving birth, their hormonal disequilibrium had probably been inherited. On the other hand, the psychiatrist believed, their temporary psychoses were also partially psychologically based. Because the twins were from a large family, both may have had unmet dependency needs so that the challenge of taking charge of another human's life was overwhelming to them. Or they might have been afraid of childbirth because of some deep-seated fear about sex and reproduction. Neither twin had been prepared for menstruation, and both had engaged as adolescents in incestuous relations with their brothers.

The Criminal Biotype

A petite sixty-five-year-old woman was found lying on her stomach in bed, in a heavily blood-stained nightgown. A towel was wrapped around her neck and the left portion of her face. She had been raped, then brutally choked to death.

"Who would commit such a crime?" an outraged public demands. In this case it was an upper-middle-class, handsome, charming, flamboyant nineteen-year-old boy named Jeff E. Jeff's brutal act had its origins in his earliest childhood.

During Jeff's first months of life his father lost a job and was then jailed for burglary. Meanwhile Jeff's mother moved with him and an older sister and brother to another state. By the time Jeff was one year old, his mother was hospitalized three days for minor surgery, and during this time his father, who was now out of jail, forced Jeff to switch from a milk bottle to a cup and to become completely toilet-trained—drastic measures, to be sure, since babies usually become gradually accustomed to a cup and then to a toilet between their first and second year. To counter her husband's excessive strictness with Jeff, Jeff's mother was extremely permissive. "I can't stand angry behavior!" she lamented. There is also reason to believe that Jeff's mother seduced him as a young boy. And if these experiences weren't devastating enough for Jeff, his father killed himself when Jeff was only eight years old.

Indeed, there is ample evidence that most criminals usually had psychologically traumatic childhoods, even more so, in fact, than suicide victims, schizophrenics, and numerous other disease personalities. Such a childhood often includes, like Jeff's, not only parental loss or separation, parents being too harsh or protective, but exposure to violence and brutality, parental crime, seductiveness, and/or mental illness. In other words, criminals tend to come from extremely impoverished psychological backgrounds. What's more, future criminals are often an only child or the oldest son in a family, suggesting that they are driven, through these birth positions, to achieve—but to achieve in an antisocial manner, thanks to their families' psychological pathology.

Another hallmark of many future criminals is that they usually show evidence of psychological disturbance at an early age, compared to schizophrenics who may not necessarily reveal it until later in life. Such disturbance may take the form of outbursts of violent aggression (the result of early childhood deprivation and an undeveloped ego), abnormal sexual development, bedwetting, setting fires, or being cruel to animals.

Jeff E., for instance, started to show psychopathology at age seven. He shared a bedroom with his older sister and, when he thought she was sleeping, caressed her breasts and vagina. At age eight he started window peeping. At age fourteen, he came home from private school to visit his mother on weekends. During these visits he slept in a twin bed in his mother's bedroom and, when he thought she was asleep, would caress her genitalia. At age fifteen, he entered homes at night and fondled the thighs and vaginas of sleeping women. At age sixteen he was hospitalized after being arrested for entering into women's homes and, during his hospitalization, slipped female teen-age patients into his room. At age seventeen Jeff married. During his one year of marriage he argued frequently with his wife and broke into homes, allegedly for monetary, not sexual, reasons. On one occasion he was observed and shot at by the man of the house. Later, after an argument with his wife, he returned to the man's house and burned it to the ground.

By the time criminals-to-be approach, or reach, adulthood, certain characteristics of their personality are often blatant. They are probably hostile, angry, suspicious, or otherwise antisocial. As David Berkowitz (the "Son of Sam" murderer who slew six New Yorkers between March 1976 and August 1977) had said shortly before his crimes, "I went there to look for a friendly face and found none," and "I have dedicated myself to murder and promise to drive all my neighbors to death by the cruelest means." Berkowitz also had on file, in his apartment, meticulous notes on times, locations, alarm box numbers, and weather conditions pertaining to fires and even claimed in his notes that he had set blazes. Future criminals are also often impulsive and aggressive. Jeff E., for instance, once held a gun to his wife's head and once threatened another employee with a knife. Furthermore, prospective criminals are often, although not always, lonely and secretive. As Berkowitz said after his arrest for his multiple slayings: "I only wish I had a machine gun, then I could make people notice me."

Still another apparent common denominator of the criminal biotype is sex problems and separation or divorce from the spouse. Jeff E. is a prime example. And in the case of David Berkowitz, since he had saved addresses and phone books of his dead mother and had sought to kill young women, it appears that he was suffering from sexual pathology. Criminals-to-be also tend to be extremely mobile, to change jobs, residences, and lines of work frequently. This is even truer of college graduate criminals-in-the-making than of lesser-educated ones. Further, prospective criminals are apt to be frequently fired from jobs and to have numerous financial problems. They may, although not necessarily, be anxious and depressed. Four months before Berkowitz shot his first victim, for example, his father had written a friend: "It seems he [David] is not happy about living where he is. He says he doesn't get much sleep, and it is too noisy. This night work is no good for him. It is affecting him physically and mentally. Will you please do me a favor and make him go see a doctor? I am worried about him." Future criminals, like schizophrenics, may be subject to bizarre, delusional, dissociative thoughts or persecution ideas. Berkowitz's apartment, for instance, contained pages of poems and declarations that indicated a disturbed mind. To wit:

> Old Mother Hubbard
> Sitting near the cupboard
> With a hand grenade under the bed
> What have me, the people, done to you?

> Today is Friday, blood day. Today I spill blood
> for the people. . . .

> I, like the dogs, are trained to kill. I kill
> on command.

Other adult criminals-to-be, however, do not give evidence of psychosis. This was the finding of a 1976 study of fifty-one death-row inmates in North Carolina, convicted of first-degree murder, rape, or burglary. Not one of those criminals, psychiatrists found, gave any evidence of persecutory or delusional ideas, such as "Someone has control over my mind," "Somebody has been trying to poison me" or "At one or more times in my life I felt that someone was making me do things by hypnotizing me."

Finally, prospective criminals tend to commit their crimes in the wake of stressful life events. A study reported in a 1978 *Archives of General Psychiatry* found a mounting accumulation of stressful life events in the year prior to the imprisonment of 176 male inmates of a federal prison and state penitentiary in Washington, compared to the previous nine years in the prisoners' lives. The prisoners were serving terms for a variety of offenses—murder, armed robbery, grand larceny, forgery, drug violations, burglaries, assaults, and sexual offenses. The prisoners included whites, blacks, Native Americans, and other races, in that order. What kinds of life events proved stressful for the criminals-to-be? Often those that reflected their psychological instability or antisocial outlook on life—being fired from a job, breakup of a marriage, change of residence, fight with one's boss—rather than loss of a loved one or illness, which often trigger other kinds of mental disorders than crime and various physical diseases. Thus it should come as no surprise that being fired from a job and receiving legal notice of his wife divorcing him were the two events that helped prompt Jeff E., discussed above, to rape and murder.

A still unanswered question, of course, is whether criminal behavior, and the character traits that seem to predispose a person to such behavior, are solely the result of environmental influences or also partially shaped by some genetic (biological) defect in the mind. Evidence to date suggests that both are involved. For instance, adoptees having noncriminal biological fathers but reared by criminal fathers have the same rate of criminality as adoptees without criminality in either their biological or adoptive fathers. On the other hand, adoptees having criminal biological fathers but reared by noncriminal adoptive fathers have twice the rate of criminality as adoptees without criminality in either their biological or adoptive fathers. Yet the highest rate of criminality is found among those adoptees having criminal biological fathers and reared by criminal adoptive fathers. Thus it appears that genes are somewhat more implicated in molding criminals than environment alone is, but that genes plus environment are particularly potent molders.

Depression Biotypes

Although most of us feel "blue" or "down and out" when life doesn't go the way we want it to, some people take knocks especially hard and become particularly depressed as a result. Psychiatrists call these individuals reactive depressives, because their depression occurs in response to particular events. Reactive depressives tend to react to adversity the way they do because of certain childhood experiences.

They are apt to have had fathers who were unloving disciplinarians and mothers who were difficult to please, intrusive, controlling, and possibly more concerned about themselves than about their children. Reactive depressives, for instance, often say about their fathers: "I sometimes hated him as a child." "He thought any misbehavior serious." "He thought I wasn't grateful." They often say about their mothers: "Nothing seemed to please her." "She wanted to know all that happened." "She wanted to control whatever I did." "She didn't take my fears and hurts seriously." "She often made promises to give me something, but failed to keep them." "She was charming and nice with people outside the family, but angry and unpleasant at home."

Such experiences imbue future reactive depressives with hurt, disappointment, and hostility, followed by a loss of self-esteem, a sense of inadequacy, helplessness, and a general pessimism. No wonder that when events don't go their way, they feel overwhelmed and sink into gloom.

Involutional depression, on the other hand, is an acute depression that does not strike its victims till middle age. The victims, however, may have had earlier bouts of less serious depression. The hallmark of involution depressives is excessive compulsive thoughts and behaviors—that is, seriousness, over-conscientiousness, scrupulous honesty, morality, frugality, lack of a sense of humor, intolerance of others' imperfections, tendency to self-punishment. Their interests are narrow, their habits stereotyped, they care little for diversion, and they have few close friends.

How such traits predispose a person to serious depression in middle age hasn't been explored to any degree. Nonetheless, the obsessive-compulsive person rarely lives up to his own standards. Thus, by middle age he may feel like a failure in life and succumb to serious depression as a result. Or possibly, obsessive-compulsive thoughts and behaviors lead to serious depression because the person with such traits is too rigid to adapt to stressful events in his life. The following case history suggests that this might be the case.

Jill E., age forty-eight, went to a psychiatrist because she was experiencing a depression far more severe than any she ever had before, and she had been depressed on and off for some years. The reason for this severe depression, it turned out, was that she was married to a charming and gifted professional man, but one who for some months had shown some unpleasant psychopathic behaviors. Rather than see her husband declared psychiatrically ill, Jill had tried to ignore the problem for as long as possible. "I didn't want a change in our lives," she flatly declared. The price of ignoring the problem, however, was a deep depression.

But why should obsessive-compulsive persons subject to involutional depression be obsessive-compulsive in the first place? Possibly to compensate for deep feelings of inadequacy arising from parental loss, a broken home, or other trauma during childhood, because such early stresses have been linked with melancholia in later life.

As for manic depression, it is so severe that it creates a temporary psychosis, frequently requiring hospitalization until the attack is past. Persons subject to this kind of depression are often subject to pathological "highs," or manias, as well. Between depressions and manias, however, manic-depressives tend to be pretty normal psychologically, that is, hardworking, successful, warm, affectionate, and sexually responsive.

Unlike reactive depression and involution depression, manic depression appears to have a strong genetic basis. For instance, identical twins are often concordant for it, and it often runs in families. On the other hand, environmental factors are crucial too, notably parental loss at an early age, or parents with serious psychiatric problems. This loss tends to lead to an extreme vulnerability to hurt, a loss in self-esteem, helplessness, and dependency. The latter characteristic is especially evident during manic phases—when the patient is "hungry for love" and would "like to eat everything up," whether people, music, or paintings—and during his depressions, when he especially needs emotional support. Dependency needs still exist between depressive and manic attacks, though, and one manic depressive, Bill D., consciously fights them. For instance, he combats his passive wish to stay in bed in the mornings by "whipping" himself up at 6 A.M. to shower and work or by imagining business enemies he has to fight down. During his depressions, though, such initiative collapses.

Possibly in an attempt to counter unmet dependency needs, a number of manic depressives engage in marked obsessive-compulsive thoughts and behaviors, such as preoccupation with certain thoughts, orderliness, excessive cleanliness, scrupulosity, stubbornness, stinginess, punctuality, and so forth. A tendency toward such thoughts and behaviors, on the other hand, might be inherited or learned, because they also are apt to run in families in whom manic depression is also rampant. The following three-generation case history makes the point.

Ernie and Martha P., a married couple, were both manic depressives and alternately spent time in mental hospitals during their depression and mania attacks. Ernie was also known for certain obsessive-compulsive traits, especially stinginess. Ernie and Martha had two children—Lissie and George. Lissie became manic depressive at age thirty-one and eventually committed suicide during a depressive phase. George, on the other hand, never developed a psychotic depression, but he was excessively stingy like his father and suffered morning depressions. Every morning while he was showering, he felt like cutting his throat. But after breakfast the depression subsided, and during talks in the evening he largely expressed optimistic thoughts. George's only child, Linda, did not have to be hospitalized for psychotic depressions, either. But, like her father, she was subject to daily morning depressions and also to stinginess.

A pressing question, though, is what sparks depressions and mania in manic depressives. Stressful events generally do not seem to be the decisive factor as in reaction depression and involutional depression. So the triggers might be some genetic (biological) abnormality in the brain. Or they might be the frustration that obsessive-compulsive manic depressives feel when they don't meet their grandiose expectations of themselves, or what one researcher called "compulsions with strong emotional reaction." In brief, manic depressives are fertile ground for more research.

The Child Abuse Biotype

The person who batters his children usually comes from a psychologically disturbed background. His parents were either excessively harsh and unreasonable—let him cry when he was a baby unless something was obviously wrong, punished him for screaming, put him on a rigid feeding schedule, got upset when he didn't eat, punished him if he showed aggressive behavior, and beat him if he didn't obey instantly—or fluctuated between extreme discipline and excessive permissiveness. As a result, he probably became nervous, was given to nightmares, sucked his thumb, wet his bed, was afraid of the dark, had trouble in school, and generally grew up feeling unloved, insecure, hostile, and depressed. Even as an adult, he undoubtedly has retained such traits, and they especially show up in marriage problems. Then he has a child of his own and takes his immaturity, anger, and unhappiness out on the child, just as his own parents took their frustrations and anger out on him, by excessively harsh and unreasonable or inconsistent treatment, laced with considerable physical abuse.

A prime example of how the child abuse personality is passed from one generation to the next can be found in the case of child batterer Emma D.: "I never felt really loved all my life. When my baby was born, I thought he would love me. But when he cried all the time, it meant he didn't love me, so I hit him."

More often than not, though, child abusers will deny that they abuse their children unless caught doing it. Take the case of Henry J., speaking of his sixteen-month-old son Johnny: "He knows what I mean when I say 'Come here.' If he doesn't come immediately, I go and give him a gentle tug on the ear to remind him what he's supposed to do." One of Henry's "gentle tugs," however, once pulled Johnny's ear partially away from his head. Thus one psychiatrist has dubbed child batterers "sick but slick." Nonetheless, child abusers are often less intelligent than nonbatterers from the same socioeconomic level. They may have acquired intellectual deficits when their own parents beat them and gave them head injuries.

8

HOW
BIOTYPES
BREAK DOWN

PERSONALITY, WE HAVE SEEN, can cause, or help cause, diseases by essentially three routes—via thoughts, emotions, and behavior. The means by which thoughts might alter the body in order to set the stage for disease are virtually unexplored, since scientists still aren't sure precisely what physiological form cognition takes. Nonetheless, one study did show that when a person thinks specific words, different electrical signals are given off from his brain for each, illustrating that there are specific electrical processes in the brain for every thought and word and that thinking takes place in specific areas of the brain. Similarly, the physiological pathways by which obsessive-compulsive behaviors lead to disease have been virtually unexplored beyond some superficial observations. For instance, those areas of the brain involved in obsessive-compulsive behaviors do not seem to be the same as those involved in anxiety, suggesting that some emotion other than anxiety prompts such behaviors. In contrast, investigators are now making considerable progress in delineating the physiological pathways by which emotions are expressed in the brain and how emotions might alter the body in order to open it to disease. Let's examine what is known in some detail.

First, how might a traumatic experience early in life, such as the loss of a parent, prepare a person physiologically for disease later on? Such an experience, as we've seen, appears capable of setting the stage for a variety of diseases and disorders. Although this question has not yet been explored to any great degree, there is evidence that early-life experiences can leave lasting physiological imprints on the body that could open it to disease. For instance, rat pups deprived of enriching early-life experiences such as handling and stimulation were found later to have lower levels of disease-protecting antibodies than were rat pups that had received such experiences. Army recruits who had lost their mothers during childhood later showed higher levels of the adrenal steroid hormone 17-OHCS (17-hydroxycorticosteroid) than did recruits who had not suffered this early loss. The probability of these results occurring through chance would be only one in two thousand. Although precisely what a higher 17-OHCS level means in terms of disease defense or susceptibility remains to be determined, emotional elevation of adrenal steroid hormones has been shown to depress the immune system's ability to fight disease.

Second, because negative emotions often seem to prepare people for disease, and positive emotions to generally keep them healthy, negative emotions affect the body differently than do positive emotions and thus open it to disease via these differences. Positive emotions are known to lower adrenal steroid hormones while negative emotions are known to raise them, and elevated adrenal steroid hormones, we've just seen, are capable of depressing the immune system's ability to fight disease. What's more, a feeling of helplessness, which is a powerful predisposer to disease, has been shown to impair the body's immune system, whereas the opposite emotion—belief that one can cope—does not have this effect. Depression and grief, two other well-documented predisposers to disease, have likewise been shown to depress the immune system.

Third, because repressed negative emotions appear to prep people for disease far more than expressed negative emotions do, might the former affect the body differently, and might such differences lead to disease susceptibility? It seems so. For instance, levels of a particular antibody called IgA have been found to change drastically in persons who suppress their anger, whereas they do not do so in those persons who express anger. Such an antibody alteration may make individuals who suppress anger more susceptible to disease. Mothers of leukemic children who denied their anxiety were found to have experienced suppressed levels of the adrenal steroid hormone 17-OHCS, whereas mothers who admitted their anxiety were found to have elevated levels of this hormone. But whether suppression of 17-OHCS would lead to greater disease susceptibility is questionable, since elevated, not depressed, levels of adrenal steroid hormones seem to depress the immune system.

Finally, because powerful, usually negative emotions experienced as a result of a traumatic event often trigger a great diversity of diseases, how might these emotions alter the body so that it falls prey to disease? This question has been explored much more than the previous ones have. To see what's known about it, let's use Laura L. as our model.

Let's imagine Laura as she was when she found her mother dead from a self-inflicted knife wound. Her mother lies slumped over against the floorboard, her eyes rolled toward the ceiling, blood bathing her chest and forming a crimson pool around her. Laura's eyes take in this gory scenario and convey the visual message to the visual cortex of her brain, which is located toward the back of her skull. The visual cortex probably then relays the sensory message to the limbic lobe, a primitive area of Laura's brain surrounding her brainstem. All sensory inputs coming into the brain appear to have the ability to make contact with this terrain. Also, there is ample evidence that the limbic lobe is the place in the brain where emotions (whatever they are, physiologically speaking) are manufactured. One man, for instance, whose limbic lobe had been damaged in an accident was given to prolonged outbursts of howling and teeth baring whenever he encountered specific sights, smells, or tastes.

What emotions will Laura's limbic lobe then conjure up in reaction to the scene she has just witnessed? Probably shock, horror, disbelief, and fear—in essence, powerful negative emotions. The limbic lobe then undoubtedly transmits these emotional messages, by a means yet to be determined, to Linda's hypothalamus, a cluster of cells tucked away not far from the limbic lobe. The limbic lobe is known to have connections with the hypothalamus, and the hypothalamus is known to be intimately involved in emotional behaviors. Destruction of a particular area of the hypothalamus, for instance, can alchemize a gentle, docile dog into a wild, aggressive one.

Having received messages of her shock, horror, disbelief, and fear, Laura's hypothalamus now appears to act as an executive switchboard to various parts of Laura's body. First it appears to notify Laura's sympathetic nervous system, which is known to hook up directly with the hypothalamus. Laura's sympathetic nervous system then sends "fight or flight" signals to the smooth muscles it innervates. These muscles are found in Laura's organs and also surounding her blood vessels. As a result of stimulation by sympathetic nerves, these organs and vessels set up a number of reactions. What's more, the sympathetic nerves also stimulate the medulla (inner core) of Laura's two adrenal glands (located above her two kidneys) to secrete the hormones adrenalin and noradrenalin. These hormones surge into Laura's bloodstream and course through her body. The net result of these organ and vessel reactions, plus adrenalin and noradrenalin action on various tissues, is a set of physiological changes preparatory for fight or flight, such as a racing heart, clammy hands, cold feet, dry throat and mouth, increased demand for oxygen, a mobilization of fats and other nutrients into the bloodstream, stepped-up metabolism of nutrients, shallow breathing, a tensed-up neck and back, a rigid pelvis, a knotted stomach, and a tight anus (Laura obviously will have no time for eating or defecating if she has to fight or flee.)

Shortly after these physiological changes have been activated by Laura's hypothalamus, it appears to send emotional messages of shock, horror, disbelief, and fear to Laura's pituitary gland. This gland is located at the base of her brain, not far from her hypothalamus, and is about the size of a cherry. The pituitary's size belies its importance, however, because it is the master hormone gland of Laura's body. The pituitary then appears to react to the emotional messages coming from the hypothalamus by either increasing or decreasing its output of various pituitary hormones. The increased or decreased levels of these hormones then probably make contact with the target hormone glands in Laura's body, and these organs then probably alter their hormonal outputs to target tissues accordingly. For instance, the cortex (outer layer) of each adrenal gland undoubtedly increases the production of adrenal steroid hormones. The result? More physiological changes preparing Laura for fight or flight, such as nervousness, high blood pressure, and facilitated energy metabolism.

Now there is no doubt that Laura's physiological responses so far serve a useful purpose. She's ready for fight or flight from the devastating scene she just witnessed. But what if Laura continues to feel shock, horror, disbelief, or fear after her mother has been buried? This is quite plausible. Laura's body would then be maintained for some days in an ever-ready stage for fight of flight. As a result, Laura's body would become exhausted, its biological rhythms would be upset, its organs and tissues would become worn down, and it would become especially vulnerable to disease.

There is yet another reason why Laura's body will be more open to disease as a result of the above emotions, and particularly if she continues to feel them for some days. After Laura's hypothalamus notified her sympathetic nervous system and pituitary gland of her emotional state, it then appeared to signal her immune system as well. (Whether it did this via sympathetic nerves, the pituitary gland, or both, however, is not clear.) In any event, Laura's immune system has probably become less competent as a result of this notice. When areas of the hypothalamus known to be influenced by emotions are damaged, the immune system is also impaired. What's more, psychological stress is known to shrink the thymus gland and lymphatic tissues throughout the body, both of which are the body's major source of immune cells and antibodies. Still another reason we can be pretty sure that Laura's immune system became depressed as a result of signals from the pituitary gland is that adrenal steroid hormones, which are under the control of the pituitary, are known to be capable of dampening the immune system.

A pressing question now, of course, is why does Laura's body succumb to psychologically induced bruising in the wake of her emotional distress? Why not cancer, heart disease, ulcer, or some other condition? This is where the biotype personality often comes into play with disease-causing microorganisms or chemicals, a genetic predisposition toward a particular disease, diet, exercise, and other factors, for while personality alone sometimes appears capable of causing disease, in most instances it appears to conspire with other culprits as well.

Fortunately, the means by which personality—essentially, emotions—can cause, or help cause, various diseases has also been explored to a considerable degree, and we will now look at some of these insights.

How the Cancer Biotype Breaks Down

Let's tune into the typical cancer biotype. As a child, he likely lost his mother, and this loss may well have elevated his adrenal steroid hormones, which in turn depressed his immune system for life. Why might such a sequence of events take place? As we saw earlier, army recruits who had lost a mother early in life later had elevated levels of an adrenal steroid hormone, and, as we saw earlier, psychologically elevated adrenal steroid hormones in turn are known to dampen the immune system. Further, our cancer personality, as a result of his early loss, probably felt extremely deprived of love. This deprivation in turn undoubtedly robbed him of immune protection against disease later in life. Why? As we saw earlier, rats deprived of handling and stimulation early in life later had low levels of antibodies.

The cancer personality then continues to feel negative emotions as his life progresses—notably helplessness and despair, which undoubtedly undermine his body's immune system further, because, as we've seen, helplessness and grief have been shown capable of impairing the immune system. In addition, our cancer personality suppresses these negative emotions, which can further alter his immune system. A chronic upset in the antibody IgA, in fact, has been found to be present in cancer patients who suppress their anger, whereas it is not present in those cancer patients who let their anger out.

Now comes a particularly traumatic event in our cancer personality's life. What happens to him physiologically so that cancer can take hold of him? His immune system and adrenal steroid hormones have already been disturbed for years by traumatic early life experiences and long-term repression of helplessness, despair, and other negative emotions. Now a new complement of overwhelming negative emotions sweep through his limbic lobe and into his hypothalamus, which are then capable of weakening his immune system and of raising his adrenal steroid hormones even more.

Let's say our cancer personality has a cancer-causing virus in his bloodstream. His immune system will undoubtedly no longer be able to fight it off, because psychological stress has been shown to increase susceptibility to cancer of mice injected with a cancer virus, and because impaired immunity has been well demonstrated to make both humans and animals more susceptible to cancer. His raised adrenal steroid hormones will probably help the cancer virus get established in his body as well, because such hormones are known to increase the production of breast cancer viruses in both mice and in cell cultures. Cancer viruses are now capable of moving into our cancer personality's cells and turning them into malignant cells. These malignant cells will then probably spread to other areas of his body, possibly with the aid of the powerful emotions he has just experienced. How is this? Emotionally activated sympathetic nerves may stimulate the smooth muscles they innervate. Stimulated smooth muscles might then help tumor cells escape from their primary site and spread to new ones.

Now, let's return to the point at which our cancer personality has just experienced powerful emotions that have disturbed his immune system and hormones. Might he also be more likely to fall prey to a cancer-causing chemical at this time than otherwise? Very likely. We know that damage to the hypothalamus, which is known to channel emotions into the body, made mice more susceptible to chemically induced cancer than they were before, and a weakened immune system is known to make animals more susceptible to chemical carcinogens. However, precisely how emotionally depressed immunity and emotionally altered hormones might allow a chemical carcinogen to alchemize healthy cells into cancer cells is not known at this point.

To return to our cancer personality, might the powerful emotions he has just experienced, and which have drastically altered his immune system and hormones, also interact with a genetic predisposition to cancer to trigger cancer? Probably, although such interactions have not yet been probed to any degree, for a very simple reason. Cancer scientists still aren't sure what genetic susceptibility to cancer means in biological terms. Does a person inherit some hormonal abnormality or some immune defect that might make him particularly susceptible to a cancer virus or a chemical carcinogen? Only when the precise defects reflecting a genetic susceptibility to cancer have been identified can researchers attempt to see how psychologically altered immunity and hormones might interact with them to allow cancer to move in.

How the Heart Attack Biotype Breaks Down

The hallmark of the heart attack biotype, as we've already seen, is a great need to achieve and compete in the shortest possible time span, a trait usually acquired early in childhood. How might this constant drive prepare the body for a heart attack later in life? It probably keeps the body continually mobilized for fight or flight. As a result, adrenalin and noradrenalin levels would be elevated. They in turn would release fatty acids into the bloodstream and would also enhance the forming of blood clots. What reasons are there to believe that this actually happens? Investigators have shown that persons with a strong need for power, which presumably applies to the heart attack personality, have elevated levels of adrenalin, that psychological stress can rapidly move fats from body tissues into the bloodstream, and that psychological stress, via adrenalin and noradrenalin, can increase blood clotting.

Increased fats in the blood and an increased ability to form blood clots prepare our heart attack personality for a heart attack. Since there are excess fats in his blood, they probably carry a lot of cholesterol as well. In fact, psychological stress is known to raise levels of cholesterol in the bloodstream. This excess cholesterol is then probably deposited in the coronary arteries, making the heart increasingly susceptible to deprivation of oxygen and death of heart muscle, which is a heart attack. At the same time, as we've just seen, the heart attack personality is very likely to form blood clots. One of these clots could lodge in a coronary artery clogged with cholesterol, depriving the heart of oxygen and leading to a heart attack.

There is still another pathway, however, by which constant mobilization for fighting or fleeing might help our heart attack personality incur a heart attack—by raising his blood pressure. Adrenalin and noradrenalin are known to be capable of raising blood pressure for fighting or fleeing, and blood pressure is a major heart attack risk factor in that it can hasten the clogging of coronary arteries with cholesterol.

So our heart attack personality is undoubtedly continually mobilized for fight or flight for months or even years on end, raising his blood pressure, clogging his arteries with cholesterol, and increasing his risk of blood clots—factors spurring him toward a heart attack. Meanwhile, all the tension he generates in his constant mobilization may very well also encourage him to smoke a lot of cigarettes, drink a lot of alcohol, and eats lots of foods rich in cholesterol—more heart attack risk factors stacked on top of those he already has. Then comes an especially traumatic event in his life. His fight-flight mechanisms, which have been stretched to the breaking point for months or years, will probably go berserk. His blood pressure will zoom skyward, his arteries will be flooded with cholesterol, and his blood will clot. It's almost inevitable that one of these clots will lodge in a major artery supplying his heart, an artery already suffocating with cholesterol, thus depriving his heart of needed oxygen. The result? Death to part of the heart muscle, which is a heart attack.

However, it's generally not a heart attack per se but heart arrhythmias following on the heels of a heart attack that are the cause of death. In fact, life-threatening arrhythmias sometimes occur without a heart attack preceding them. Is the heart attack personality also predisposed physiologically to heart arrhythmias? Yes, it seems so. If a dog is forced to enter a chamber it greatly fears, the dog has a much better change of experiencing heart arrhythmias than if it wasn't filled with such anxiety, and simply stimulating the dog's sympathetic nervous system also increases its chance of heart arrhythmias. So it's quite likely that the heart attack personality, being constantly mobilized for fight or flight and particularly so in the wake of an especially traumatic event, is directly courting heart arrhythmias.

Now, how about the angina biotype who is subject to frequent chest pains over his heart for purely psychological reasons? How does his personality lead to his symptoms? His personality, if you'll recall, is quite different from that of the heart attack biotype. He has strong dependency needs that he covers with aggressive bravado and is given to fantasy. Nonetheless, he may acquire his heart pains in much the same manner that the heart attack personality acquires a heart attack or heart arrhythmias—via fight-flight mechanisms mobilized by intense emotions. What happens in many cases of psychologically induced angina, it seems, is that fight-flight mechanisms raise blood pressure and speed heart rate, increasing the heart's need for oxygen. At the same time, adrenalin and noradrenalin cause a spasm of coronary arteries, decreasing oxygen reaching the heart. Thus the heart has an increased need for oxygen on one hand, yet is getting even less oxygen than usual on the other. The result? Angina pains. In fact, if oxygen deprivation is severe or lengthy enough, the angina personality can go on to experience a heart attack or even fatal arrhythmias.

Other cases of psychologically induced angina, however, result from hysterical conversion rather than from fight-flight activation depriving the heart of needed oxygen. In other words, the angina personality, by a psychological pathway yet to be determined, converts his emotional upset into angina pains. His heart isn't deprived of oxygen at all; he only thinks it is. Thus he is not in danger of a heart attack or of heart arrhythmias. If angina pains are due to the heart being deprived of oxygen, the electrocardiograph machine will usually show up heart arrhythmias or other heart disturbances.

How the Ulcer Biotype Breaks Down

The small-intestine ulcer victim, you'll recall, may have lost a parent early in life or perhaps experienced an otherwise emotionally disturbed childhood. But what is sure is that by the time he becomes an adult, he will have unmet dependency needs with frequent conflicts over whether to be dependent or independent. In addition, he is probably hardworking, meticulous, and ambitious, possibly to bolster a weak self-image; tends to repress negative emotions; is unduly sensitive to stress; and gets an ulcer in the throes of a particularly trying life event. How might these experiences and traits change him physiologically so that he gets an ulcer?

Let's say our ulcer personality had a less-than-satisfactory childhood that left him with unmet dependency needs later in life. These experiences might permanently alter his stomach's ability to secrete acid, because two infants who experienced emotional deprivation during their first year of life were secreting stomach acid erratically by the time they were toddlers. In contrast, a third infant who had enjoyed a happy, healthy first year did not secrete stomach acid erratically by the time she was a toddler. In other words, the former two toddlers were particularly prone to overproduction of acid when they felt strong emotions like joy or irritation.

Now our ulcer personality is an adult. Because of his early childhood conditioning, his stomach probably produces more acid in the wake of strong emotions than a nonulcer-prone individual would. He may also be prone to excessive acid secretion following intense emotions because of inheritance. Precisely how might emotions make his stomach secrete lots of acid? Emotions are undoubtedly manufactured in his limbic lobe and shunted to his hypothalamus, just as emotions are so processed in the cancer and heart attack personalities. The ulcer personality's hypothalamus, however, probably then sends the emotional messages along a nerve called the vagus nerve to his stomach, which then makes acid. Emotions are known to influence the stomach via the vagus nerve, but it's also possible that emotions might reach the stomach via pituitary and adrenal hormones.

Regardless of the means by which emotional messages reach our ulcer personality's stomach, however, there is no doubt that they can influence his stomach acid production. How can we be sure of this? There was once a fellow named Tom (now famous in ulcer literature) who destroyed his esophagus by swallowing scalded soup. As a result, surgeons cut a hole in Tom's stomach. This way Tom could taste and chew his food, then spit it into a tube which fed into his stomach, and his stomach could then proceed to digest the food just as if it had arrived through his esophagus. But the hole in Tom's stomach also gave gastrointestinal researchers what they had long dreamed of—a window into the human stomach, and particularly a window for visualizing the effects of emotions on the stomach. And one of the most valuable insights they obtained along these lines was that whenever Tom grew anxious about something, the mucous membranes of his stomach became swollen and red and markedly increased their production of stomach acid.

So here we have our ulcer personality who is probably churning out even more stomach acid when he feels joy, irritation, or anxiety than nonulcer individuals would. Does his tendency to repress negative emotions also make him even more prone to acid production? Probably, because hostility and resentment are repressed forms of expressed anger, and such emotions also made Tom's stomach secrete lots of stomach acid. And does our ulcer biotype's tendency to work, work, work and to be a perfectionist also increase his stomach acid production? One would think so, because obsessive-compulsive behaviors would undoubtedly make him feel frequently anxious about meeting deadlines and doing a perfect job. And would our ulcer biotype be prone to put out still more acid because he is especially sensitive to stress? Very likely, because he would probably feel harassed in many instances where a less sensitive personality would not.

Now our ulcer personality is pouring out excessive stomach acid on a more or less regular basis because of early life experiences and particular personality traits and possibly also because of inheritance. Then comes a traumatic event, very possibly one that threatens to deprive him of a person on whom he depends. He will probably feel overwhelmingly anxious as a result. This anxiety then probably sweeps from his limbic lobe into his hypothalamus and via the vagus nerve to his stomach. His stomach then probably releases a flood of acid. The acid probably makes its way into his small intestine, eats away at the lining, and creates a bleeding ulcer. On the other hand, should our ulcer personality feel helpless instead of anxious in the wake of his threatening event, it's hard to say whether or not he will get an ulcer. Why is this? The infants described earlier secreted less stomach acid, not more, when they felt helpless; and monkeys helpless to do something about being shocked did not get ulcers, whereas monkeys able to do something about being shocked got them. Another study, however, has shown that helpless rats experienced more stomach lesions than did rats with some control over their fate.

How the Asthma Biotype Breaks Down

Now we come to the asthma biotype, who because of a dominating mother and weak father, or harsh, rejecting parents, grows up with unmet dependency needs. He also tends to repress negative emotions and attempts to redeem his low self-esteem through neatness, conscientiousness, self-sacrificing works, and other obsessive-compulsive behaviors. He is unusually sensitive and has his asthma attacks triggered by stressful events or by stressful events combined with an allergy, respiratory infection, cold, or some other physical factor. How might these experiences and traits predispose him physiologically to asthma? Since the physiological events underlying asthma have not been clearly identified, the answers are hard to come by.

Because of his less-than-satisfactory childhood and repressed negative emotions, our asthma personality, like other disease personalities with such experiences and traits, might well have an impaired immune system later in life. Whether such an impairment contributes to his asthma is doubtful, though, because, if anything, asthma is an excessive immune reaction, certainly not an impaired one, as we'll see further on. As a result of his obsessive-compulsive behaviors and extreme sensitivity, our asthma personality probably also feels anxious, frustrated, and hurt quite frequently. Whether such emotions might help prepare him for asthma is not known, but it's a possibility.

Now our asthma personality is faced with a particularly trying event. How might it trigger an asthma attack? He may feel overwhelmed with anxiety and helplessness, since he is a dependent person by nature. The anxiety and helplessness are manufactured in his limbic lobe and shunted to his hypothalamus, as any emotions would be. So what happens next? His anxiety and helplessness do not seem to lead to physiological changes preparatory for fight or flight, as one might expect. How do we know this? Asthmatics' levels of the hormone adrenalin are low during asthmatic attacks and also during periods of psychological stress. So if this hormone is not present in our asthma personality's body in very large amounts, then what is making his bronchial tubes (lung airways) constrict, thus narrowing the passage of air through them, and what is making the mucous membranes lining the inside of his bronchial tubes swell, further narrowing air passages? These two physiological events have been well documented as underlying an asthma attack.

It seems that our asthma personality's hypothalamus sends messages of anxiety and helplessness not to his sympathetic nervous system and adrenal glands but rather to his parasympathetic nervous system and specifically to his vagus nerve. Why should we suspect that this is what happens? Even back in 1935 a stimulation of the vagus nerve produced constriction of bronchial tubes in guinea pig lungs; the vagus nerve is known to innervate the bronchial tubes, and both human and animal experiments have shown that psychological stress precipitates asthma attacks via the vagus nerve.

So our asthma biotype's hypothalamus undoubtedly orders his vagus nerve to stimulate his bronchial tubes. The vagus nerve may release its nerve-transmitting chemical acetylcholine into smooth muscle cells wrapped around the bronchial tubes. The stimulation could result in excessive contraction, or spasm, of the tubes, and thus asthma. Or acetylcholine released by the vagus nerve might stimulate cells in the lungs called mast cells to release histamine. The histamine might then make the bronchial tubes contract and create asthma. Histamine is known to be released from mast cells in the lungs during an asthma attack and to be capable of both constricting bronchial tubes and making their mucous membrane linings swell.

But there's still another possible route by which anxiety and helplessness might cause bronchial tube contraction. The excessive release of acetylcholine from the vagus nerve into the bronchial tubes might create an imbalance of acetylcholine in those tubes compared to adrenalin secreted into the tubes by sympathetic nerves. Why is this? There is ample evidence of a parasympathetic-sympathetic nervous system imbalance in asthmatics.

As if these three possible routes by which anxiety and helplessness could trigger an asthma attack in our asthma personality are not confusing enough, suppose an allergy, respiratory infection, or cold also helped trigger his attack? Such complicity is quite possible. Unfortunately, the physiological paths by which an allergy or infectious agent might conspire with emotions in constricting the bronchial tubes and swelling their membranes have not been very well explored. However, it's possible that while emotions might contract the tubes via the vagus nerve, an allergen or infectious agent might contract the tubes indirectly, that is, by contacting lung mast cells that then release histamine into the bronchial tubes. Allergens are known to be capable of making mast cells release histamine, and infections are known to release histamine at the tissue level. Let's use asthma victim Armand Trousseau, described in an earlier chapter, to see how the interplay of allergen and emotion might work:

Trousseau, if you recall, was known to be allergic to dust. Whenever he entered his stable, his lung mast cells probably encountered dust and released histamine into his bronchial tubes, causing them to contract. This contraction was not sufficient to bring on an asthma attack, however. One day Trousseau spied his coachman in the stable stealing oats. Trousseau became very angry. This anger probably sped from his hypothalamus along his vagus nerve and further contracted his bronchial tubes. Now his tubes were so constricted by the double insult of allergy and emotion that air passing through them was severely cut off. Trousseau succumbed to an asthma attack.

What is known for sure, though, is how cold helps bring on an asthma attack. Cold stimulates the vagus nerve, which then makes the bronchial tubes contract and the mucous membranes lining the tubes swell. Thus, if both emotions and cold were to contribute to our asthma personality's asthma, the two factors would undoubtedly bring on the asthma by the same route—the vagus nerve.

How the Rheumatoid Arthritis Biotype Breaks Down

Rheumatoid arthritis, you'll recall, is the most serious of all forms of arthritis, not only inflaming and crippling joints but attacking other tissues and organs as well. RA can even kill by attacking the lining of the heart and causing heart failure. What are the physiological mechanisms underlying this disease?

First, a person probably has to have some genetic predisposition to rheumatoid arthritis to get it. Why is this? RA has been shown to cluster in certain families; some 70 percent of rheumatoid patients have been found to share certain genes, and all rheumatoid patients, as well as some 25 percent of their first-degree relatives, have ample amounts of a molecule called rheumatoid factor in their blood. Rheumatoid factor is an antibody attached to another antibody instead of to some foreign protein—hence it is an autoimmune phenomenon.

A genetic predisposition to rheumatoid arthritis doesn't seem to be sufficient to get the disease, however, because relatives with rheumatoid factor don't necessarily come down with RA. Something else— probably emotions in most instances, or an infectious agent in others—appears necessary to send rheumatoid factors into the joint linings and get rheumatoid arthritis underway. What happens after the factors enter the joint linings? Various immune cells appear to detect the factors, consider them foreign bodies, and attack them, inadvertently destroying joint tissue in the process of attack. Whether rheumatoid factors might be capable of initiating RA in other kinds of tissues and organs than joint tissue isn't known. However, once rheumatoid arthritis gets underway, it is known to be capable of depositing tiny nodules in the heart and thus creating heart failure.

Let's now take a look at the life experiences and traits of the RA biotype to see how they might interact with a genetic predisposition to rheumatoid arthritis and physiologically prepare the body for this disease. The rheumatoid biotype, you'll recall, had a harsh, dominating parent or otherwise traumatic childhood experience that left him feeling timid, submissive, conforming, and helpless. How might such emotions prepare him for RA? They might impair his immune system because, as we've seen earlier, early life experiences can alter the immune system later in life; negative emotions can dampen the immune system; subjects with rheumatoid factor but without rheumatoid arthritis showed an ability to cope with life that rheumatoid arthritis victims did not display, and an ability to cope does not lower the immune system the way that helplessness does. But how might inhibition of our rheumatoid personality's immune system help lead to rheumatoid arthritis? Researchers aren't sure. But provided that our rheumatoid biotype is already manufacturing rheumatoid factors due to a genetic predisposition, an impaired immune system might now allow the factors to enter joint linings whereas before this it destroyed such factors in the bloodstream.

In addition to chronically feeling negative emotions that probably impair his immune system and help open him to rheumatoid arthritis, our rheumatoid biotype also tends to repress these negative emotions. Might such repression further erode his immune system and prepare him for rheumatoid arthritis? Possibly. Antibody levels, as we've already seen, can change dramatically in persons who suppress anger. To compensate for his low self-worth, our rheumatoid biotype also engages in martyrlike, obsessive-compulsive behaviors. Might such behaviors further impair his immune system and prepare him for rheumatoid arthritis? There is no scientific evidence on this point. Such behaviors might help hasten disease by reinforcing our rheumatoid personality's negative emotions rather than alleviating them. On the other hand, such behaviors might help delay disease by releasing psychic and physical tension that comes from repressed negative emotions.

Now our rheumatoid personality is faced with an exceptionally traumatic event with which he feels helpless to cope. His helplessness and distress do not seem to activate disease via fight-flight mechanisms, because adrenal steroid hormones are known to help prevent rheumatoid arthritis, not launch it. However, helplessness and distress might well step up the production of rheumatoid factors in his body. Rheumatoid factors have been found to increase in the blood of healthy players after an emotionally charged game. This excess production of rheumatoid factors might then swamp the joint linings of our rheumatoid biotype because his immune system, undoubtedly impaired by longstanding repressed emotions, isn't capable of destroying the factors before they enter joints. Nonetheless, his immune system will probably make a last-ditch effort to destroy the factors inside of joints. And it is undoubtedly during this effort that it inadvertently destroys joint tissue. Thus rheumatoid arthritis is underway.

How the Migraine Biotype Breaks Down

The migraine biotype is given, if you'll recall, to excessive pursuit of duty, which often leaves him feeling frustrated, unfulfilled, guilty, and exhausted. How might such emotions and physical depletion predispose him physiologically to a migraine? The emotions probably prepare him by activating fight-flight mechanisms. Psychic stress is known to activate such mechanisms, notably the release of the hormone noradrenalin; noradrenalin has been found to shoot up in the blood of migraine patients several hours before they have a migraine attack; noradrenalin is known to be capable of constricting arteries; and constriction of skull arteries is known to precede migraines. The exhaustion resulting from excess duty might then cause constricted skull arteries to dilate and thus move our migraine personality closer to a migraine attack. Exercise is known to dilate skull arteries, and dilation is known to underly a migraine.

Our migraine personality, then, is probably prone to constriction then dilation of skull arteries, which are prerequisites for migraine headaches. Then along comes an especially trying event, which produces especially strong emotions in him. These emotions would undoubtedly cause his skull arteries to constrict even more than usual and would undoubtedly then lead to physical exhaustion and even more dilation of his skull arteries than usual. This excessive constriction then dilation of skull arteries would probably now be sufficient for a migraine to occur. Similarly, removal of tension would probably be capable of triggering a migraine for the same reason: excessive constriction of skull arteries would be rapidly followed by their excessive dilation.

Constriction and dilation of skull arteries doesn't appear to be sufficient for a migraine to take place, though. Chemicals that act on dilated skull arteries, notably serotonin and bradykinin, also appear to be necessary. Serotonin alone, or serotonin plus bradykinin, has been shown to produce pain in blood vessels; a substance like bradykinin has been identified around scalp arteries during a migraine, and serotonin is known to be released from body stores during a migraine. How strong emotions might activate these chemicals to spark a migraine isn't known. However, persons with low aggression have high levels of serotonin in their spinal fluid. So it's conceivable that if our migraine personality represses powerful negative emotions, which he is prone to do, it might raise serotonin in his spinal fluid, and this serotonin might in turn contact already dilated skull arteries, creating excruciating head pain.

Obviously, vastly more remains to be learned about how thoughts, emotions, and behaviors can trigger disease. Fortunately, though, we don't have to wait for all the mechanisms to be understood before patients with different diseases and disorders can start altering their personalities in order to improve their health. What patients can do to lessen their disease status, or perhaps even cure themselves, will be discussed in the next chapter.

9

BIOTYPE
MODIFICATION
CAN HEAL

The body is not so fragile
as we sometimes fear. It is capable
of forceful resistance. It can be
pushed far, very far, and still find
resources to recover unless the spirit is
broken or the body tissues are worn out....
True recovery is . . . in our hands
if we have the will.

—Arnold A. Hutschnecker, M.D.
The Will to Live

As WE HAVE SEEN in preceding chapters, a striking personality pattern underlies many diseases. A traumatic childhood can lead to insecurity, helplessness, or even hopelessness. These thoughts, emotions, and difficulties, however, are generally repressed, resulting in a Pollyanna stance that "everything is fine," or are channeled into obsessive-compulsive thoughts and behaviors, which are essentially efforts to compensate for a deep sense of personal worthlessness. And once these repressed negative thoughts, emotions, and behaviors are coupled with a particularly stressful event, especially the loss of a loved one, illness can appear anywhere from three weeks up to ten years later. The illness is sometimes even a literal translation of the negative body image that a person held. In brief, years of unhappiness and negativism can trigger many different diseases.

If such a common psychological thread runs through numerous disorders, might altering such a psychological profile improve the health of patients suffering from various diseases? Ample scientific studies and clinical observations suggest a resounding yes! There is evidence, for instance, that while a patient cannot alter early life events that predisposed him to his disease, discharging his feelings about these events can speed his recovery. Take the case of Teddy S., described in an earlier chapter, who was a childhood asthma victim until his parents died and he went to live with his aunt and uncle. Later in life, however, at age sixty, Teddy's asthma dramatically flared up again. He had considered himself a failure beside his physician father and other members of his family, and now he feared that he and his wife weren't going to have enough money to retire on. Since medications were not sufficient for controlling Teddy's increasingly severe bouts of asthma, his allergist urged him to see a psychotherapist and discuss his problems. Teddy did, and told his psychotherapist all about his past and about the compromises he had made to get the nurturing care he craved. After this catharsis, Teddy finally realized for the first time in his life how angry he felt over the lack of love he had received from his parents in childhood and the price he had paid for this deprivation in subsequent years. He stopped needing asthma drugs almost immediately and plunged into a more active, fulfilling life than he ever had the courage to pursue before.

There is even more evidence that if patients change their helpless, hopeless outlooks on life, they can become healthier and maybe even disease-free. Rheumatoid arthritis patients with greater ego strength, for instance, have a better prognosis than do rheumatoid patients with lesser ego strength, two different studies have revealed. Rheumatoid patients whose joint tenderness correlates with anxiety and hostility have a better health outlook than do rheumatoid patients whose joint tenderness relates to hopelessness, yet a third investigation has shown. Breast cancer patients with positive emotions have a better chance of remissions than do those with negative emotions, a 1969 study found. Asthmatics who are mature, extroverted, and capable of handling stressful situations are more likely to improve than are asthmatics who are immature, introverted, and not capable of handling stressful situations, researchers reported in 1978. Women who do not menstruate have a better chance of a spontaneous cure if they are active and extroverted than if they are not, scientists found in 1977.

In the early 1970s heart attack patients who survived exceptionally long in spite of life-threatening disease were compared psychologically to heart attack patients without such track records. The former were found to be much less anxious and depressed than the latter and also to get immense satisfaction out of their lives, even engaging in activities that their cardiologists hadn't recommended in view of their grave state of health. The authors of this study, a psychiatrist and a cardiologist, concluded: "If it is indeed true that the continued high function [of the long-surviving heart attack patients] contributed to psychological health, it might even lead to a prolongation of life by way of decreased neural or hormonal stress on the cardiovascular system."

Yet another investigation has shown that more outgoing, independent anorexics have a better prognosis than those who are introverted and dependent, and a particular case history illustrates how psychotherapy can help anorexics gain self-confidence and hope and thus modify the disease. Early in psychotherapy, nineteen-year-old anorexic Polly R. confessed, with tearful despondency, her deeply entrenched sense of inadequacy: "I can't do anything, I have nowhere to live; I'm in a rut." With support from her therapist and behavior modification techniques, however, she started to put on weight, and as she gained weight she began to express pride in herself for the first time in her life. A year later she weighed 105 pounds (only five pounds below her ideal weight). And while she still had a tendency to undereat or overeat in times of stress, her eating habits were otherwise normal. She was also engaged in several social and avocational activities and even planned to move into her own apartment—steps toward independence.

Still another study documenting the value of overcoming helplessness and hopelessness in fighting disease was conducted in 1949 at a Veterans Administration hospital on some three hundred neurologically damaged patients who had been immersed in a monotonous hospital environment from three to ten years. A rehabilitation team attempted, as part of the study design, to raise the morale of the patients and instill in them the goal of returning to the community and even of becoming self-supporting. The team also solicited the support of the patients' families toward these ends. The result? Seventy percent of the patients were able to leave the hospital in subsequent months, and 40 percent of the 70 percent became self-supporting.

Undoubtedly the toughest and most provocative data that a banishment of helplessness and hopelessness can fight disease and sometimes even cure patients comes from a physician specializing in cancer radiation treatments—Dr. Carl Simonton—and his psychotherapist wife, Stephanie. Back in the 1960s, Carl, then a radiation oncology resident at the University of Oregon Medical School, noticed that patients who asserted that they wanted to live often really acted as if they did not. For instance, lung cancer patients refused to give up smoking, liver cancer patients wouldn't cut down on alcohol consumption, and patients whom doctors had reassured that they could live many more years if they tried showed more apathy, depression, and giving up than did some patients whom doctors had labeled terminal. On the other hand, Carl noted that certain patients whose conditions had been dubbed terminal were still returning for follow-up exams several years later and appeared to be in quite good health. When Carl asked them why they thought they were doing so well, they would invariably reply, "I can't die until my son graduates from college," "They need me too much at work," or give some other response revealing a strong will to live and the conviction that they couldn't die because they still had something to offer their families and society. Thus, by the time Carl was board-certified as a radiation oncologist and working as chief of radiation therapy at Travis, California, Air Force Base, he decided to explore scientifically whether cancer patients with a positive outlook on life respond better to radiation treatment than do cancer patients with a negative perspective. With the help of other colleagues, he rated cancer patients on their attitudes toward the therapy, then evaluated their physical responses to it over the next eighteen months. The results were clear: cancer patients with positive views responded better to treatment than did the negative patients. In fact, of the 152 patients tested, only two who had revealed a negative perspective toward therapy actually profited physically from it. The most compelling revelation of this study, however, was that a positive stance toward treatment was an even better predictor of disease outcome than was the severity of the disease itself!

Meanwhile Carl's wife, Stephanie, as a psychotherapist, had become involved in motivating people toward outstanding achievements. She and Carl wondered, might they be able to use certain psychotherapy techniques, such as relaxation, mental imagery, positive thinking, and biofeedback, to instill a demand for life in cancer patients? And if they succeeded in so motivating them, would the patients' enhanced investment in living make their disease retreat and extend their lives? The Simontons decided to test these bold hypotheses, first at Travis Air Force Base, and then later at their own Cancer Counseling and Research Center in Fort Worth, Texas, where they are now located.

They first tried their techniques back in 1971 on a sixty-one-year-old throat cancer patient, George N., whose prospect for survival looked grim. While Carl gave George radiation treatments for cancer, he also pointed out that George himself could assist the course of radiation with relaxation exercises and with mental imagery of radiation and his immune system smashing his cancer cells to death. What happened to George over the next few weeks was even beyond what the Simontons had deeply hoped for. George's cancer regressed rapidly; he gained weight and strength. Two months later he showed no sign of cancer, and he is still alive and well to this day.

This exciting result prompted the Simontons to try similar psycho-therapy techniques combined with radiation on more patients diag-nosed for medically incurable cancer. By 1978 they had so treated 159 patients, 63 of whom were still alive, with an average survival time of 24.4 months since their diagnosis. Life expectancy for this group, based on national norms, was only twelve months. The Simontons, asserts Dr. Jerome D. Frank of the Johns Hopkins University School of Medi-cine in Baltimore, have "observed spectacular remissions in some pa-tients with far advanced disease. At the very least, these therapists have raised the strong possibility that psychotherapy can sometimes beneficially affect the course of cancer."

"We do not deny the possibility of death," the Simontons insist, in speaking of their results. "Indeed we work hard with our patients to help them confront it as a possible outcome. [But] we also work to help them believe that they can influence their condition, and that their mind, body and emotions can work together to create health."

There is also evidence that venting negative emotions can modify the disease. A psychologist at Johns Hopkins Medical School recently surveyed thirty-five breast cancer patients. He found that women who expressed anger not only toward their diseases but toward their phy-sicians as well lived longer than women who were pleasant and coop-erative. Of patients successfully operated on for malignant melanoma, patients who relapsed tended to minimize the significance of their ill-ness, whereas patients who remained well faced up to the gravity of their situation. The study of long-surviving heart attack patients, cited above, found that such patients do not deny the possibility that they are close to death. This finding was actually the opposite of what the scientists conducting the study had expected. The scientists had thought that denial, rather than admission of negative emotions, might prove to be an effective defense mechanism against a life-threatening disease.

Similarly, one of the factors that helped Polly R., discussed earlier, to overcome her anorexia was mourning the loss of her father for the first time since his death and expressing anger at her family for bully-ing her into eating. She related a dream to her psychotherapist in which one sister and the sister's boyfriend were eating steadily and continued to expand until they were huge; they pushed her around the house, forcing food down her throat. During her therapy and hospital stay, Polly also showed an increased ability to confront people, and she came to realize that her weight loss was due, in part, to directing anger meant for others onto herself. An allergist reported, in 1977, that urticaria victims have trouble weeping but that when they do, their symptoms often vanish. And even back in 1943, an internist wrote that rheumatoid arthritis patients who vent negative emotions experience improved health.

Altering obsessive-compulsive thoughts and behaviors can also mitigate disease. Heart attack victims with long survival rates, cited above, have been found to be less obsessive-compulsive in their behaviors than heart attack victims without such survival rates. Colorado researchers reported in 1975 that a two-week behavior-modification program helped heart attack patients alter their frenzied life-styles and thus lower levels of fats and cholesterol in their bloodstreams. This program, wrote the investigators, "may prove to be the first meaningful approach to reducing the psychological risk factors associated with heart disease." According to a 1977 study, psychotherapy can help chronically depressed persons who have devoted their lives to pleasing a dominant spouse, parent, or sibling learn how to revamp their behavior so that it is more meaningful and gratifying to them, and such behavioral changes in turn can lift depression. Migraine sufferers who avoid undertaking excessive amounts of work in a given time and being too perfectionistic and who learn to delegate duties can become spontaneous and productive and less tense and less subject to headaches, a British researcher wrote in 1973. Psychotherapy and relaxation exercises can help migraine sufferers achieve these aims, other British scientists wrote in 1975. Geraldine S., one of the migrainers helped by their therapy and relaxation exercises, comments: "After consultation I was sent for 'relaxation exercises.' I found the very term insulting as I had considered myself to be extremely easygoing. Only to be proved wrong! I think it was the fifth treatment that made me realize the benefit of relaxation exercises. My mind and body felt soothed as never before. And as a result of psychotherapy and relaxation exercises, my migraines have become much better. Often two or three weeks pass without my getting one at all."

When banishment of obsessive-compulsive behaviors leads to a profound new commitment to life, it can even help cure patients of potentially fatal diseases, reports Dr. Lawrence LeShan. Take the case of Phillip the engineer described in an earlier chapter. Phillip appeared to be leading a happy and successful life. He lived with an attractive wife and three children in a luxurious suburban home and had a position in his father's firm. But Phillip was not really pursuing the life he wanted. As a child, he had shown exceptional musical ability but was timid and withdrawn. As he grew older, he became an engineer to satisfy his father and even married the girl his mother had picked out for him. He despised his work, and his marriage was empty of love and fulfillment. At the age of thirty-five Phillip contracted a massive brain tumor; physicans said it was too late to do anything for him and gave him only a few months to live. But paradoxically, the imminence of death seemed to release an inner strength in Phillip. Having read about Dr. LeShan's psychotherapy for terminal cancer patients, combined with the then-new technique of chemotherapy, he contacted Dr. LeShan and was enrolled in his program. Dr. LeShan convinced him that he himself could alchemize his helplessness and hopelessness into a yen for life, provided that he start living the way he wanted, not the way others dictated, and that a kindling of his spirit would not only make the days remaining to him more fulfilling but might possibly even extend his life. So Phillip began working seriously on his music and divorced his wife. He came to realize that people would love him just as much if he did what he wanted as if he did what they desired. Even more dramatic, Phillip's supposedly incurable brain tumor re-treated as he continued to receive chemotherapy and change his philosophy and behavior. Phillip is alive to this day, twelve years after he had been diagnosed as a terminal cancer patient, and working as a professional symphony musician—his long-repressed dream.

Finally, there is also indication that once patients learn how to cope with stressful life events, their health can improve. In 1973, for instance, Gilberto de Aranjo of the University of Washington School of Medicine and his colleagues probed the association between psychosocial assets, the number of stressful events, and severity of chronic asthma in asthmatics ages nineteen through seventy-four. They suspected that patients with high psychosocial assets and lots of stressful events in their lives would have less severe asthma than patients with low psychosocial assets and numerous stressful events. Their expectations were confirmed. Thus they concluded: "This study supports the concept that development of certain enduring methods of coping results in varying ability to adjust to life situations and has a significant influence on the clinical course of subsequently developed disease processes." Similar findings have also been reported on patients with chronic kidney disease. Patients with high coping ability in the face of stressful life changes experienced fewer symptoms than did patients with low coping ability in the thrust of difficult events. Another investigation noted that emphysema patients with a strong ego in the wake of stressful experiences lived longer than did emphysema patients with a weak ego under similar conditions.

Given that personality changes can help modify or get rid of disease, how might a patient revamp his personality in order to improve his health? The first responsibility a patient has to himself is to seek the best medical care available and to strictly follow his physician's orders, especially if he has an acute, critical illness. The suggestions offered here are not a substitute for professional medical care, but they reflect the possibilities for patients to actively participate in their own healing.

First, try to honestly see whether you fit the disease personality that matches your particular problem, or if your disease is not discussed earlier, whether you match the general disease personality profile recapped below. Maybe you don't. But keep in mind that a common characteristic of many disease personalities is to deny negative emotions and thus to have trouble viewing themselves objectively. If you cannot evaluate yourself accurately, then perhaps friends or a psychotherapist can help you do so.

For instance, did you have a traumatic childhood, such as the loss of a parent? Were your parents too authoritarian, protective, cold, or neglectful? If so, did these experiences scar you with a sense of inferiority, worthlessness, rigidity, conformity, reluctance to change, a negative body image, sex problems, a sense of helplessness or even hopelessness—in sum, the deep conviction that fate has control over your life and that you cannot achieve what you want out of it? Do you repress such negative convictions and emotions, acting as if "everything is fine" and sacrificing your own interests to those of others, as if to compensate for your sense of worthlessness? Was your illness preceded by a particularly stressful event or events?

If your answer to most or all of these questions is "Yes," or if you find that you closely parallel a specific biotype discussed in previous chapters, then it is quite likely that your illness has a strong personality component to it. But if this is the case, don't feel guilty! There is a vast difference between having "participated" in your disease and "being to blame for it," because most people are not attuned to the link between personality and health and don't bring on their illnesses consciously.

The next step toward improving your health, provided that you agree that your disease has psychological inputs, is to try to alter those components of your life that helped trigger your illness. If you had a traumatic childhood, for example, obviously you cannot change it at this date; nor will you profit from feeling angry or chastising yourself about it. But a psychotherapist can help you probe those remote experiences and come to realize how they have contributed to your present mental distress and disease state. Intellectually grasping the connections should lessen your anguish and improve your health to a certain degree. What's more, calling up the ghosts of a childhood past will undoubtedly also discharge your long-repressed, excruciatingly painful reactions to them. Such an emotional catharsis will unleash even greater healing forces, for as a psychotherapist wrote, "If a patient really wants to profit from psychotherapy, he must be viscerally touched by what he learns during therapy and change as a result."

If you have feelings of helplessness stemming from a psychologically impoverished childhood, as do many disease victims, they too can be overcome. Try to go off alone someplace where you won't be expected to play accustomed roles, where you can get in touch with yourself. Take stock of your past achievements in life. You'll be surprised to see how an assessment can bolster your self-image and prepare you for more independence and self-fulfillment in the future. To further your self-assurance and self-sufficiency, feel your feet planted squarely on floor or earth. Inhale, and while inhaling, imagine yourself an eagle soaring high in an indigo sky; exhale, and while exhaling, continue to be that eagle, gliding on a stream of success. Now probe deep into your heart: What do you really want to do with your life? Don't agonize over why you haven't done it up to now but map out a plan of action for accomplishing this goal, and take a first step in that direction the very same day. Sound foolish? Maybe. But you'd be surprised how one small behavioral change in the right direction can lead to more dramatic behavioral changes and how these alterations in turn can lead you back to health. Infantile dependency, or helplessness, is really nothing other than an evasion of action.

Take the case of Mary S., a cancer patient undergoing psychotherapy with Dr. LeShan. Mary had been working for twenty years at a profession she despised because she had always felt it was impossible to change. Dr. LeShan, however helped convince her that a change was feasible. But then Mary had to motivate herself to pursue what she really wanted to do, and she finally took a modest, but nonetheless significant, first step toward achieving it. She bought a stamp on her way home from therapy in order to send off for a college catalog listing evening courses available in her field of interest.

Now suppose you are hopeless as well as helpless—a characteristic of a number of disease victims, particularly those with severe, life-threatening conditions. How can you banish this hopelessness, especially if death is imminent and your body is throbbing with pain? You must mobilize your will to live, and swiftly, because you are literally as well as psychologically fighting for your life. Sound like an overwhelming challenge? Certainly, but it is humanly possible, as the following case history testifies.

Ron J. was a plebe midshipman, star varsity end, and honor student at the U.S. Naval Academy in the fall of 1973. Just before the Academy's Michigan game, Ron's stomach was "killing" him, he couldn't sleep, and he had a large lump in his groin. So the coach sent Ron to the infirmary. Ron learned that he had cancer and was operated on that very night. However, the surgeons found that the cancer had spread to both his lungs and lymph nodes and that it was too late for surgery to save him.

Thus Ron undertook intensive radiation and chemotherapy treatments. Although they, along with cancer, inflicted his body with intense pain, and although they made him extremely nauseous and lose lung capacity and hair, Ron persisted. He had a fervent will to live. His treatment progressed and, finally, under remission, he returned to the Academy in August 1974. Encouraged by his physicians and coaches, Ron began running and weight-lifting. Although one of his lungs had been burnt 95 percent by radiation, Ron built it up 65 percent. He practiced endlessly, often dragging his wasted body onto the field and crawling back upstairs at night. He fought valiantly for a health comeback, and he made it. By the spring of 1976 Ron was hopeful that he would be able to return to the Academy's football team and that he would eventually even be able to pass the Academy's physical. In fact, Ron not only managed to pass the physical but to graduate from the Academy and, by 1979, to receive his first naval assignment in North Carolina. He appears to have completely conquered his cancer.

"Before, when people said 'cancer,' I just thought, 'too bad,'" Ron says. "Now I don't automatically think death; it's an ordeal you have to go through and you'll make it. The worse part of my treatments was sitting there listening to the ladies talking at Bethesda Naval Hospital. They'd say, 'He's going to die.' I didn't want to hear it. I *wasn't* going to die."

But how, if you're a seriously ill patient, particularly if inflicted with pain, can you motivate yourself to live? Like a helpless patient, you must have a goal or goals for the future that are profoundly important to you. But what gives you a desire for a goal or goals? You must deeply believe that your life has meaning and that you have something to contribute to both yourself and society. Whether or not you arrive at such convictions is nothing less than an existential (philosophical) decision beyond sheer reason, deriving from intuition, gestalt, faith, the very fabric of your mind.

But even if you transform existential despair into a profound joie de vivre, can it really help you physically? Yes, it can, not only on the basis of evidence presented above but on the grounds presented in a fascinating article published by psychiatrists in a 1973 issue of the *Journal of Nervous and Mental Disease*. According to the article, a number of patients "born again" spiritually have experienced physical healing in subsequent months, and the healing was not only of chronic, less severe disorders like backache and ulcers but also of life-threatening diseases like cancer and tuberculosis.

There is no guarantee, of course, that a renewed mind (spirit) will be potent or swift enough to save a person's diseased body. But even so, mental (spiritual) refurbishment is a worthy aim for a patient to strive for, because it can enrich the days, weeks, or months left to him and make the prospect of death far less formidable. As Dr. Elizabeth Kübler-Ross, a physician who has helped many terminally ill patients face death, writes: "If you have not loved well, death will always come too soon and be too terrible to face."

Take the case of cancer victim Amy, discussed in Chapter 1. During psychotherapy with Dr. LeShan, Amy became convinced that in spite of her cancer, she must make an effort, for the first and possibly the last time in her life, to pursue what impassioned her, which was ballet. So Amy decided to write a book about the history of ballet in New York City. Dr. LeShan and her children provided her with the research materials she needed while she was being treated for cancer in the hospital. Her bed and nearby tables and chairs were piled high with library books and yellow pads. Each day she read and wrote until she was exhausted, slept, then worked some more. Her orientation toward life changed dramatically; she became exuberant and fulfilled. Medical reports indicated that her treatments were proving much more effective and the growth of her tumor appeared to have stopped.

Then the weather turned unbearably hot, and as the hospital was not then air-conditioned, a number of patients died due to the heat combined with their frail conditions. Amy was one of them. "But Amy," Dr. LeShan writes, "did not die in despair, consumed by self-contempt. As both she and her children attested, the last months of her life were full of zest and pleasure in life. Even on the day of her death, she was looking to the future."

As for the venting of negative emotions—another way that patients can help heal themselves—it too can be learned with effort. First of all, think about what negative emotions you might be repressing. For one patient it might be anxiety and depression, for another anger and resentment. Once you've decided what emotion or emotions you should let out more, try different approaches toward doing so. Keep in mind, though, that this is something you should go about slowly, because you can't change unhealthy behaviors overnight.

For instance, if you tend to repress anxiety or depression, you might set aside a period each evening where you can pour out your frustrations to your spouse or roommate, and where your companion, understandably, can also do the same with you. If you're apt to withhold anger, it might be cathartic for you, whenever someone makes you mad, to confront him as soon as possible. How do you go about this? If you're really furious, you might let a torrent of rage pour out. However, if you still find it difficult, or undesirable from your point of ethics, to give people "what for," you can confront them in a more civilized, low-keyed manner. For instance, you might say, "Hey, George, I've got a bone to pick with you." George asks, "What about?" You then proceed to tell him what has upset you, and as you do this, you'll feel considerably better. Still another way to vent anger if you don't want to confront an offender directly is to go about the house screaming. Psychologists George R. Bach and Herb Goldbert, authors of *Creative Aggression,* call this the "Vesuvius" ritual. It is a means, they explain, "by which individuals can vent their pent-up frustrations, resentments, hurt, hostilities and rage in a full-throated, screaming outburst."

As for relieving yourself of resentment, which is really chronic, bottled-up anger and a sentiment commonly harbored by disease victims, you might finally pluck up the courage to pour forth your emotions on the offender and, in the process of deluging him, feel extremely refreshed. Or you might try using a tactic that the Simontons encourage cancer patients to use. Sit in a comfortable chair, feet flat on the floor, eyes closed. Create a picture in your mind of the person toward whom you feel resentment. Picture good things happening to that person. See him or her receiving love, attention, money, or whatever you think he likes. If you have trouble visualizing nice things happening to him, it's perfectly natural, but it will become easier with practice. Also think about the part you might have played in a stressful interaction with the person and how the interaction might have looked from his point of view. Be aware of how much more relaxed and less resentful you now feel. Promise yourself that you will carry your new insights with you. Now open your eyes and resume your usual activities. "After using the process repeatedly," the Simontons report, "our patients have shown—both through subjective reports and objective psychological tests—*less* tendency to repress and deny their feelings."

How about obsessive-compulsive behaviors? How can you alter them in order to improve your health? Get away from your demanding daily routine to where you can do some hard, clear thinking about what *you* want out of your life, not what parents, spouse, children, friends, or employer want. Now draw up goals that coincide with what you want in the way of a career, personal growth, or relationship with others. Chances are, if you're an obsessive-compulsive type, that you've been grossly neglecting those goals for other duties which you may find tedious and unfulfilling. Now write down goals for recreation and physical exercise as well. As an obsessive-compulsive person, you undoubtedly discover that you've been neglecting recreation and exercise for work. All the goals you set, of course, should be realistic and within your power to grasp. You should also write down specific steps required to reach those goals.

Now use mental imagery devised by the Simontons to reinforce these goals in your mind and to motivate yourself to accomplish them. In your mind's eye, visualize yourself with a goal already met. Experience the feelings you will have when your goal is fulfilled. What will people say to you? What will you be doing? What will you look like? Visualize significant people in your life responding to your achievement. Be happy and grateful for having reached the goal. Gradually drift back to the present. Now open your eyes and take the first step leading to the goal.

As you continue to picture yourself achieving your goals, you will increase your expectancy that you can achieve them. You will also begin acting in ways that are compatible with bringing them about and give up frustrating, unrewarding, and health-eroding behaviors.

Another valuable therapy, if you're an obsessive-compulsive patient, is to force yourself to relax on a daily basis, using meditation or relaxation exercises that have been shown to lower blood pressure and quell the fight-flight reactions, for as we saw in the previous chapter, obsessive-compulsive behaviors appear to chronically activate such mechanisms, and as we saw earlier in this chapter, relaxation can definitely improve the health of chronically compulsive patients. You might try the progressive relaxation technique devised by Dr. Edmond Jacobson back in the 1930s and refined by the Simontons for use by cancer patients:

> Go into a quiet room with soft lighting. Shut the door and sit in a comfortable chair, feet flat on the floor, eyes closed.
>
> Become aware of your breathing.
>
> Take a few deep breaths, and as you let out each breath, mentally say the word, "relax."
>
> Concentrate on your face and feel any tension in your face and eyes. Make a mental picture of this tension, which might be a frown or a tic in your jaw, and then picture it relaxing.

Experience your face and eyes relaxing. Feel a wave of relaxation emanating through your body.

Tense your eyes and face, squeezing tightly, then relax them and feel the relaxation spreading through your body.

Apply the previous instructions to other parts of your body, moving slowly down your body, until every part is relaxed.

Once you have relaxed each part of your body, rest quietly in this comfortable state for two to five minutes.

Then let the muscles in your eyelids lighten up, get ready to open your eyes and become aware of the room.

Now open your eyes, and you're ready to go on with your usual activities.

As for successfully coping with acute stressful events in your life and thus improving your health, keep in mind that any disturbing life change that occurs after illness has already set in can aggravate that illness. Thus it deserves your immediate attention if you are to even preserve your present health state, much less improve your health under such conditions. Then assess the situation as quickly and objectively as possible. If you're upset by what has happened, which is probably the case, the relaxation exercises described above can calm you and help you think objectively. Now decide: How should you deal with the stressful event? Although fight-flight responses are inappropriate for chronically dealing with life's challenges, they are the only appropriate means of coping with acutely distressing events. If you've just been fired from a job, for instance, an appropriate action might be fight, that is, getting out immediately and looking for a new position. Or if your spouse has just died, a healthy response might be fleeing, that is, getting away from your usual environment and painful memories for a while. Whether you decide on fight or fleeing, either will be healthier for your mind and body than denying the stress or doing nothing about it. As psychotherapist Arnold A. Hutschnecker writes in his book *The Will to Live: "Resignation is not adjustment.* The only true adjustment, the one for which the human mind and body are equipped, lies in the choice between fight, which is an effort at adjustment, and flight, which is the act of getting out of an unwholesome situation."

Once you've dealt effectively with an acutely distressing event, of course, you should then switch off your fight-flight mechanisms so that they will not erode your already less-than-desirable health state, and this is where relaxation exercises can once again prove useful. During an acutely distressing experience and in the wake of it, you should also go to great pains to take good care of your body, that is, get extra sleep and eat well, since illness has already depleted your body resources, and stress has weakened your immune system. In other words, it's a tough challenge not getting sick in the first place in the wake of a stressful event; it's an even tougher challenge not to erode your health further under similar circumstances if you're already sick; and it's an even vaster challenge if you want to improve less-than-ideal health under such "wartime" conditions. But it can be done, as studies cited earlier in this chapter indicate.

Altogether, then, as a patient whose disorder has personality inputs, your challenge is to become a happier person, because happy people tend to be healthy people. As psychologist Leslie D. Weatherhead has written, "More people are sick because they are unhappy than unhappy because they are sick."

Here are still other suggestions on what some specific disease victims can due to improve their health, particularly if personality helped cause their conditions in the first place.

Biotype Changes for Healing Cancer

If you believe that your cancer is partially or entirely due to life experiences and personality traits of the cancer biotype, follow the suggestions offered above to counter a traumatic childhood, overcome helplessness and hopelessness, learn to express negative emotions, and learn to cope with stressful events. Such personality changes can counter cancer dramatically, as you saw earlier in this chapter. Whether your cancer was caused by personality or not, however, you can use mental imagery three times a day to bolster the effects of any physical treatments you are receiving. For instance, if you are getting chemotherapy, picture the drug rushing into your bloodstream, then poisoning cancer cells, while immune cells, like an army, rush to the sites of cancer cells to finish them off. Visualize your tumor or tumors shrinking until they are all gone. Imagine yourself healthy and free from cancer and pain. Even better, reinforce your mental images with drawings. Drawings will also give you a yardstick for measuring your progress in thinking away your disease.

Such imagery for cancer patients is being encouraged not only by the Simontons but by two Dallas psychologists—Jeanne Achterberg of the University of Texas Health Science Center and G. Frank Lawlis of North Texas State University. Although the actual effects of such imagery on cancer have yet to be scientifically demonstrated, clinical impressions suggest that it does help cancer patients strengthen their belief that they can recover from cancer, and this belief in turn toughens their immune systems and thus helps lead to tumor regression. Cancer patients also report reduced side effects from cancer treatments as a result of their developing more positive attitudes to such treatments through mental imagery.

Whether you believe your cancer was caused by personality or not, exercise can also help it regress. The Simontons have observed that most of their patients with the most dramatic recoveries from cancer were physically very active; exercises have been shown to bolster the body's immune system, and even as far back as 1921, researchers noted that death rates from cancer were highest among persons in sedentary occupations and lowest among persons with physically demanding occupations. Still other studies reveal that persons engaged in regular exercise tend to become healthier psychologically—to have an improved self-image, greater self-sufficiency, less depression, and less tendency to blame others—precisely those personality characteristics vital for the cancer personality to conquer cancer. "Our experience," the Simontons write, "has shown us that cancer patients are capable of far more physical activity than most people usually assume." In fact, not only a vibrant will to live but vigorous exercise probably helped midshipman Ron J., described above, to overcome his cancer.

Biotype Changes for Countering Heart Attacks

If you're a heart attack biotype who has had a heart attack, you may still, after a successful convalescence and returning to work, yearn to achieve and compete in the shortest possible time—factors that can obviously open you to still another attack and death. How can you abort such unhealthy behavior? First, set clear, limited goals for yourself, goals that please *you*, not other people. In deciding whether this or that pursuit should be included among your goals, seriously ask yourself: "Is it worth dying for?" If it is, include it. If it isn't, exclude it. Allow yourself twice as long to accomplish these goals as you would otherwise be prone to do. Force yourself to delegate more duties at work, a habit which heart attack personalities are loathe to do, and don't let yourself be interrupted by just any phone call, which heart attack personalities are apt to do because of insecurity. Keep in mind that slow, careful work, not a hasty pursuit of ill-defined goals, is what has led to your successes in the past. Stop wearing a watch if at all possible, so that you won't be constantly glancing at it. Try not to hurry the speech of others, to do two or more things at the same time. If you're in a traffic snarl, don't swear and honk, but use the time to listen to soothing music or to savor past successes and pleasant events in your life. Recall the study of long-term survivors of heart attacks cited earlier in this chapter. A hallmark of these patients was that they got keen satisfaction out of their lives.

Also force yourself, as a heart attack biotype and heart attack victim, to practice relaxation exercises, such as those described above, daily, in order to quell unnecessarily activated flight-fight mechanisms in your body—dangerous stresses for an already damaged heart. Group therapy for heart attack patients, provided you have access to it, can likewise help you pursue a more relaxed, fulfilling life-style. One study, for instance, had forty heart attack patients attend some five group therapy sessions in order to change their frenzied behavior, whereas twenty heart attack patients didn't attend these sessions. The results? The former patients experienced considerably fewer rehospitalizations than the controls.

To enhance the quality of your life and give your heart a rest, become more interested in your surroundings, something that heart attack personalities usually ignore. Make your office a pleasant environment. Top executives, you will notice, usually have orderly tasteful offices. Set aside a room or a corner of a room at home where you can retreat, unwind, and savor your daily accomplishments, because to live a truly fulfilling, healthier life, you must first live beautiful days, and to live beautiful days you must think beautiful things. You don't have to tell other people what you think.

As a heart attack personality who has had a heart attack, you probably also resent people who stand in your way of success. To banish this sentiment practice visualizing good things happening to these people, as suggested above. You can also rid yourself of hostility by learning how to accept affection and love, which is generally not easy for the heart attack personality, and how you might fill other people's needs as well rather than always being egotistically wrapped up in your own pursuits. To reduce your risk of incurring another, possibly fatal heart attack, also strive diligently to lessen other obsessive-compulsive behaviors—overeating, heavy smoking, drinking too much alcohol, coffee, or other liquids, not getting enough sleep, and engaging in no physical activity at all or too much. In other words, strive for moderation in these habits. Regular walking, for instance, would undoubtedly benefit you if you've already had a heart attack, but jogging against your doctors' orders when you have a heart condition could prove fatal.

As a heart attack biotype, you have undoubtedly also neglected the private side of your life for your work. Building it up might very well help save your life, because whereas social isolation and lack of companionship have been shown to increase the risk of heart disease, the smallest psychosocial interaction has been shown to dramatically help the diseased heart. Buy yourself a pet. People who have a dog, cat, bird, gerbil, or even an iguana are more likely to survive a heart attack than people who do not have a pet, a Pennsylvania biologist reported at the 1978 annual meeting of the American Heart Association.

Because heart attacks are often triggered by stressful life events, especially negative ones, be particularly attuned to such events in your life, as you've already had one heart attack and certainly don't want to bring on another. If you're a heart attack biotype, your body will easily gear up for fight-flight reactions in the face of such events, which is healthy for coping with them. However, the health danger for you, as a heart attack biotype who has had a heart attack, is to remain physiologically charged up even after you've coped with the events. To get rid of superfluous, heart-damaging fight-flight responses, you can use the relaxation exercises described above. As the Colorado cardiac stress management program cited above indicates, heart attack patients can indeed learn to control their reactions to stressful events.

Biotype Changes for Reducing Asthma

As we've seen earlier in this chapter, when asthma biotypes discuss early life experiences and vent pent-up emotions about these experiences, they have fewer asthma attacks. Thus, if you believe that your asthma partially had its origin in traumatic childhood experiences, try to decondition your feelings about these experiences. A psychotherapist would probably be the most effective in helping you, but even a compassionate physician without psychotherapy training might be of some assistance. If you believe that your asthma partially derives from passivity and dependency, follow the advice given earlier in this chapter on how to overcome helplessness and thus in turn become more healthy. Also try to become more assertive in your daily life. For instance, learn to say "No" to authority figures, to request favors from people, to initiate and terminate conversations. Asthmatics trained along such lines by a psychiatric team were found to experience an improvement in their asthma.

Daily relaxation exercises, such as the ones described above, can also ameliorate your asthma, whether your condition derives from personality or not. Meditation can help you too. In one study, asthmatics practiced transcendental meditation, whereas other asthmatics did not. After three months, the two groups switched for another three-month period. During the total six months, all of the patients kept daily records of their asthma attacks and medication needs and had their lung resistance to air passage measured periodically. The results were dramatic: Subjective reports from the patients as well as objective lung resistance tests revealed that meditation reduced asthma symptoms and airway obstruction while both groups of patients were using it, compared to when they were not using it.

Biofeedback training, which consists of giving a person immediate and continuing signals of changes in a bodily function of which he is usually unaware, can also reduce your asthma, whether your condition derives from personality or not. A 1973 study revealed that some contol over bronchial tube constriction is possible through biofeedback training, and that this control is acquired primarily through variations in the tone of muscles in the lungs. In 1976 four children hospitalized for severe asthma largely due to parental strictness or other psychological trauma in the home environment were hooked up to a biofeedback machine that continually measured the resistance of their lungs to breathing. Each patient heard a tone of constant volume whose pitched varied as a function of his lung resistance to air passage, yet also a sound simulating breathing. He was asked to match his own breathing pattern to the sound and told that if he succeeded, the tone reflecting his breathing would become lower in pitch. After such biofeedback training, all four patients showed less lung resistance to air passage comparable to the improvement seen after bronchodilation inhalation therapy. The pediatrician conducting the investigation concluded: "This pilot study gives promise that asthmatic children can lower airway resistance in short biofeedback training sessions. One may speculate on the future therapeutic significance of this finding. Some children might learn to control airway reactivity completely, while others might use biofeedback training for symptomatic relief." A biofeedback test conducted on college students with mild asthma likewise revealed that biofeedback can decrease asthmatics' total lung resistance to air passage. Yet a fourth investigation demonstrated that whereas relaxation training is effective in reducing mild to moderate asthma, it is particularly effective if combined with biofeedback.

The drawback of biofeedback training for improving asthma or any other disease, however, is that it is still largely experimental and only available through a few physicians or medical centers. True, biofeedback machines can now be purchased for use at home, but a patient must first be trained by the proper personnel in how to use a machine for his particular condition, and while there are some effective biofeedback instruments on the market, there are also some which are ineffective.

Another personality change that might mitigate your asthma if your asthma has personality inputs is to lessen stressful events in your life, since asthmatics with fewer life changes have been shown to have less disease. You cannot control all the stressful events in your life, of course, but you do have power over some of them. For instance, if you've just experienced a death in the family, it would be unwise from a health viewpoint to take on a new job or move into a new home until your mind and body have recovered from the loss.

If you have a child whose asthma has a psychological component, you can encourage his independence and thereby help reduce his asthma by making him fit in with his peers as much as possible. For instance, let him ride the schoolbus or walk to school if that is what his friends do, rather than driving him. Encourage him to play tennis, swim, or engage in other sports where he can progress at his own pace and thus bolster his ego and health rather than to participate in team sports, which may be too fatiguing for an asthmatic, which may erode rather than build up his ego and health because of his less-than-robust asthmatic condition, and which may expose him to dusty exercise mats, overheating, showers, and then going out in the cold—physical stressors that can help bring on an asthmatic attack.

If you suspect that your child's asthma might be partially due to you or your spouse dominating or overprotecting him, send him away to boarding school for a while, or to one of the special rehabilitation centers for asthmatic children situated throughout the United States. Such facilities have brought about dramatic improvement in children with severe asthma, both because the children are separated from their usual home environments and because the parents of these children are guided in how to handle their children once they return home. "In the vast majority of instances," a physician who pioneered one of these centers reports, "we can help the child recover from the state of intractable asthma and help develop either complete freedom from asthma or substantial relief from his condition."

Biotype Changes for Countering Rheumatoid Arthritis

If, as a rheumatoid arthritis victim, you suspect that your disease had its origin in a traumatic childhood, deconditioning your feelings about these experiences might help improve your condition. Follow the advice along the lines given earlier in this chapter. Although a psychotherapist could probably help you achieve this goal best, a compassionate physician might help you release painful, unhealthy emotions.

If you believe that your disease was partially triggered by helplessness or hopelessness, as is the case for many rheumatoid victims, overcoming such emotions can benefit your health. As we saw earlier in this chapter, rheumatoid patients with ego strength have a better prognosis than do rheumatoid patients without such strength. A 1969 study also revealed that rheumatoid patients with a positive self-image and with an interest in the world and other people respond better to treatment than do rheumatoid patients who have a poor self-image and who are pathologically preoccupied with themselves.

Has a tendency to repress negative emotions also contributed to your arthritis? If so, learning to express such emotions can likewise lessen your rheumatoid flareups, a 1978 study showed. You might also ask your physician whether he knows of any group therapy for rheumatoid patients. Group therapy sessions conducted at the Veterans Administration Hospital in Philadelphia had rheumatoid patients engage in role playing. This way the patients came to discern alternate ways of dealing with negative emotions other than simply repressing them.

Whether or not your RA was triggered by particularly stressful events, keep in mind that flareups in the rheumatoid condition are often triggered by such events, and try to keep such events in your life to a minimum. You should try to improve your ability to cope with such events, as detailed earlier in this chapter, because rheumatoid patients who learn how to better cope with stressful events have been found to experience an improvement in their conditions.

But undoubtedly the greatest personality challenge facing you as a rheumatoid biotype is giving up obsessive, compulsive, largely masochistic behaviors, because they further the joint damage and symptoms of rheumatoid arthritis. However, if you truly want to improve your health on a long-term basis, you should retire to your bed until your joint inflammation and systemic manifestations subside, which may be anywhere from several weeks to several months, and then get enough rest daily to prevent fatigue, a common symptom of rheumatoid arthritis. What is the scientific basis for such drastic advice? In a 1974 study, sixteen rheumatoid patients stayed in bed at least thirteen hours a day for a month, whereas fourteen other rheumatoid patients went about their usual activities. The former patients experienced a significant decrease in pain, duration, and severity of morning stiffness and joint tenderness, and increased grip strength, whereas the latter did not. Clinical observations reveal that rheumatoid patients can particularly profit from bed rest early in their disease, when they are especially likely to resist it. Rheumatoid patients who get enough rest have also been found to show greater improvement and to require less medication than those who do not get enough rest. "The aims of treatment of rheumatoid arthritis," rheumatologists wrote in a 1978 issue of the *Mayo Clinic Proceedings,* "are to reduce pain and inflammation, preserve joint function and insofar as possible, prevent deformity. Pathophysiologic, biophysical and clinical evidence supports the thesis that rest of inflamed joints and related tissues is beneficial, and that use of inflamed parts is harmful. No better way has yet been devised for resting the musculoskeletal system than by limiting its activity."

But does this mean that, as a rheumatoid patient, you must become almost totally incapacitated in order to prevent further deterioration in your condition or to improve your health? No, it does not. But it does mean taking to your bed when you are tired and when your joints are inflamed and painful, and it does mean pursuing activities that can help, not aggravate, your rheumatoid condition. For instance, a physical therapist recommended by your physician can teach you exercises to help your condition, not hurt it.

Finally, if you find it tough to totally give up rheumatoid-aggravating, obsessive-compulsive behaviors, try restructuring such behaviors toward healthier ends. For instance, rather than knocking yourself out and aggravating your arthritis by keeping your house spotless, use your obsessive-compulsive energies to maintain a precise daily schedule of physical exercises that can improve your rheumatoid.

Biotype Changes for Healing Gastrointestinal Conditions

If you're an ulcerative colitis biotype who has ulcerative colitis, you probably grew up in an emotionally repressed atmosphere or had a dominating mother. Deconditioning your feelings about these early life experiences, as prescribed earlier in this chapter, would probably improve your condition. And if, as an ulcerative colitis victim, you are a dependent, immature person, you should not only follow the advice offered above in overcoming helplessness but seriously consider psychotherapy in order to become more independent and thus improve your health. A study compared fifty-seven ulcerative colitis patients treated with both psychotherapy and medical management to fifty-seven ulcerative colitis patients treated only with medical management and found that the former patients showed a greater health improvement, and that this greater improvement lasted at least five years. Thus, "psychotherapy has a demonstrably favorable effect on the somatic curse of the disease," the researchers conducting the investigation concluded.

As an ulcerative colitis biotype with the disease, you undoubtedly also repress negative emotions and have obsessive-compulsive habits. Follow the suggestions offered earlier in this chapter for overcoming these traits and becoming healthier, because as a study cited in Chapter 3 showed, healthy siblings of ulcerative colitis patients tend to be more rebellious and less obsessive-compulsive than their sick brothers and sisters.

And finally, if your ulcerative colitis was triggered by stressful events, shore up your ability to cope with more such events in the future. This is because ulcerative colitis is often triggered by stressful events in the first place, as we discussed in Chapter 3. It's quite likely that such events would also aggravate ulcerative colitis if it already exists. Also as we saw above, learning how to cope with stressful events can help patients combat disease.

If you're an ulcer personality with an ulcer, on the other hand, you probably have conflicts over whether to be dependent or independent. To overcome them, follow the suggestions given above on how to overcome helplessness and thus to become more independent. If you do so, you should become less prone to an ulcer, because as we saw in Chapter 3 and in the last chapter, stomach acid secretion may be due to dependency needs, and such acid is necessary for ulcers of the small intestine. As an ulcer personality with an ulcer, you are probably also prone to repressing negative emotions. Following advice given earlier in this chapter on how to vent negative emotions should make you less prone to acid production and an ulcer, for, as we have seen, repressed negative emotions make the stomach secrete a lot of stomach acid, and lots of stomach acid helps set the stage for an ulcer.

As an ulcer biotype, you are also undoubtedly ambitious, hardworking, and meticulous and are particularly sensitive to stress. Thus you probably feel harassed in many instances, and such feelings probably heighten your stomach acid production and aggravate your ulcer, since anxiety is known to increase stomach acid production and to be capable of producing ulcers in animals. To counter such feelings and get rid of your ulcer, you might try relaxation exercises. Such exercises should quell anxiety messages which course along your vagus nerve to your stomach, because relaxation exercises are known to decrease sympathetic nerve activity, and a sympathetic nerve called the vagus nerve is known to send emotional messages from the brain to the stomach. Still another way to improve your ulcer is to set priorities in your life so that you stop trying to overachieve and be such a perfectionist.

As far as especially stressful events over which you have little control go, follow advice given earlier in this chapter on how to better cope with them. The reasons? Because ulcers are often triggered by stressful events in the first place, it's quite likely that such events would also aggravate an ulcer that already exists. Also, as we saw earlier in this chapter, learning how to cope with stressful events can help patients combat disease.

If you're an anorexia nervosa biotype, you probably had a dominating mother or other childhood trauma leading to excessive dependency needs, helplessness, and worthlessness. Follow the suggestions offered above on how to decondition feelings about a distressing childhood and how to overcome helplessness and hopelessness. Studies have shown that more outgoing, independent anorexics have a better prognosis than do more introverted, dependent ones. Psychotherapy should also help you immensely in achieving these aims. Studies have also demonstrated that psychotherapy alone or combined with other regimens, such as hospitalization, tube feeding, drugs, or behavior modification, can benefit anorexics considerably and help them eventually lead healthy lives. In fact, some evidence suggests that psychotherapy is more valuable than all other treatments for the condition. As some Pittsburgh physicians put it: "We make no effort to feed these patients and direct all our efforts at collaborative psychotherapy with them and their parents. We tell them that we are concerned that death is possible, but that we will direct our attention to the feelings and unhappiness that caused them not to care about eating or living. We also tell the parents that we, just as they, cannot keep their child alive by intravenous therapy or by tube feeding for any length of time, since that would be avoiding the issue rather than confronting it."

Psychotherapy has likewise been shown to help anorexics vent negative emotions more and thus to become healthier. Thanks to psychotherapy, Edith H. learned how to better confront people and came to realize that her weight loss was due, in part, to directing anger meant for others onto herself. If you are an anorexic who represses negative emotions, also follow the suggestions offered earlier in this chapter on how to express negative emotions. And if you're obsessive-compulsive about achievement and exercise while starving, follow the advice given earlier in this chapter on how to become less obsessive-compulsive. One study showed that anorexics who are willful and manipulative have a better prognosis than do those who are compulsive and ritualistic.

Biotype Changes for Banishing Headaches

As a migraine biotype with migraine headaches, you probably are a compulsive worker, compulsive perfectionist, or both, thanks to indoctrination by a parent or other influential person while young. Will deconditioning your feelings about your relationship to this person in childhood help relieve your migraines? Possibly, although such deconditioning via lengthy psychoanalysis has not proved to be very effective, probably because migrainers need an active rather than passive approach to their health problems. However, there *is* ample evidence that changing your obsessive-compulsive behavior can mitigate your migraines, some of it detailed earlier in this chapter. How do you go about changing your behavior? Follow advice given to obsessive-compulsive patients earlier, particularly the relaxation exercises, as they have been found to reduce migraines. Also avoid being too perfectionistic, and try to complete only half the work that you ordinarily would do in a set time. Learn to delegate responsibilities. Deal with each day as it comes along rather than anxiously anticipating problems and meeting them halfway. Eventually you will realize greater spontaneity, effectiveness, and productivity, less anxiety and tension, and in turn less severe and frequent migraines. Group therapy for migraine patients might also help you become less obsessive-compulsive, as it has other migraine victims. As two physicians who have run such group therapy write: "It has been our aim to make migraine patients aware, sometimes for the first time in their lives, of their state of tension, to recognize it when it recurs during their everyday life and to provide them with a technique of reducing it without having to go to the length of getting into a hot bath, or recourse to the bottle of tranquilizers which so many bitterly resent and fight. Thus, many sufferers eventually learn to relax in the most propitious situations, e.g., being late for an appointment in a traffic jam, during persistent needling of a resident parent, during the annual audit or attending an unusually frustrating committee." How do you locate group therapy for migraine patients? Ask your doctor if he knows where the technique might be offered.

As a migraine sufferer, you may also be repressing negative emotions, for there is evidence that releasing anger and hostility can reduce migraines. Follow the suggestions above for learning how to vent negative emotions, especially anger and resentment. If you're a migrainer whose condition appears to be partially due to insecurity and immaturity, following the advice given earlier in this chapter on overcoming helplessness might help reduce your headaches. Biofeedback training has also been shown to give migrainers a sense of control over their destinies and headaches and thus to reduce their migraines.

As a migraine biotype with migraines, you should also sit down, think about what kind of situation or situations usually trigger your headaches, and decide how you might better cope with such events to reduce your headaches. For instance, if your migraines are usually brought on by suppressed anger, allowing yourself to become angry at someone might stop the attack, clinical evidence suggests. If your headaches are sparked by jealousy, becoming less helpless and hopeless about life, as advised earlier in this chapter, might help you gain self-confidence and direction in life and thus to feel less jealous and consequently to experience fewer migraines. If your migraines are set off by tension or release from tension, striving hard to eliminate obsessive-compulsive behaviors should help reduce tension and release from tension and thus also reduce your headaches. And if your migraines are set into motion by suppressed resentment against a particular person in your life, overcoming this resentment with the Simontons' mental imagery technique, described earlier, should help banish your resentment and your headaches.

Finally, you can even use positive thinking to abort migraines once they get under way, clinical evidence shows. Helen D. was a thirty-two-year-old wife and mother and frequent migraine victim. After Helen's physician convinced her that she could abort migraines with positive thinking, Helen decided to try it. One day her husband infuriated her by being cross with her and the children. Right after that she knew a migraine was coming, because she saw lights and colors and pinwheels. Immediately, she lay down on the sofa and told herself, "I *don't want* an excruciating headache and nausea." Then she thought, "Although I'm furious with Bob, I really don't want to kill him." These thoughts eased her anger and tension, and as her anger and tension evaporated, so did her pending headache. In other words, she had used thought power to switch off emotionally ordered fight-flight mechanisms that help bring on a migraine.

If you're a tension headache biotype with tension headaches, you probably are chronically despondent and angry and translate these emotions into tension headaches. Following the advice given earlier in this chapter on overcoming hopelessness should lessen your headaches. So should the mental exercises the Simontons recommend to get rid of chronic resentment. And so should relaxation exercises or just getting more relaxation on a daily basis. Take the case of chronic tension headache sufferer Richard I., discussed in Chapter 6. Whenever Richard played the guitar, his headaches eased, but when he quit playing, they returned. Biofeedback training has also been found effective for treating tension headaches, but only if followed up with relaxation practice at home.

If, as a tension headache victim, you also repress negative emotions, following suggestions on venting negative emotions given above should also help lessen your headaches. And if you tend to be disorganized and forgetful like many tension headache patients, drawing up priority lists for your daily activities might ease up your tenseness and tension headaches.

Biotype Changes for Healing Mental Disorders

Nervous tension, you'll recall, is one of the hallmarks of people who later in life succumb to schizophrenia. A 1975 study found that schizophrenics have a lot of muscle tension. Relaxation exercises or muscle tension biofeedback might thus help ameliorate schizophrenia, the authors speculated, particularly since such treatments have been found to have a positive effect on the psyche of neurotic persons (those who are anxious, depressed, insecure).

If you're a reactive depressive—a person who often gets depressed by various life events—jogging should help you. A University of Wisconsin researcher reported in 1978 that jogging a few times a week may be just as effective as, if not more so than, psychotherapy for treating moderately depressed patients (those with reactive depression rather than with the more severe involutional depression or manic depression). This investigator had twenty-four moderately depressed patients either jog three or more times a week or attend long-term psychotherapy. After ten weeks, the joggers felt only occasionally depressed, while the subjects in long term psychotherapy were still quite depressed. How might exercise combat reactive depression? Probably by giving a person a sense of achievement and providing an outlet for anger and anxiety. The reactive depressive, you'll recall, tends to be rather helpless and pessimistic by nature.

The ultimate challenge for all patients, regardless of the kind of affliction, then, is to regain soundness of mind (soul) so that a soundness of body will follow. That is what the ancient Greeks advocated. Indeed, according to Old and Middle English, "healing" means "to make whole."

10

BIOTYPE AS
PREVENTIVE MEDICINE

I assure you it is much wholesomer
to be a complaisant, good-humored,
contented Courtier, than a Grumbletonian
Patriot, always whining and snarling.

—John Adams to his wife Abigail,
The Hague, July 1, 1782

FOR QUITE A WHILE there had been something distinctive about Roseto, Pennsylvania, a town seventy-five miles north of Philadelphia.
But the first person to take public note of it, around 1960, was a Roseto
physician. He observed that Rosetans, almost all Italians, seemed to
have a remarkably low death rate, especially in heart attack fatalities.
A subsequent study of most of Roseto's population dramatically confirmed his contention.

Only one Rosetan man in one thousand died from a heart attack, the
investigation found, compared with a national rate of 3.5 males per one
thousand. The female heart attack death rate for Roseto was even less,
compared to the national average. What's more, the study revealed
that Roseto also had rates of gastrointestinal ulcers, senile dementia,
and some other disorders that were lower than that of not only the rest
of the United States but of neighboring towns as well.

These findings were all the more provocative because Rosetans were
relatively obese—a heart attack risk factor. Their diets contained at
least as much animal fat, another heart attack predisposer, as that of
nearby residents. Their incidence of high blood pressure and high
levels of cholesterol in the bloodstream—two other heart attack risk
factors—were the same as those of their neighbors. They even shared
a water supply with their neighbors, ruling out water hardness—a
heart attack protector—as the cause of their low prevalence of heart
attacks.

With physical explanations for the Rosetans' exceptionally good
health apparently ruled out, scientists turned their attention to sociological and psychological characteristics of the Rosetans for an answer. Indeed, one of the Rosetans' greatest protections against disease,

it turned out, was their outstanding ability to cope with life's stresses. This is a trait that disease personalities do not possess; otherwise they would not succumb to illnesses in the wake of stressful life events.

What particular methods did Rosetans use to manage stresses? Being a small, tightly knit Italian community, they valiantly supported each other in times of crises. Following a death in the family, for instance, the bereaved received food and money from relatives and friends, who at times temporarily assumed responsibility for the care of the chidren of the bereaved. When a Rosetan had money troubles, relatives and friends rallied to his aid, and in cases of abrupt, extreme financial loss, the community itself assumed responsibility for helping the family that was struck. As for other kinds of personal problems than money, Rosetans also tended to work them out with the help of relatives and friends and the parish priest. The elderly and mentally retarded were rarely put in institutions; their families cared for them at home if at all possible.

Other studies, too, demonstrate that ability to cope with stressful life events can prevent disease. In 1977 researchers reported that personality factors added significantly to the predictability of health changes following stressful life events. Individuals who tended to establish relationships with others, who were not particularly sensitive, and who tended intellectually and socially to conform were found to weather stressful events and hence remain healthier in the wake of such events than were persons who were more antisocial, more sensitive, and intellectually and socially nonconformist. In 1969 college students who resisted serious respiratory infections in the face of stressful events were found to cope better with these events than were students who succumbed to such infections under similar circumstances. Rather than react helplessly to the events, or angrily strike out at them, as the disease victims did, the students who remained healthy handled the crises in their lives energetically and assertively. In 1956 a scientist compared two battalions of American infantrymen from the same regiment in Korea with respect to morale and psychiatric casualties in the thrust of battle. The battalion with high morale (greater self-esteem and group cohesiveness) experienced about half the rate of psychiatric illnesses than did the battalion with low morale. Then in a 1972 study, army wives who encountered numerous trying events while pregnant but who received ample social support experienced fewer pregnancy complications than did army wives with similar trying events but little social support. And according to a 1978 investigation of eighty-two women who became mothers in Berkeley, California in 1928 and 1929, middle-class American women who learned to cope during the Great

Depression rank higher in health fifty years later than do middle-class American women of the same age who didn't learn to cope at that time. The researcher—Glen H. Elder, Jr.—interviewed the women in 1969 and 1970 and evaluated them on a variety of physical and psychological health measures. The women were also divided into working class and middle class, and into those deprived economically by the Depression and those nondeprived.

Specifically, whereas the Depression had increased the likelihood of poor health around 1970 among women from the working class, deprived women from the middle class ranked even healthier around 1970 than middle-class women who had not been economically deprived during the Depression. Why these results? Elder suggests that the working-class women had had little to start with and were completely wiped out both financially and psychologically by the Depression, leading to poor health in later years. In contrast, the middle-class women had maintained some financial reserves even in the Depression and this had helped many of them learn how to cope and thus become psychologically and physically healthier than average in later years.

Undoubtedly, the fact that Rosetans were gay, friendly, enthusiastic, and optimistic toward life helped them ward off disease just as much as their ability to cope with stresses did. According to a 1977 study, many Vietnam prisoners of war returned to the United States healthier than noncaptured servicemen. The reason? They believed that they were masters of their own fate and improved their diet and physical fitness in prison rather than allowing themselves to languish away. Healthy siblings of ulcerative colitis victims are often independent, rebellious, and adventurous, whereas those with ulcerative colitis tend to be immature, ingratiating, and indecisive. Similarly, nonulcer victims are apt to be more independent than ulcer patients are. Relatives of rheumatoid arthritis patients who have a genetic predisposition to RA but who do not have the disease tend to exhibit more ego strength than do rheumatoid patients. And nonalcoholics are likely to reject pictures reflecting an infantile need for security, narcissism, low frustration-tolerance, and reliance on external objects, whereas alcoholics are often attracted to such pictures.

Similarly, just as repression of negative emotions appears to help set the stage for so many diseases, expression of negative emotions helps prevent them. As we saw in previous chapters, noncancer victims are generally more aware of their anxiety than cancer victims are. Relatives of rheumatoid arthritis patients tend to admit angry feelings more than the patients themselves do. Headache-free individuals suppress

negative emotions less than do tension headache and migraine sufferers and are also apt to concur, more than headache victims do, that
repressed anger is the cause of much unhappiness and that if people
expressed their anger, they would feel a lot better. Persons who do not
commit suicide generally vent negative emotions while young,
whereas suicides generally hold them in. Individuals who sleep well at
night tend to let anger out during the day, while insomniacs are apt to
repress it.

Whereas obsessive-compulsive behaviors prep people for diseases,
avoiding such behaviors helps people stay healthy. Ample evidence
shows that men and women who are not excessively ambitious, competitive, hardworking, hurried, impatient, and who tend to do two or
more things at once, are much less susceptible to heart attacks than individuals who engage in such excessive behaviors. As we saw, non-
asthmatics are not as bent on excessive neatness, conscientiousness,
and altruism as are asthmatics.

A happy childhood can help protect people against diseases, just as
a traumatic childhood can make them more vulnerable to them. For
instance, a teen-ager named Charlene G., who had been a wanted
child, got on well with her parents and enjoyed good health. In contrast, her younger brother Tim had been unwanted, was physically
abused by their father, and suffered from diabetes. Similarly, Karl P.,
who had received a lot of attention from his mother as a baby, remained psychologically and physically healthy during childhood,
whereas his identical twin, Kay, who had been farmed out to many
caretakers as a baby, experienced stunting of both her psychological
and physical growth. Cancer patients generally had a problematic
childhood. Whereas asthma-free boys are not likely to be overprotected and overindulged by their mothers, boys with asthma are. Children without rheumatoid arthritis generally experience a more
satisfying home life than do youngsters with the disease. Nonschi-
zophrenics tend to have been much closer to their parents and happier
as children than schizophrenics were.

Granted that certain personality traits and experiences can help
keep people healthy, might you, then, as a presently healthy person,
exploit such traits and experiences as a form of preventive medicine?
Absolutely! Keep in mind, however, that preventive medicine is a
major challenge because it entails a serious reevaluation of one's attitudes and habits and sometimes radical changes involving one's
spouse, friends, job, environment, philosophy, or goals.

First, take the case of a disturbing childhood. If you have unresolved
conflicts stemming from your childhood, psychotherapy is probably

the best way to get them into better perspective, vent pent-up emotions about them, and hence better guarantee continuing good health for yourself. Such psychotherapy doesn't necessarily have to be lengthy, costly in-depth psychoanalysis to be beneficial. Linda N., a young New York City career woman, found herself facing some unresolved conflicts stemming from her childhood about male-female relationships, the role of women in a male-dominated professional world, and the part that the formal religion she was brought up in should play in her adult life. At the urging of a friend, Linda made an appointment with psychiatrist, Dr. Sarah G., to get some professional help with her problems. In the first session, Linda pointed out to Dr. G., "I have three problems I need help on but can only afford several months of appointments to solve them. Can you help me in that time span?" "I'll do my best," Dr. G. replied. And indeed, during the next several months, as Dr. G. probed into Linda's early childhood, Linda came to realize intellectually how her three present conflicts arose largely from interactions with a too-dominant mother—something Linda had not been aware of before. But even more vital from an emotional and physical health standpoint, Dr. G.'s probings helped Linda let long-repressed anger against her mother surface. Linda had no idea that she had been harboring such emotions. And once they poured out, Linda found herself so mad at her mother that she didn't call or visit her for another two months.

Deconditioning feelings about an unsatisfactory childhood isn't the only way to safeguard your health, of course. You should also replace any helpless and hopeless feelings you have with self-confidence and self-fulfillment (happiness). How do you get self-confidence? Go off alone somewhere, where you won't be expected to play your usual roles, where you can get in touch with yourself. Take stock of your past achievements in life. You'll be surprised to see how such an assessment can bolster your self-image and prepare you for more independence in the future.

It's also possible that a fear of failure is keeping you from attaining the self-confidence you want in life. To overcome such a fear, keep in mind the findings of a course on failure conducted at the Massachusetts Institute of Technology:

People fail, but people aren't failures.

Failures are what lead to successes.

A failure at one point in your life may be a success in the future.

Before labeling something a failure, ask yourself who considers it one. Then decide whether you do too. If you agree, determine whether you are at fault. If so, turn the defeat into a learning experience by ascertaining what went wrong and why and how you can avoid or correct your errors the next time around.

On the other hand, a fear of success might be keeping you from being as self-confident as you would like. How do you know whether you fear success? Look in the mirror. If you don't like what you see, then you fear success. Also, think about what you consider important and desirable goals in your life. Are you afraid of achieving such goals? If so, you fear success. How do you overcome the fear of success? One way is to use a technique described in the last chapter on mental imagery. In your mind's eye, visualize yourself with a goal already met. Visualize significant people in your life responding enthusiastically to your achievement. Be happy and grateful for having reached your goal; savor the sense of success. Gradually drift back to the present and take a first step toward reaching that goal.

Still another way to overcome helplessness and increase your self-confidence is to meditate regularly. A 1976 Canadian study showed that persons who do so become less anxious and more autonomous and creative than they were before. How can you meditate? You might try the technique subjects used in the Canadian investigation:

Before your morning and evening meals ritual, retire to a calm and normally lit room, somewhere between bright daylight and darkness. Try to avoid being disturbed during the exercise by the phone or other loud noises.

Sit in the most comfortable position for you, your spinal cord straight and leaning against a flat vertical surface. Be sure your abdomen is free to ease breathing.

Close your eyes and wait half a minute. Now count your respiration (count for inhalation and exhalation) from one to 10, and start again at one, and so on. If you lose count during the exercise, don't try to recall where you were but simply start over at one and keep on.

During this exercise you will notice that thoughts, feelings, and sensory distractions will appear, but you shouldn't try to fight them. Wait until it becomes easier to resume the exercise.

Perform this respiratory exercise for 20 minutes. Wait three more minutes. Now open your eyes.

After you've practiced the above technique for two weeks, you may then want to pursue a more advanced meditation ritual as well. Before you were to count your respiration from one to 10. Now you will stop counting in order to concentrate on the breathing process itself. You will breathe as usual without any effort or restraint. Your attention should be on your inhalation and exhalation. Follow the entrance of the air through the nose down to the lungs and from there toward the outside.

Your breathing may be long or short. This is not important. Breathe naturally. The only important thing is that when your breathing is short, you are aware of it, and the same when it is long.

Exercise can also increase your self-confidence. A Purdue University social scientist studied the effects of exercise on men and women ages thirty to sixty and reports that it made them more self-assured and imaginative. To conquer helplessness, you might also follow the advice of the Reverend Norman Vincent Peale of New York City:

Whenever a negative thought about your abilities comes to mind, deliberately voice a positive thought to cancel it out.

Minimize obstacles in your imagination.

Don't let yourself be awestruck by other people; they too are doubtful of themselves from time to time.

Get a psychotherapist to help you understand the origins of your inferiority, which probably stems from your childhood. Self-knowledge can lead to a cure.

Yet another way to overcome helplessness is to start believing that you, not fate, have control over your life. Finally, keep in mind what a physician wrote in a 1969 issue of the *Journal of the American Medical Association*: "Physicians long have known ... that how a man feels about himself heavily influences his health, as well as his recovery from illness. Most important among his feelings is their sum, his self-esteem."

While a person's self-esteem largely derives from his self-confidence, of course, it is also intimately caught up in his self-fulfillment and happiness. To ascertain whether you are fulfilled and content, or prone more to pessimism and hopelessness, ask yourself whether you agree with the following statements:

I look forward to the future with hope and enthusiasm.

When things are going badly, I'm helped by knowing they can't stay that way forever.

I have enough time to accomplish the things I most want to do.

My past experiences have prepared me well for my future.

I can't imagine what my life would be like in 10 years.

Things just don't work out the way I want them to.

I never get what I want so it's foolish to want anything.

If you find yourself agreeing with the first four statements and disagreeing with the last three, then you are fulfilled and content. But if you find yourself disagreeing with the first four statements and agreeing with the last three, then you're a pessimist sliding into hopelessness. Now, if you're a pessimist bordering on hopelessness, how can you become more fulfilled and happier and thus better bolstered against disease? You must have a goal or goals for the future that are profoundly important to you, because a happy life involves commitment and involvement. Or as Reverend Peale advises: "Get interested in something. Get absolutely enthralled in something. Throw yourself into it with enthusiasm." But what kind of goal or goals should you pursue? A 1978 study of some two hundred middle-aged employees working for the Bell System revealed that the happiest employees were not necessarily those with status on the management ladder but those who were satisfied with their careers, engaged in active recreation, learning, and expressing themselves creatively, and who had good friends and a close relationship with a spouse. Other studies of Americans' views of what constitutes happiness have revealed that love is the most important element and that marriage, family, friends, and children are even more vital for happiness than job satisfaction is.

In addition to having a goal or goals that are of great importance to you, still another useful technique is to lie in bed each morning before rising and deliberately think happy thoughts and visualize good things happening to you that day. Before going to bed each night, picture negative thoughts and emotions flowing out of your head. And if, during the day, you catch yourself thinking or feeling something negative, block it out with a positive thought or feeling.

You can become self-fulfilled and happy even if you had a traumatic childhood. According to Dr. Jonathan Friedman, a Columbia University psychologist, "People who led very unhappy childhoods, whose parents divorced or died, who were treated coldly, who had physical and psychological problems, still manage to be happy as adults." Note, however, that Dr. Friedman uses the word "manage," because the attainment of happiness requires a lifelong and ever-changing quest. It doesn't simply happen.

Another strong weapon of preventive medicine is learning how to vent negative emotions. One clue that you might be suppressing such feelings lies in whether or not you engage in what the French call *pensée operatoire* (operative thinking). It is where a person describes something while totally omitting emotional words. This kind of thinking received particular attention at the eleventh European Conference on Psychosomatic Research in 1976. Data were presented showing that patients with ulcers, ulcerative colitis, high blood pressure, asthma, rheumatoid arthritis, thyroid disease, and neurodermatitis used fewer emotionally laden words during interviews than did a matched group of healthy persons. Still another way to determine whether you repress negative emotions is to ask yourself whether you recall your dreams. If you rarely do, it may be because you tend to repress negative emotions. So, provided that you *are* apt to suppress such feelings, how do you go about learning how to express them?

First, decide what particular negative emotion or emotions you might be repressing. For one person it might be anxiety and depression, for another it might be anger and resentment. If you're prone to suppressing the former two, for instance, set aside a period each evening where you can pour out these feelings to a sympathetic spouse or roommate. If you're apt to withhold anger, you might try confronting as soon as possible a person who has angered you. If you don't want to confront an offender, let off steam by going around the house screaming. As for relieving resentment, you might pluck up courage to let your offender know what has been bugging you, or you might try to ease resentment out of your mind by thinking good things about the offender (the technique described in detail in the previous chapter). Another method that might help you surface negative emotions is to work at recalling your dreams right after you awaken in the morning, since frequent dream recallers have been found to repress negative emotions less than infrequent dream recallers do. Finally, another technique that should get negative emotions off your chest and help keep you healthy is enriching your fantasy life, because research shows that persons subject to disease tend to engage in pragmatically oriented mental activity to the exclusion of fantasies.

As for obsessive-compulsive thoughts and behaviors, how can you banish them from your life in order to reinforce continuing good health for yourself? If you've been working too hard to the exclusion of restorative rest and play, you must learn the art of relaxation. Try something new and different for yourself. Choose an activity you really enjoy, not something other people want you to pursue. It may be walking around your neighborhood or the woods, biking or carpentry, handball, tennis, or even belly dancing. Or you might practice relaxation exercises described in the previous chapter, or meditation described in this chapter, since it has been found to make more people more empathetic and open to experience and less aggressive and ambitious. Or maybe you simply prefer a warm bubble bath to take away mental and bodily strain. Once you select a relaxation activity, however, it's important that you pursue it on a regular basis (daily, if at all possible). Most people accept the responsibility to meet duties and deadlines imposed on them by others, but it is equally important for them to give their minds and bodies the relaxation that their minds and bodies crave.

If you find daily activities in your life "chores" or "duties" rather than pleasures, sit down and map out strategy for eliminating as many of them as possible. For instance, you're the mother of seven children and find that two hours of each day are spent running the laundromat that your husband bought as a sideline and one hour of each day is used up chauffeuring your children to school and activities; get your husband to sell the laundromat if it isn't making a good profit, or turn it over to one of your teen-age children to run if it is making a good profit. One of your teen-agers might also take over your chauffeuring duties. In other words, you must stop sacrificing yourself for others all the time and think of your own happiness and health for a change. Now, all this doesn't mean you have to become a selfish egotist. But it does mean that whatever activities you pursue in life should bring you satisfaction and joy, and as they fulfill you, they will undoubtedly benefit other people as well.

Doing away with health-eroding, obsessive-compulsive thoughts and behaviors could, in fact, require a frank appraisal of the role that religion plays in your life. According to an article in a 1976 issue of *Preventive Medicine*, active religious faith promotes health by establishing a sense of well-being, an investment in health care for oneself and others, and a willingness to accept human limitations and death. Health indexes are also dramatically better among the Mormons of Utah than among comparative populations. The Amish and the Lutheran farmers of the Midwest rarely suffer from depression compared to Americans in general, thanks to their wholesome way of life. In a 1972 study, American men who attend church regularly were found to run only half the risk of getting a heart attack as were American men who didn't worship in church regularly. And back around the turn of the century, the famous Swiss psychiatrist Carl Jung noted a markedly low rate of neurotic and psychotic illness among Roman Catholics in Germany and Switzerland. Jung attributed this low illness rate to the routine opportunity for repentance and restitution (being put right with God and the world) that the confessional afforded Catholics. However, when a religious person becomes excessively bent on leading a pure or perfect life, his impulses can degenerate into health-eroding, obsessive-compulsive thoughts and behaviors.

Lucy C., a young mother and housewife, became obsessed with disease largely because of her attraction to the tenets of Christian Science. Such an obsession was hardly rational, of course, since Christian Science holds that disease does not exist. Nonetheless, Lucy's fear of botulism led her to adopt a severely restricted and costly diet for her family in which only fresh meats and vegetables were prepared and to prohibit her children from eating at friends' homes. So great was her anxiety over contracting tetanus that she rushed to the doctor's office demanding a tetanus shot if she as much as pricked her finger. Then one day her son was knocked to the ground by a stray dog. Although Lucy knew it was impossible for him to contract rabies from the dog's paws, she dwelled so much on the incident that she awakened her son in the middle of the night to bring him to the hospital emergency room for a rabies shot. A hospital psychiatrist interviewed her at that time and referred her to a psychotherapist for treatment.

Lucy went to the therapist for twenty-four sessions. The first session was spent discussing her various living problems. The therapist made no attempt to deal directly with her obsessive-compulsive thoughts and behaviors. Then, during the nineteenth session, Lucy reluctantly brought up involvement with Christian Science, which she had previously avoided mentioning, and it became clear to both her and her therapist that this attraction was the source of her excessive concerns about disease. The therapist didn't advise Lucy to reject Christian Science, however, since he respected her religious needs, but he did give her guidance in how to shuck off her excessive strivings toward perfection. He prescribed relaxation exercises to reduce her anxiety by day and to help her sleep at night. He also taught her a procedure for stopping obsessive thoughts. And by the time Lucy finished her therapy, she had overcome the urgent, irrational fears that had haunted her before she started therapy.

What about health-threatening, stressful life events? How can you deal with them so that you don't become ill? First, become aware of what kinds of situations can endanger you. Undesirable occurrences that can most imperil health include death of a spouse, divorce, marital separation, a jail term, or a death of a close family member. Undesirable events that can endanger health to a much lesser degree include trouble with one's boss, trouble with one's inlaws, or anxiety about a minor mortgage or loan.

Next, become aware that it is the accumulation of stressful life events within a few months' period that has been found to be *at least twice as powerful* a factor in eroding people's health as any specific unwholesome reactions that people might make to those situations. Thus your major resistance against health-threatening crises is to try to keep them to a minimum or at least to try to keep them from bunching up in your life. For instance, if you've just lost a spouse through death—generally the most devastating stress that people encounter in their lifetime—don't sell your house, switch jobs, or take out a mortgage or make any other immediate major life change, so as to allow your mind and body to recover from the enormous blow it has received and to spare yourself illness or even death in that time period. (Widows and widowers have been found much more likely to fall ill or even die in the six-to-twelve-month period following the death of a spouse than are persons of similar age who have not lost a spouse through death). Or let's say your mother has just died, a stress that is not quite so devastating to most people as death of a spouse, but nonetheless a great potential threat to health. This is not the time for you to switch jobs, become pregnant, get into a fight with your inlaws, or instigate other major changes in your life.

After keeping potentially devastating events in your life to a minimum or at least staggered, your next most potent tool against these situations is to cope effectively with them. This means taking action (fighting or fleeing), not being passive and doing nothing (which might consist of retreating into self-pity, guilt, hostility, denial, or drinking). There is significant evidence that action is the healthy way to cope. A group of navy psychologists studied the reactions of pilots and their flight officers during jet aircraft carrier-landing practice. Because the pilots had control over the practices and the flight officers did not, the former suffered less anxiety and bodily symptoms during the flights. Similarly, soldiers on a special combat unit in Vietnam who were anticipating an enemy attack experienced less anxiety and depression than basic trainees did because they were engaged in a furor of activity while waiting for the attack—building defenses and maintaining equipment.

You should try to take carefully thought-out, constructive action, not impulsive, defiant action in coping with trying incidents. Why is this? As cited earlier in this chapter, persons who handle crises energetically and constructively tend to stay healthy, whereas those who react defiantly or passively are apt to become ill. A good example of an individual who handled a challenging event assertively and constructively was Ken E., a college sophomore who was oriented toward what he wanted to do in life and who was already married. But Ken had a problem. His mother-in-law objected to her daughter having to work while Ken continued school. So Ken discussed the situation with his wife's mother and came up with a solution that was satisfactory to both her and him. He would work during the summers, taking a big part of the financial burden off his wife.

You can learn to handle stressful events assertively and constructively even if you had a traumatic chidhood. Take the case of student Charlie W., whose background had been unpleasant in that both his parents were rigid, controlling, cold people. Nonetheless, Charlie had managed to extricate himself from them and embark on a life of his own. He had laid out precise schooling and career plans for himself. Then came a crisis: Charlie was turned down by the graduate school of his choice. How did he handle the situation? He took action which was, in a sense, both fighting and fleeing. He did not give up plans to go to graduate school but decided to put it off for a year and meanwhile to accompany a scientist and his family around the world. This decision undoubtedly not only spared Charlie the health-eroding effects of the crisis that had assailed him but even gave him an opportunity to grow personally from the event. (Interestingly, the Chinese word for "crisis" is written by combining the symbols for the words "danger" and "opportunity.") Stressful life events, then, are precisely that: if you don't cope effectively with them, they can make you sick, but if you do effectively grapple with them, you can not only preserve your health but grow personally as well.

Using action to cope with stressful events also helps you achieve what should be your next step in coping with such events, and that is switching off physiological fight-flight mechanisms after you've coped so that they will not erode your health. As we saw in Chapter 9, activated fight-flight mechanisms can help set the stage for disease, particularly if they are chronically activated. An interesting study was conducted on two groups of American infantrymen participating in the Korean War. One was an attacking company, the other a defending company. The former's fight-flight mechanisms were back to normal six days after combat, whereas the latter's were only back to normal thirteen days later, showing that activity was better able to quell unhealthy, chronically activated fight-flight mechanisms than was passivity. Another way besides action to reduce health-threatening, chronically activated fight-flight mechanisms following stressful events is to engage in relaxation exercises such as those described in the previous chapter, or in meditation, as described in this chapter, because they have been shown to reduce such mechanisms. And if the stress you are experiencing is loss of a loved one, crying can help you safeguard your health in the weeks and months that follow because it has been shown to reduce fight-flight mechanisms, notably adrenaline in the bloodstream.

One vital measure you can take to deal with life's trying circumstances is to make sure that you have sufficient social supports to help you get through them before they actually occur. As we saw earlier, a major reason that folks in Roseto, Pennsylvania, had such remarkable health was that they supported each other in times of crisis. Army wives who receive ample attention from spouse and friends while pregnant experience fewer pregnancy complications than do army wives with similar difficult events but little attention from spouse and friends. Other studies have shown that social buttressing can protect people in crisis from a wide variety of pathological states—low birth weight, depression, arthritis, tuberculosis, alcoholism, and even death. How do you know whether you have enough social props to cushion you adequately during stressful events? You should have a spouse or at least one close friend in whom you can confide at the time and whom you can ask for assistance if necessary. It would be even better for your health if you had a large network of relatives, neighbors, and casual friends as well on whom you could call for help in the time of a crisis. Being active in a church, club, or special-interest group is still another reservoir of social support that can help you safeguard your health in times of emergencies.

If you are a liberal intellectual, skeptical about religion, or emotionally sensitive, you are likely to be more vulnerable to stressful events and should work especially hard at combating them when they come into your life. Keep in mind that people with high self-esteem—people who are married, have ample education, or have a good occupation—are better buffered against life's health-threatening crises than are persons with low self-esteem—those who are single or divorced, or with limited education, or with not very satisfying or remunerative occupations. Thus you might consider shoring up on these particular preventive-medicine assets if you don't already possess them.

A final piece of advice on how to deal successfully with health-threatening life events: avoid boredom! It has been found to arouse physiological fight-flight reactions that can lead to disease just as exceptionally stressful events can.

You will hear a great deal more during the next several years on how to alter your biotype in order to preserve your health, because increasing attention is being given to preventive medicine. Psychosomatic-medicine centers are starting to help people draw up potential-stress profiles so they know their strengths and weaknesses in the face of life stresses and thus are better able to cope with them. Physicians are being educated in how to diagnose stress in patients and help their patients cope with it. Researchers are currently trying to learn more about which mechanisms of coping with stress can prevent illness. A study is being conducted throughout the United States to document whether changes in diet, smoking, and exercise can prevent heart attacks; the investigation started in 1973 and will run to 1982, and is the most extensive trial ever conducted by the National Heart, Lung and Blood Institute. The Canadian Government has launched a major campaign to get Canadians to engage in more healthful behaviors. The campaign consists of educating the public about the advantages of giving up smoking, becoming physically fit, driving safely, and so forth, as well as legislation and regulation. The campaign has already brought about some dramatic improvements in Canadian health. In a "Walk a Block a Day" campaign, hordes of Canadians walked a distance they would otherwise not have done. Even patients in hospitals used crutches and wheelchairs to pace out their block. Canadian housewives are fighting flab with the government's "Fit-Kit." Canadian men are working out in gyms.

The challenge for both present and future preventive medicine, in other words, depends on convincing every individual that he has control over his health and inspiring him to do something about it. Or as Dr. Hutschnecker puts it: "We can learn to guard our emotional health as we guard our physical health. We can make every effort to develop our fullest capacity as human beings. We can strengthen every link that joins us to work, to other human beings, to the world around us. Those are our safeguards against illness and against premature death. They are the deeper roots of the will to live."

11

PREPARING
YOUR CHILD
FOR A
HEALTHY LIFE

I've had parents in my office and
we would just be chatting and I would
happen to say, "Tell me something
about your experiences when your mother
or father died," and they would burst
into tears. Even though the death may have
occurred 30 years ago, when they were five
years old, they still felt responsible for it."

—Dr. Morris A. Wessel, clinical
professor of pediatrics,
Yale University of Medicine,
in *Emergency Medicine*

As YOU'VE NOW SEEN, certain traumatic childhood experiences can
predispose a person to illness later in life—such as the death of, or separation from, a parent or loved one and parental domination or rejection. Such experiences can make a child feel insecure, unloved,
helpless, or even hopeless. They can destroy his self-image and render
him incapable of coping with life's challenges. Such personality scars
can then predispose him to illness when he is faced with numerous, or
extremely harassing, stresses or if he engages in obsessive-compulsive
thoughts and behaviors.

Now, let's flip the coin. If a child is spared the loss of a loved one or
some other major childhood trauma; if his parents give him a sense of
self-esteem (self-confidence plus happiness), teach him how to meet
life's stresses, show him how to express negative emotions, and dis-
courage him from engaging in obsessive-compulsive thoughts and behaviors, will he be assured a healthy life? Chances are strong that he
will, as the evidence from previous chapters reveals.

Cancer-free persons are much more likely than cancer patients to have had a satisfactory childhood, that is, not to have lost a parent through death, and to have had parents who were warm, steady, and companionable. Healthy persons are also more apt than cancer victims to have had ample time being the youngest or only child in the family, thus getting ample parental attention and love. Similarly, healthy individuals are much more likely than mentally ill patients to have been close to their parents as a child and not to have lost a parent through death. When identical twins discordant for schizophrenia are compared, the co-twins without schizophrenia are twice as likely to have had normal births as are the co-twins with schizophrenia. Youngsters who escape juvenile rheumatoid arthritis generally come from happy homes, whereas youngsters who fall prey to the disease often do not. And healthy, well-adjusted members of society are far less likely to have experienced the exceptionally distressing childhoods that criminals are likely to have incurred.

What evidence is there that self-esteem acquired during childhood can help secure health? Healthy siblings of schizophrenics tend to have been more independent and happier from ages two to five than the schizophrenics. Similarly, healthy identical twins of schizophrenics are apt to have been more independent, carefree, and outgoing. Persons with lots of stomach acid but without excessive oral needs acquired in childhood (such as wanting to be fed, lean on others, and have close bodily contact) are less prone to getting an ulcer than are those individuals with lots of stomach acid and excessive oral needs. Nonasthmatic boys tend to be less overprotected and overindulged than are asthmatic boys. According to a 1970 British study, youngsters with high self-esteem are less prone to juvenile delinquency than are youngsters without it. Whereas healthy children are apt to have a good self-image, youngsters who are hyperactive and who have learning problems tend not to. In fact, children who are happy and relaxed are much less liable to colds than are unhappy and tense children, according to no less an eminent child authority than Dr. Benjamin Spock.

What evidence is there that learning to cope with life's stresses while young can preserve health later? Children who learn to adapt themselves to various stresses have been found to be better protected against psychiatric illness than those who have not learned to adapt. Take the case of seventeen-year-old Cindy D., versus seventeen-year-old Ryan O. Both had undergone, during the previous year, an exceptional number of stressful life events, such as the marital separations of their parents, death of a close friend, difficulties in their peer relationship, and academic problems. Although Cindy did experience temper outbursts because of such stresses, she remained healthy, but

Ryan suffered a nervous breakdown. Comments a psychiatrist who counseled both Cindy and Ryan: "The one truly striking difference between these two young people was the obvious psychological maturity in the girl and the immature, premorbid personality of the boy."

Healthy adults tend to have been much less prone to nervousness and tension while under stress when young than were suicidal victims. Students who resist serious respiratory infections in the throes of trying events are apt to cope better with these events than are students who succumb to serious respiratory illnesses under similar circumstances. The former tend to handle crises energetically and assertively, whereas the latter are likely to react helplessly to them or to strike angrily out at them. In fact, thanks to a fascinating study reported in a 1978 issue of *American Psychologist,* there is reason to believe that children can learn to deal successfully with life stresses, and thus preserve their health later in life, even if they experienced parental loss or other major trauma during childhood.

This investigation found many more successful persons have experienced parental loss during childhood than have the average population. So why do some persons become successful in spite of early parental loss, whereas other individuals succumb to disease as a result? The study in *American Psychologist* suggests that the former learned from their early childhood loss how to cope with life stresses, reacting to a major personal loss or other kind of stress with excessive productivity and creativity rather than with helplessness and hopelessness. In other words, these successful individuals reacted to early parental death energetically and assertively. Thus one can conclude from the *American Psychologist* study as well as from other evidence presented earlier in this book that if a person learns during childhood to react to stresses with energy, assertion, productivity, and creativity, rather than with helplessness and hopelessness, he will be much more likely to be not only healthy but successful later in life.

Learning how to express negative emotions during childhood can safeguard health then and later in life. Adolescents who do not harbor resentment tend to be less at risk of getting ulcerative colitis than are those who do. Take the case of Robert K., age twenty-eight, and his fraternal twin, Charles, cited in Chapter 3. Robert is healthy, whereas Charles has ulcerative colitis. Whenever Robert and Charles had childhood fights, Robert recalls, Charles would brood about them and recall all the details months later, whereas Robert would usually forgive and forget. According to a 1978 study, children of Jews who survived the Nazi Holocaust do not fall prey to psychiatric problems if their parents discuss their wartime experiences in an open but non-horrendous way, whereas those children of Holocaust survivors do tend to have such problems if their parents refuse to discuss their experiences.

Finally, there is evidence that avoiding obsessive-compulsive thoughts and behavior during childhood can assure individuals healthy lives later. Adults resistant to ulcerative colitis, as we saw in Chapter 3, were much less likely to have engaged in goody-goody, perfectionistic, and idealistic behavior as youngsters than were their siblings with this disease. Take the case of Maxine P., age thirty-four and healthy, and her forty-one-year-old sister, Vera, victim of ulcerative colitis. Maxine reports that Vera had always been more idealistic, perfectionistic, worrying, and anxious to please than Maxine herself has been. Or take the case of Robert K., cited above. Robert had been much less obsessive-compulsive as a youngster than had his brother Charles, an ulcerative colitis victim later in life.

Given that being spared major trauma during childhood, and that certain thoughts, emotions, and behavior can help protect a child against disease both during childhood and later in life, how can you safeguard your youngster against such trauma and encourage such personality traits in him? First, try to reproduce late enough in life to have the maturity to be a good parent. A 1975 study found that the older the mother, the healthier her relationship with her child. On the other hand, try not to reproduce so late that there is a serious chance of your dying before you have seen your child through to maturity, since parental loss early in childhood often helps set the stage for disease later in life, as we've seen time and again, and because suicidal victims often had fathers who were extremely far along in years, as we saw in Chapter 7.

It is important to get your child off to a healthy start in life both psychologically and physically. Want your child, because wanted children are more likely to be happy and healthy than unwanted children are. A 1975 Czech study found that children who are unwanted—especially boys—are more liable to acute illness, hospitalization, and antisocial behavior (an illness predisposer in its own right, as we've seen) than are children who are wanted. Other studies show that if you want a baby at the time it is conceived, it has a much better chance of being of normal weight at birth and healthy than if you don't want it. Charlene G. had been a welcomed child, had had a normal birth, and had gotten on well with her parents, whereas her brother Tim had been unwelcome, had had a difficult birth, and was abused by their father. Charlene grew up healthy, but Tim succumbed to diabetes at age eleven.

If you're a woman, bearing your child when you are not under exceptional stress can also help get him off to a healthy start in life and keep him healthy. Studies have shown that pregnant women under excessive stress have more complications of pregnancy, labor, and delivery than do those who are not and that they are also less likely to have healthy babies than women who do not conceive under such circumstances.

According to an investigation reported in a 1966 *Annals of the New York Academy of Sciences*, potent negative maternal emotions during the last three months of pregnancy, particularly grief, fear, and anxiety, were found to adversely affect the health of unborn children. Although these infants were not born with major birth defects, they were more irritable, hyperactive, and given to feeding problems than were children gestated under less distressing emotional conditions. A study reported at the 1977 annual meeting of the American Association of Psychiatric Services for Children found that an unusually high percentage of mothers of autistic children had been subject to stress while pregnant, such as being separated from their husband, being harassed by a former husband, or frequently arguing with their husband. Yet another investigation revealed that mothers who had been disturbed late in pregnancy tended to have children who by age four were more intense, less adaptable, and more negative in their outlook on life than did mothers who had been content late in pregnancy, and as we've already seen, nervousness, nonadaptability, and a negative outlook on life are disease predisposers.

It is important for a woman to receive adequate support from husband, family, and friends during pregnancy. As we saw in the previous chapter, wives who get ample social buttressing during pregnancy tend to have fewer pregnancy complications than those who do not.

Women should take exceptionally good care of themselves physically during pregnancy. They should eat healthy foods, get plenty of exercise, and give up smoking, preferably long before they become pregnant. Women who smoke and cough heavily during pregnancy have been found to give birth to more nervous, insecure infants than women who do not, and nervousness and insecurity are disease predisposers, as we've already seen. According to a nationwide study reported in 1979, women who smoke cigarettes during pregnancy are more likely to have miscarriages, stillbirths, complications during labor, or an infant who dies from crib death. In fact, this study revealed that even if women give up smoking before becoming pregnant, their offspring are still more subject to *placenta praevia* than if they had never smoked at all. This is a condition where the placenta is attached abnormally low in the womb and thus can lead to dangerous complications during labor and birth.

Another means of launching your child into health and keeping him there is to deliver him at a hospital that attempts to reinforce parent-infant bonds as soon as an infant pops into the world. A hospital can do this by having a newborn emerge into a delivery room with soft rather than harsh lighting, being placed immediately on his mother's abdomen, then put in a warm bath or perhaps in his father's arms, being given to his mother so he can start suckling at her breast, and being allowed to room in with his mother in the hospital. Such efforts have been shown to make children mentally and physically healthier than they would have otherwise been. One-, two- and three-year-old children who have been "bonded" right after birth to their mothers, French investigators showed, were better protected against colic than average and also displayed less trouble in self-feeding and toilet training than toddlers usually do. Early maternal-infant bonding, Tennessee scientists demonstrated, also reduces incidences of child abuse.

Just as crucial to the immediate and long-term health of a child is self-esteem—self-confidence and happiness versus the helplessness and hopelessness that set the stage for so many diseases. How do you give your child self-confidence? First off, strive for "benevolence" rather than for "domination" or "rejection."

Domination may take the form of overcontrol—manipulative, intrusive, interfering behavior. Or, as one adult disease victim recalls about her mother, "She wanted to know all that happened." Domination, on the other hand, may take the form of overprotection—infantilizing, overconcern, overwatchfulness, oversolicitous behavior. Or, as one adult patient says about her mother, "She wanted to control everything I did." Domination can even take the form of seductiveness—possessiveness or erotic behavior. As for rejection, it may consist of abandonment—cold, indifferent, remote behavior or actual physical withdrawal from a child. As one adult disease victim recollects about her father, "He didn't take my hurts and fears seriously." Rejection, on the other hand, may take the form of punishment—harsh, overly hostile, or cruel behavior. As one adult patient remembers her father, "He thought any misbehavior serious." And as another adult patient recalls about her mother, "Nothing seemed to please her." And as still another adult disease victim asserts about her mother, "She thought I wasn't grateful." The ideal parenting behavior is warm, interested, concerned behavior, behavior which is neither overly controlling, protective, indifferent, or harsh. It is intermediate between domination and rejection, involving not so much closeness and control as to stifle a child nor so little as to make the child feel unwanted. Benevolence gratifies and satisfies a child's ego and builds self-confidence, whereas domination and rejection erode the ego and make the child helpless and dependent.

Some specific examples of benevolent, self-confidence-building, health-building parenting are breastfeeding and cuddling. Particularly keep in mind that breastfeeding may help protect people psychologically from cancer later in life. Breastfeeding also makes an infant work hard for a meal, filling him with a sense of accomplishment, and thus with self-confidence to move onto other challenges in life. Another example of this type of parenting is taking a positive view toward your child, because babies whose mothers saw them as better-than-average at one month of life had fewer emotional disorders later in life than did infants whose mothers saw them only as less than average. Yet another instance of right parenting is satisfying your child's infantile and childish needs. This way he will come to feel loved and to trust other people and to become self-confident rather than grow up with unmet childhood dependency needs that can later open him to disease.

Probably the most vital way you, as a benevolent parent, can give your child self-confidence and preserve his or her health, however, is to know what you want out of life, what you expect from your child, and then firmly to let your child know it. A California psychologist found little connection between self-esteem and family social status and income. But he *did* find a strong link between self-esteem and parents who set strict standards of behavior for their children and then consistently enforced them. Or as the esteemed Dr. Spock puts it: "If the parents know what they believe, have no embarrassment about expressing it and yet have no need to overcontrol their children (you might say they respect themselves and their children), then youths have relatively little trouble in achieving independence without making their parents and themselves miserable."

So how do parents go about setting strict standards and consistently reinforcing them? Around six months of age, place limits on where your infant can crawl and consistently reinforce these rules. Babies enjoy discipline more than most people realize, because they are constantly trying to see how far they can go in life, what the acceptable boundaries are. On the other hand, if you are a benevolent parent anxious to instill self-confidence and health in your infant, you will also give your child an ample, stimulating environment to explore and will not constantly harass him with "No's." If you doubt whether too many "No's" to a toddler can erode his self-confidence later in life, take the case of twelve-year-old Larry T. Larry was abnormally anxious every time he wandered into unfamiliar territory, so much so that he saw a psychiatrist, and the psychiatrist soon learned why. As a toddler, Larry's mother had always responded to his meanderings with an adamant "No!"

You can further build self-confidence and health in your child by making the youngster feel like a success from an early age on. Rather than criticizing your daughter after she has forgotten to brush her teeth, which is liable to make her feel like a failure, remind her to do so right after a meal; then she'll feel like a success. And if your son doesn't rake the lawn the way you ordered, don't call him a "dummy" but say, "I guess I didn't teach you that very well. Let's go over it again." Keep in mind that mothers of healthy children were found to praise their children far more than they scolded, slapped, or severely punished them, whereas mothers of children with failure-to-thrive problems were more likely to do the latter. Also, don't expect too much from your child; otherwise he'll fail and fail again and start feeling like a failure rather than like a success and keep from developing self-confidence. For instance, if your daughter isn't doing well in school, don't punish her or dump more homework on her but encourage her at what she is good at, say tennis, crafts, or scouting.

Yet another way, as a benevolent parent, to instill self-confidence and health in your child is to respect and trust him. If your toddler drags a dirty, tattered security blanket around the house, it could shatter his ego far more than you realize to wash it, or even worse, throw it away. As for your teen-age son, keep your distance from him but also let him know you care and are available to him if he needs you, because teen-agers need room to acquire self-confidence and to become independent, and because they prefer to choose their own moments for intimacy. And by all means trust your teen-ager if you want him to develop self-confidence! As sixteen-year-old Ken E. rightfully complains: "My parents are always worrying about whom I'm going out with, is she a good girl, will we be good, or will there be trouble. They say they know I'm grown up, but they don't really believe it."

What about the effects of a working mother on her child's self-confidence and health? If you, as a mother, want to work, it is probably better for your child's self-confidence and health for you to do so than not to. But if you do become employed away from home, make sure that your youngster has a competent, stable substitute caretaker. One study showed that mothers who work tend to have happy children, whereas mothers who gave up their desire to work "out of duty" tend to have unhappy ones. Another investigation revealed that while inadequate or unstable substitute care can erode a child's self-confidence, children with stable substitute care are even more self-assertive than children whose mothers don't work.

Finally, in order to make your child self-confident and thus to insure his health for life, be careful about the playmates, teachers, and other persons you expose him to, because, depending on the kind of people they are, they can profoundly enhance, or erode, his self-confidence. If you have any doubts that this is the truth, consider the case of Kay P., who was severely stunted in her psychological and physical growth because of maternal neglect. Yet Kay shot up both in height and I.Q. during her first year in school because of a compassionate, interested teacher and a concerned school nurse. A most revealing study was conducted in 1968, in conjunction with Head Start, the federal program designed to give disadvantaged youngsters a chance to overcome their environment. Teachers were told that, according to testing, one group of disadvantaged children would succeed in school, whereas another group would not. What was the outcome? Seventy-five percent of the children predicted to succeed did, whereas only 13 percent of children predicted not to did, emphasizing that the teachers' expectations from the students dramatically influenced the students' self-confidence and achievements.

Happiness is a potent health protector for your children. Many of the things you can do to give them self-confidence are also the things that can fill them with happiness. Just as benevolent parenting can foster self-confidence in them, therefore, so can it instill happiness, since research has shown that the better parent-child relationships are, the happier the child. Dr. Spock underscores this point: "I'm quite convinced that not only the best-behaved children but also the happiest and most successful ones are those whose parents present their beliefs unequivocally and leave no doubt that they expect their children to live up to them. I don't mean stern parents. I mean affectionate but firm parents."

However, there are some other ways you can instill happiness in your child as well. For one, try to avoid making him feel guilty, because children who feel guilty have been found to be less optimistic and happy as adults and more likely to experience loneliness, worthlessness, anxiety, and insomnia—disease predisposers, as we've seen again and again. For another, your child can acquire happiness by learning how to give and take with other children and by forming lasting relationships with other people. Novelty and creativity can help a child become positively involved in life and hence happy as well.

Many of the things you can do to give your child self-esteem, as you might expect, can also help your youngster learn how to cope successfully with life's stresses—another potent health protector. As we saw earlier, wanting a child gives him a better chance of achieving a normal birth weight than if he isn't wanted. Children with normal birth weights tend not only to be healthier but more easygoing than those with light birth weights; and a relaxed approach toward life, in turn, can help a person cope with life stresses better than nervousness and tension can. What's more, whereas benevolent parenting can give a child self-esteem and thus increase his chance for a healthy life, it can also help him master life's challenges and guard his health through that route as well. How is this?

Let's say you have a toddler, and you set certain limits on where she can roam in your house. These limits will not only make her feel secure and happy but also build her ability to cope with frustrations later in life. At the same time, though, you provide her with ample, diverse environments to explore. Such stimuli will not only build her self-confidence and contentment but also provide her with lessons in how to cope with challenges later in life. An animal study especially underscores this point. Some infant rats were treated to a new environment each day, whereas other rat pups were always kept in the same environment. The former rats learned how to adapt to different situations later in life, whereas the latter rats did not.

The ideal here, really, is to give a child challenges just tough enough to stimulate him to find solutions to them but not so rough as to overwhelm him and make him feel unable to cope. In other words, any new, demanding situation leads to a sense of distress in a child. But if the situation is within the child's ability to cope, then his distress is quickly replaced by conquest and a deep sense of pride. He is then ready to tackle another, larger challenge and, with each victory, will feel less and less distress and more and more capable of coping. Such a slow but sure accumulation of conquests and coping ability is absolutely imperative if a youngster is going to successfully grapple with the ample stresses of adolescence and the even greater ones that can threaten a person's happiness and health in later years. In brief, it is vital that an individual starts to learn, even during the first few months of life, to react to stressful situations with energy, assertion, productivity, and creativity rather than with helplessness and hopelessness, because as we have already seen, persons who employ the former tactics are apt to stay healthy and be exceptionally successful in this life, whereas the latter tactics are apt to lead to disease and even early death.

There are also specific ways you can prepare your child to cope with life's most health-challenging events—separation from loved ones, particularly through death. Although many parents believe they are doing a child a favor by shielding him from death, the opposite is really the case. Only if a person learns in his younger years what death is and how to react to it will he be truly capable of coping with it in later years, and particularly when the deceased is someone he deeply loves. The child should be given exposure to the concept of death from a very early age, and this exposure should be slowly intensified as he grows older. For instance, the game of "peek-a-boo" (a name derived from the Old English words meaning "alive or dead") can give an eight- to twelve-month-old child some idea of what it is like to be separated, however briefly, from a loved one. Teaching a toddler to flush the toilet can give him a grasp of the concept of "all goneness." As for a somewhat older child, encourage him to hold a little funeral for a beloved pet that has died and let him bury it himself, rather than whisking the dead animal away so that he doesn't see it. Yet another way a child ages three to six years can get used to the idea of being separated from a loved one is to spend the night at a friend's house. Let your child decide when the time is right, though, because if a youngster isn't ready for such a separation, it can upset him rather than strengthen his ability to cope with apartness. Stints with babysitters and attending nursery school or kindergarten can also get children used to being away from loved ones.

Explain to your child what death is, even at an age as young as three or four years. For instance, you might tell your child that when a person dies, he no longer feels, smells, sees, laughs, or talks, that his arms and legs will move no more, and that his heart stops beating. Also tell your child that the departed person will not return to this life, even though a youngster is not really able to grasp the finality of death until nine years of age. If a friend or a family member dies, you can also prepare your child to cope with death by taking him to the funeral home with you and including him in the funeral rites and mourning process. Such an experience, even for a child of three or four years, can be a profoundly moving and positive experience in how to cope with death. It can give him a sense of the dignity of death, of its rightful sequence to a life fully lived, and of how a person can go on living in the minds and hearts of others even after he has departed this world.

How should you handle the question of an afterlife with a child? If you believe that a deceased person's mind (soul) does not end when his body dies, tell your child so, and it will undoubtedly strengthen his ability to cope with death. However, if you aren't sure what you believe on this issue or are convinced that there is no afterlife, tell your child that. As Rabbi Joshua Lieberman wrote some years ago in his book *Peace of Mind,* "A child can stand tears, but not treachery; sorrow, but not deceit." It would probably be wise, regardless of your honest response, though, to emphasize that your reply reflects what you believe and that other people hold other views. This way your child will realize that there is no certainty about what happens to people's minds (souls) after the death of their bodies, and he will thus be better prepared to eventually arrive at his own belief about it.

Early exposure to death, funerals, and mourning is valuable to a person's future health in that it teaches him at an early age that it is acceptable to vent negative emotions—particularly grief, which is one of the most health-damaging if repressed. In fact, if a person whom a child loves dies, it is absolutely necessary that the child be included in the bereavement process so that he can deal not only with the grief but with any feelings he harbors that might have caused that individual's death. If this is not done, unresolved grief and guilt will become imbedded in the child's subconscious mind and in the years to come may erode his health. Dr. Morris A. Wessel, a pediatrics professor at Yale University School of Medicine, has written: "I've had parents in my office and we would just be chatting and I would happen to say, 'Tell me something about your experiences when your mother or father died,' and they would burst into tears. Even though the death may have occurred 30 years ago, when they were five years old, they still felt responsible for it. No one had paid much attention to their feelings; they had been left out of the mourning process."

It doesn't take the death of a loved one, however, to teach a child to vent grief, guilt, and other emotions. A youngster can be taught such expression from an early age on, and in simple ways. For instance, an infant should be allowed to scream and thrash about when frustrated; a toddler to throw temper tantrums and express negativism and resistance; an adolescent to let a parent know he is angry without fearing verbal or physical punishment. Otherwise children will still experience these emotions but simply sublimate them, and such sublimation may open them to disease either while young or later in life. A prime example underscoring this point is the case of fifteen-year-old Tara N., who tried to kill herself with an overdose of sleeping pills. Tara later explained to a social worker one of the reasons she tried to commit suicide: "I wish I was the sort of person who could tell people when I'm mad at them without being scared of what they would do to me if I did." Further, if youngsters are deprived of the expression of emotions when young, they will not know how to vent such feelings as they grow older, and such repression will help open them to disease as well.

And, for heaven's sake, if you have a son, don't tell him that "Big boys don't cry." Big boys *do* cry if they are "man" enough to do it in a culture that takes a dim view of such emotional expression, and they are a lot healthier for such bravery, too.

Avoid being a parent who believes that "children should be seen but not heard." Include your child in mealtime conversations. Ask her, "Jane, what do you think?" or "How do you feel about that?" before autocratically making decisions that affect her well-being. Be sensitive to her moods. If you suspect that something is troubling her, ask her, "Jane, is something bothering you? Can you tell me what it is?" (According to a 1975 study, *only 10 percent* of suicidal adolescents feel that they can talk to their parents when troubled). Encourage your child to fantasize and to recall her dreams, because as we saw in the previous chapter, fantasies and dream recall can help people de-repress emotions. Probably the best way you can teach your youngster to express emotions, though, and thus help safeguard his health, is to do it yourself. That way your child is reassured that such expression is acceptable and will imitate the ways you go about it.

Parental example is also the best way to bring up your child to avoid health-eroding obsessive-compulsive thoughts and behaviors, both in childhood and later in life. If you doubt whether this is the case, recall certain studies and case histories cited earlier in this book. Hardworking, competitive boys in the San Francisco area were found to have fathers with the same traits. Achievement-oriented mothers tend to have achievement-oriented children. Anorexics usually have mothers who place great emphasis on having "perfect" children and who expect too much from their youngsters because they have sacrificed their own dreams to be "perfect" mothers. Women who continually miscarry for psychological reasons often feel like failures beside their "hardworking, efficient, self-sacrificing mothers." As migraine sufferers often recall: "Dad was irritated as hell whenever he caught us reading a book instead of working." "Mother considered sitting down such a waste of time we boys were not allowed to sit down for meals." "Mother would beat me every time I made a fuss about working." According to one rheumatoid arthritis patient, "Our home was open to anyone, even strangers, you were always welcome. Mother would give anyone anything and go without herself."

Now, all this doesn't mean that you should be nonproductive, lazy, inefficient, sloppy, and selfish and thus preen your child to be the same. But it does imply that you should not put extravagant importance on work, neatness, cleanliness, perfection, and self-sacrifice, in order to keep your youngster from acquiring such traits to an abnormal degree and thus opening himself to disease at some later point in life.

To discern whether you are encouraging immoderate achievement and impatience in your child, ask yourself whether you urge him to do better when he is already performing adequately and also hurry him all the time. A National Institute of Mental Health study found that women with the heart attack personality traits of "workaholism" and impatience are apt to push their children to greater performance when they are already doing well and to rush them. Also watch for signs of such characteristics in your child's personality. A 1977 study revealed that these traits can surface in children even by eight years of age, and one of the most blatant characteristics to surface is a tendency to be impulsive rather than reflective and inhibited in one's initial impulses. A 1976 investigation also disclosed that whereas extreme emphasis on work and impatience has a modest genetic component, they are mostly learned from one's parents and begin as early as five years of age. Other research similarly demonstrated that while youngsters who start life with more energy output are particularly open to "workaholism" and hurrying, these traits are otherwise learned, and especially from the parent of the same sex—that is, mother-daughter molding and father-son molding.

Another way to tell whether you are placing undue weight on health-eroding obsessive-compulsive behaviors and encouraging the same traits in your child is to ask yourself these questions: "Do I keep a spotless house and expect my daughter to keep her room spotless?" "Am I always 'doing my duty' to the exclusion of mind-enriching or leisure activities, and do I require my son to do likewise?" "Am I always sacrificing my own interests to those of other people, and am I encouraging my daughter to do the same?"

To keep from inculcating health-threatening obsessive-compulsive thoughts and behavior in your child, also become aware of the fact that children generally develop a conscience (superego) between six and twelve years of age and are particularly prone to obsessive-compulsive thoughts and behaviors during those years—for example, they take the view that "black is black and white is white"; they scold their fathers for driving thirty-eight-miles-per-hour in a thirty-five-miles-per-hour zone; they have a compulsion about stepping on a crack for fear of "breaking their mother's back." In other words, this is the time in a person's life when he will particularly incorporate the values, ideals, and views to which he is exposed, and which is necessary if he is to develop a sound, happy, and healthy character. But at the same time, this is also the period when he is particularly vulnerable to the acquisition of an excessive conscience, one that can hurt his health. So during these years particularly, try to keep your youngster from falling prey to obsessive-compulsive thoughts and behavioral patterns that can threaten his health either in childhood or later in life.

Also keep in mind, from previous chapters, that children of a particularly sensitive nature are especially vulnerable to the acquisition of health-damaging obsessive-compulsive thoughts and behavior. For instance, suicide victims were often extremely sensitive and idealistic from their earliest years. Ulcerative colitis patients have been generally sensitive, ingratiating, helpful, compliant, and always anxious to please ever since they were children, whereas their healthy siblings have tended to be much less sensitive, helpful, and eager to please and far more independent and rebellious. So if your youngster is sensitive, try especially hard to keep him from acquiring health-threatening obsessive-compulsive thoughts and behavior. And if you have a child who is a "model" child—that is, always neat, clean, compliant, and anxious to do what you want—don't be too quick to congratulate yourself on good parenting. Such traits may make your life as a parent easier, but your youngster's immoderate zeal to do what you want, rather than what he wants, may erode his health later.

You can also keep society at large from instilling health-eroding obsessive-compulsive thoughts and behavior in your child by becoming aware of such influences, and then trying to counter them with your private example. Keep a lookout for children's stories that push immoderate achievement and "nice" little boys and girls, television commercials that overly emphasize excessive neatness and cleanliness—for example, spray cleaners and deodorant ads; teachers and sports coaches that place undue emphasis on achievement, perfection, haste, and always "winning." If you live in a large city, your child will probably be more likely to hurry than if you live in the suburbs or a small town. On the other hand, moving to a remote village isn't really going to spare your child from obsessive-compulsive thoughts and behavior that are encouraged by society at large. One study showed that while rural students are less rushed than suburban students are, they are just as bent as suburban youngsters on achieving and competing.

Of the many ways you can prepare your child for a healthy life, however, probably the most crucial of all is to have a strong passion for life yourself—to find ecstasy in sun-tinted snow; in silence with a friend before low-burning embers; in work that is self-fulfilling and other-fulfilling; in human sexuality; in running, backpacking, flying, diving, and other feats that suspend you from your ego. By seeing you become enthralled and letting yourself go, your child also learns how to immerse himself in life and to become eager to commit himself to it and to contribute to it. Such joy, such yearning, will then, in turn, be a mighty buffer against illness in the years to come.

12

IS THERE
A DISEASE-FREE
BIOTYPE?

*... most people who have worked with centenarians
have the impression of a psychosomatic component
—that these are people who have aged without
illness because they never let the bastards
grind them down.*

—Dr. Alex Comfort
A Good Age

THE CAUCASUS MOUNTAINS OF the Soviet Union are a land enchanted since remote antiquity. The Golden Fleece, famous in Greek mythology, was supposed to have been sheared there. The ten-thousand-foot-high peaks are slashed by deep, narrow ravines and turbulent streams and boast exquisite alpine meadows, fruit trees, and grapes. But probably the Caucasus Mountains' greatest claim to fame is that they are inhabited by some of the oldest, healthiest people in the world. Folks who live there commonly survive into their eighties, nineties, or even their hundreds, and when they die, it's from old age, not disease.

Similarly, on the other side of the world, in South America, can be found the Andes Mountains, also mesmerizing since remote times with their snowcapped peaks, stark canyons, verdant valleys, sacred springs, and agriculture dating back to the Inca Indians. Local legend holds that one of the valleys was the true Paradise from which Adam and Eve were expelled. The Andes also claim some of the oldest, healthiest people in the world—individuals who survive into their eighties, nineties, or even their hundreds and who die not from disease but because they have lived out their genetically programmed life-span.

But there are also persons in civilized areas of the world as well who enjoy long, healthy lives and who die not from disease but from old age. Some thirteen thousand Americans are one hundred years old, and 14 percent of all Americans over age sixty-five are healthy.

All of these individuals dramatically document that, whereas humans' immune systems deteriorate with chronological aging and thus open them more to disease than when they were young, some people still manage to live long, disease-free lives. What's more, the key to these persons' exceptional life-spans appears to lie more in their personalities and life-styles than in their genes or environment (the Caucasus Mountains, for example, are one of the most ethnically diverse areas of the world). As British gerontologist Alex Comfort has written: "... most people who have worked with centenarians have the impression of a psychosomatic component—that these are people who have aged without illness because they never let the bastards grind them down." In other words, there is such a thing as a disease-free personality.

Although the study of the aging process (gerontology) is a relatively new area of research, limited studies have already been conducted on individuals who have managed to live long, healthy existences. These studies imply that such persons possess essentially the same personality traits as do younger, healthy people. For instance, investigations of centenarians of the Caucasus suggest that a major key to their health and longevity is their profound involvement with life from an early age up to the time they die. Helpless, hopeless, disease-prone persons they are not! They work hard at agriculture and pastoral activities, are encouraged by younger members of society to remain productive and to serve as respected heads of extended families, and maintain active sex lives well into their eighties, nineties, or even hundreds. They have been found to be much happier and more active than people living in nearby plains and to suffer ten times fewer strokes and six times fewer heart attacks. As for the centenarians of the Andes, they too are deeply engaged in vigorous, physical work; are lean, dynamic, even tigerlike in their movements; and are said to be passionate in their lovemaking. One centenarian in the village of Vilcabamba, for instance, had had seven wives, and his sexual escapades with married and single women were legendary, leading one time to his nearly being shot. Investigations of healthy older Americans have produced similar findings.

In 1978 a California professor of medicine reported several reasons why male symphony conductors live unusually long, healthy lives. (Leopold Stokowski survived to ninety-five, Arturo Toscanini to ninety, Walter Damrosch to eighty-eight, Ernest Ansermet to eighty-six, and Bruno Walter to eighty-five.) They have a passion for self-fulfillment, are engrossed in their music until they die, and are gratified by the recognition they receive for their efforts. "My conclusions," this researcher wrote, "do not necessarily conflict with evidence for a heart attack personality, for the lives of conductors are filled with gratifying stress, not frustrating stress." Similarly, a 1973 Special Task Force to the Secretary for the U.S. Department of Health, Education and Welfare found that the strongest predictor of longevity is job satisfaction, and the second-best predictor is overall happiness. A Michigan study also noted that the more a person is satisfied with his work, the longer he is likely to live. And yet a fourth investigation of four hundred and fifty persons who had lived to be one hundred showed that two of the reasons for their longevity were that they kept busy and got a great deal of fun out of life.

Individual case histories, too, underscore the profound ability of enthrallment with life to ward off disease even in later years. Take the case of Bertrand Russell, British philosopher, champion of individual liberty, and one of the most influential thinkers of the twentieth century. He died at age ninety-seven. In his autobiography, which was published in 1969, the year before his death, he wrote: "Three passions, simple but overwhelmingly strong, have governed my life: The longing for love, the search for knowledge and unbearable pity for the suffering of mankind." Or take Pablo Picasso, one of the most influential artists of all time. He remained, to the end of his ninety-one years, full of vigor and zest for life, particularly for his work, and exhausted younger companions with his energy and enthusiasm. And then there was the famous American primitive painter Grandma Moses, who was still busy painting at age one hundred and who died at age one hundred and two. Or how about Helena Rubenstein, who created, over seven decades, a beauty empire that stretched across six continents? In her memoirs, written when she was in her nineties, she said: "But work has indeed been my beauty treatment. I believe in hard work. It keeps the wrinkles out of mind and spirit. It helps to keep a woman young. It certainly keeps a woman alive." Then there was the black Ragtime pianist Eubie Blake who, at ninety-six years of age in 1979, was still practicing the piano three hours a day. "I try to do my best," Blake said.

What a contrast between these zestful, healthy older individuals and a 1977 study revealing that feelings of uselessness and inability to enjoy leisure time is a major cause of declining health among retired Americans! What a difference between these exuberant, robust older persons and multibillionaire Howard Hughes, who might be considered an archetypal disease personality plus. Both of Hughes's parents died at an early age, scarring him deeply. He developed, perhaps as a result of this psychological devastation, obsessive-compulsive thoughts and behaviors—an inordinate thirst for monetary success, a need to repeat orders twenty to thirty times, and a great fear of germs. The latter phobia was so great, in fact, that he became a recluse, his secretaries had to wear white gloves, and his furniture had to be draped to keep it sterile. By the early 1970s Hughes was worth $2½ billion, but "I'm not very happy," he conceded. What's more, his health was poor, and he was confined to a wheelchair. But he excused his condition with this comment: "How in the hell is anybody's health at 66 years of age?"

Still other evidence, too, suggests that a moderate life-style rather than extreme thoughts and behavior can promote healthful longevity. For a few years now, a California proponent of preventive medicine and his colleagues have been studying some eleven thousand adults and have concluded that certain simple health habits are associated with a long life. These habits include three meals a day, with particular emphasis on breakfast; ample exercise; seven to eight hours of sleep a night; no smoking; moderate weight; temperate use of alcohol. According to this study, a thirty-five-year-old man who practices three or fewer of these health habits can expect to live to age sixty-seven, whereas a man who practices six or seven of them can expect to live to seventy-eight years of age. In the mid 1970s a Maryland scientist studied the death rates of twenty-five thousand American ministers between 1950 and 1960, and as he reported in 1978, their death rates during this period were about 30 percent lower than those of all white males of comparable age in the United States. The clergy had particularly low mortality rates from tuberculosis, stomach and lung cancer, suicide, and accidents and moderately low ones from heart disease and strokes. The investigator attributed the ministers' healthful longevity largely to a temperate, regular, and hence healthy life-style.

Moderation and regularity, too, characterize the lives of people in the Caucasus Mountains and is probably one of the reasons for their healthful longevity. This includes a low-fat diet, eaten slowly and sparingly; consumption of only dry red wine and in limited amounts; abstention from cigarette smoking; vigorous physical work but without competition; and with ample time out for horseback riding, swimming, feasting, and other leisure activities. Says one centenarian, "I'm never in a hurry." For them, wealth and success do not lie in money, fame, or material possessions but in numerous loyal, devoted friends and family members. Invariably, when Caucasus centenarians are asked why they think they have lived such long, healthy lives, they don't credit fate, or Providence, but "the good life." The centenarians of the Andes, too, tend to pursue a rhythmic life-style; they rise with the sun and go to bed with it. Although they work hard physically, they find time for guitar playing, seranading, lovemaking, and other leisure activities. (However, the men do not show the restraint in smoking and drinking that the centenarians of the Caucasus do.)

Still another reason why Caucasians and people high in the Andes claim such exceptional health and longevity is that they keep negative stresses in their lives to a minimum. The Caucasians are taught from a very early age to confront stresses rather than to react helplessly to them. For instance, Caucasian children learn that excuses are not acceptable; they must look for solutions to problems. When a child is afraid of ghosts, he may have to sleep in a cemetery until he learns to overcome his fear. When something is broken, it must be mended, whether a vase or a friendship. Ceremonies and rituals, too, appear to be among the reasons why healthy, older people have arrived where they are in life. Centenarians of both the Andes and Caucasus, for instance, are highly revered by younger people in their communities, asked to head up feasts and to mediate disputes.

If you want to live out your entire life disease-free, then, imitate the Bertrand Russells and Grandmas Moses, not the Howard Hughes, of this world. You have nothing to lose other than several billion dollars and everything that really matters to gain—a life happily, fully, and healthily lived.

SOURCES

Chapter 1

Abse, Wilfred, et al. "Personality and Behavioral Characteristics of Lung Cancer Patients." *Journal of Psychosomatic Research.* Vol. 18, 1974, pp. 101–113.

Anon. "The Psychological Aspects of Cancer—A Summary of Research by Dr. Bahnson and his Research Group." *American Cancer Society's 13th Science Writers' Seminar,* April 2–7, 1971.

Anon. "Loneliness Tabbed as Factor in Cancer." *The Choice.* September, 1976, p. 17.

Anon. "Cancer and the Mind: How Are They Connected?" *Science.* June 23, 1978, pp. 1363–1365.

Arehart-Treichel, Joan. "The Mind-Body Link." *Science News.* December 20, and 27, 1975, pp. 393–394.

Arehart-Treichel, Joan. "Mental Patterns of Disease." *Human Behavior.* January, 1976, pp. 40–43.

Arehart-Treichel, Joan. "Can Your Personality Kill You?" *New York.* November 18, 1977, pp. 62–67.

Bahnson, Claus Bahne. "Psychophysiological Complementarity in Malignancies: Past Work and Future Vistas." *Annals of the New York Academy of Sciences.* Vol. 164, 1969, pp. 319–334.

Bahnson, Claus Bahne. "Basic Epistemological Considerations Regarding Psychosomatic Processes and Their Application to Current Psychophysiological Cancer Research." *International Journal of Psychobiology.* Vol. 1, no. 1, 1970, pp. 57–69.

Bahnson, Claus Bahne, and Bahnson, Marjorie Brooks. "Role of the Ego Defenses: Denial and Repression in the Etiology of Malignant Neoplasm." *Annals of the New York Academy of Sciences.* Vol. 125, 1966, pp. 827–845.

Bahnson, Claus Bahne, and Bahnson, Marjorie Brooks. "Personality Variables and Life Experiences Predicting Specific Disease Syndromes." Presented at the 82nd Annual Convention of the American Psychological Association, September 1, 1974.

Bahnson, Claus Bahne, Bahnson, Marjorie Brooks, and Wardwell, Walter I. "A Psychologic Study of Cancer Patients." Presented at the Annual Meeting of the American Psychosomatic Society, April 2–4, 1971.

Bahnson, Marjorie Brooks, and Bahnson, Claus Bahne. "Ego Defenses in Cancer Patients." *Annals of the New York Academy of Sciences.* Vol. 164, 1969, pp. 546–559.

Booth, Gotthard. "General and Organic-Specific Object Relationships in Cancer." *Annals of the New York Academy of Sciences.* Vol. 164, 1969, pp. 568–575.

Brock, A. J. *Galen in the Natural Faculties.* Cambridge, Mass.: Harvard University Press, 1916.

Crombie, William J. "Personality Is Linked to Cancer Vulnerability." *Enterprise Science News.* February 18, 1975.

Day, Emerson. "Preface to Conference on Psychophysiological Aspects of Cancer." *Annals of the New York Academy of Sciences.* Vol. 125, 1966, pp. 775–776.

Forer, Lucille, and Still, Henry. *The Birth Order Factor.* New York: David McKay, 1976.

Galen. *De Tumoribus Naturum Praeter,* trans. Thomas Gale. London: 1567.

Greenberg, Joel. "Stress May Damage Cell Immunity." *Science News.* March 11, 1978, p. 151.

Greene, William A. "The Psychosocial Setting of the Development in Leukemia and Lymphoma." *Annals of the New York Academy of Sciences.* Vol. 125, 1966, pp. 794–801.

Greene, William A., and Swisher, Scott N. "Psychological and Somatic Variables Associated with the Development and Course of Monozygotic Twins Discordant for Leukemia." *Annals of the New York Academy of Sciences.* Vol. 164, 1969, pp. 394–408.

Grinker, Roy R. "Psychosomatic Aspects of the Cancer Problem." *Annals of the New York Academy of Sciences.* Vol. 125, 1966, pp. 874–875.

Grissom, Julie J., Weiner, Barbara J., and Weiner, Elliot A. "Psychological Correlates of Cancer." *Journal of Consulting and Clinical Psychology.* Vol. 43, 1975, p. 113.

Hagnell, Olle. "The Premorbid Personality of Persons Who Develop Cancer in a Total Population Investigated in 1947 and 1957." *Annals of the New York Academy of Sciences.* Vol. 125, 1966, p. 846.

Hamby, W. B. *Ambroise Paré–Surgeon of the Renaissance.* St. Louis, Mo.: W. H. Green, 1967.

Harrower, Molly, Thomas, Caroline Bedell, and Altman, Ann. "Human Figure Drawings in a Prospective Study of Six Disorders: Suicide, Mental Illness, Emotional Disturbance, Hypertension, Coronary Heart Disease and Malignant Tumor." *Journal of Nervous and Mental Disease.* Vol. 161, No. 3, 1975, pp. 191–195.

Hobson, Janet. "Social Stress and the Immune System." *Science News.* February 1, 1975, pp. 68–69.

Katz, Jack, et al. "Psychoendocrine Considerations in Cancer of the Breast." *Annals of the New York Academy of Sciences.* Vol. 164, 1969, pp. 509–515.

Kavetsky, R. E., et al. "Induced Carcinogenesis Under Various Influences on the Hypothalamus." *Annals of the New York Academy of Sciences.* Vol. 164, 1969, pp. 517–519.

King, Lester S. *History of Medicine.* New York: Penguin Books, 1971.

Kissen, David M. "The Significance of Personality in Lung Cancer in Men." *Annals of the New York Academy of Sciences.* Vol. 125, 1966, pp. 820–826.

Kissen, David M. "The Value of a Psychosomatic Approach to Cancer." *Annals of the New York Academy of Sciences.* Vol. 125, 1966, pp. 777–779.

Kissen, David M. "Personality and Psychosocial Factors in Lung Cancer." *Annals of the New York Academy of Sciences.* Vol. 164, 1969, pp. 535–545.

Kissen, David M., and Rao, L. G. S. "Steroid Excretion Patterns and Personality in Lung Cancer." *Annals of the New York Academy of Sciences.* Vol. 164, 1969, pp. 476–481.

LaBarba, Richard C. "Experiential and Environmental Factors in Cancer." *Psychosomatic Medicine.* Vol. 32, 1970, pp. 259–276.

LeShan, Lawrence. "Emotional Life-History Pattern Associated with Neoplastic Disease." *Annals of the New York Academy of Sciences.* Vol. 125, 1966, pp. 780–793.

LeShan, Lawrence. "Cancer and Character." *Psychology Today.* September, 1976, p. 4.

LeShan, Lawrence. *You Can Fight for Your Life—Emotional Factors in the Causation of Cancer.* New York: Evans, 1977.

LeShan, Lawrence, and Worthington, Richard E. "Some Recurrent Life History Patterns Observed in Patients with Malignant Disease." *The Journal of Nervous and Mental Disease.* Vol. 124, No. 5, 1956, pp. 460–465.

Marcus, Mary. "Cancer and Character." *Psychology Today.* September, 1976, p. 4.

Marcus, Mary G. "The Shaky Link Between Cancer and Character." *Psychology Today.* June, 1976, pp. 52–85.

McQuerter, Gregory. "Cancer: Clues in the Mind." *Science News.* January 21, 1978, pp. 44–45.

Mezei, Árpád, and Németh, György. "Regression as an Intervening Mechanism: A System-Theoretical Approach." *Annals of the New York Academy of Sciences.* Vol. 164, 1969, pp. 560–567.

Muslin, Hyman L., Gyarfas, Kalman, and Preper, William J. "Separation Experience and Cancer of the Breast." *Annals of the New York Academy of Sciences.* Vol. 125, 1966, pp. 802–806.

Pettingale, Keith W., Greer, Steven, and Tee, Dudley E. H. "Serum IgA and Emotional Expression in Breast Cancer Patients." *Journal of Psychosomatic Research.* Vol. 21, 1977, pp. 395–399.

Prehn, Richmond T. "The Relationship of Immunology to Carcinogenesis." *Annals of the New York Academy of Sciences.* Vol. 164, 1969, pp. 449–453.

Rabkin, Judith G., and Struening, Elmer L. "Social Changes, Stress and Illness." Presented at the American Association for the Advancement of Science Symposium, "Brain Functions and Physical Well-Being," January 27, 1975.

Riley, Vernon. "Mouse Mammary Tumors: Alteration of Incidence as Apparent Function of Stress." *Science.* August 8, 1975, pp. 465–467.

Schmale, Arthur, and Iker, Howard. "The Psychological Setting of Uterine Cervical Cancer." *Annals of the New York Academy of Sciences.* Vol. 125, 1966, pp. 807–813.

Solomon, George F. "Early Experience and Immunity." *Nature.* November 23, 1968, pp. 821–822.

Solomon, George F. "Emotion, Stress and the Central Nervous System and Immunity." *Annals of the New York Academy of Sciences.* Vol. 164, 1969, pp. 335–342.

Southam, Chester M. "Emotions, Immunology, and Cancer: How Might the Psyche Influence Neoplasia?" *Annals of the New York Academy of Sciences.* Vol. 164, 1969, pp. 473–475.

Stein, Marvin, Schiavi, Raul C., and Luparello, Thomas J. "The Hypothalamus and Immune Process." *Annals of the New York Academy of Sciences.* Vol. 164, 1969, pp. 464–470.

Stern, Elizabeth, Mickey, Max R., and Gorski, Roger A. "Neuroendocrine Factors in Experimental Carcinogenesis." *Annals of the New York Academy of Sciences.* Vol. 164, 1969, pp. 494–507.

Temkin, Owset. *Galenism.* Ithaca, N.Y.: Cornell University, 1973.

Thomas, Caroline Bedell. "Precursors of Premature Disease and Death—The Predictive Potential of Habits and Family Attitudes." *Annals of Internal Medicine.* Vol. 85, 1976, pp. 653–658.

Thomas, Caroline Bedell. "What Becomes of Medical Students: The Dark Side." *The Johns Hopkins Medical Journal.* Vol. 138, 1976, pp. 185–195.

Thomas, Caroline Bedell, and Duszynski, Karen R. "Closeness to Parents and the Family Constellation in a Prospective Study of Five Disease States: Suicide, Mental Illness, Malignant Tumor, Hypertension and Coronary Heart Disease." *The Johns Hopkins Medical Journal.* Vol. 134, No. 5, 1974, pp. 251–270.

Thomas, Caroline Bedell, and Greenstreet, Richard L. "Psychobiological Characteristics in Youth as Predictors of Five Disease States: Suicide, Mental Illness, Hypertension, Coronary Heart Disease and Tumor." *The Johns Hopkins Medical Journal.* Vol. 132, No. 1, 1973, pp. 16–43.

Thomas, Caroline Bedell, et al. "A Prospective Study of the Rorschachs of Suicides: The Predictive Potential of Pathological Content." *The Johns Hopkins Medical Journal.* Vol. 132, No. 6, 1973, pp. 334–360.

Chapter 2

Anon. "Ambition and Disease: The Chicken or the Egg? *The Lancet.* December 19, 1970, pp. 1291–1292.

Appels, A. "Het hartinfarct een cultuurziekte?" *Tijdschrift Voor Sociale Geneeskunde.* Vol. 50, 1972, pp. 446–448.

Arehart-Treichel, Joan. "Emotions and High Blood Pressure." *Science News.* July 26, 1975, p. 58.

Benson, Herbert. "Can Hypertension Be Induced by Stress? *Journal of Human Stress.* March, 1977, pp. 4–11.

Bishop, Louis F., and Reichert, Philip. "Emotion and Heart Failure." *Psychosomatics.* November–December, 1971, pp. 412–415.

Bortner, Rayman W., Rosenman, Ray H., and Friedman, Meyer. "Familial Similarity in Pattern A Behavior." *Journal of Chronic Disease.* Vol. 23, 1970, pp. 39–43.

Briggs, Kenneth A. "U.S. Catholics Finding Bearings After a Long Period of Upheaval." *The New York Times.* January 29, 1979, pp. D1, D8.

Caffrey, Bernard. "Behavior Patterns and Personality Characteristics Related to Prevalence Rates of Coronary Heart Disease in American Monks." *Journal of Chronic Disease.* Vol. 22, 1969, pp. 93–103.

Connolly, Joseph. "Life Events Before Myocardial Infarction." *Journal of Human Stress.* December, 1976, pp. 3–17.

Davies, Martin. "Blood Pressure and Personality." *Journal of Psychosomatic Research.* Vol. 14, 1970, pp. 89–104.

Dongier, M. "Psychosomatic Aspects in Myocardial Infarction in Comparison with Angina Pectoris." *Psychotherapy and Psychosomatics.* Vol. 23, 1974, pp. 123–131.

Eliot, Robert S., and Forker, Alan D. "Emotional Stress and Cardiac Disease." *Journal of the American Medical Association.* November 15, 1976, pp. 2325–2326.

Engel, George L. "Sudden and Rapid Death During Psychological Stress—Folklore or Folk Wisdom?" *Annals of Internal Medicine.* Vol. 74, 1971, pp. 771–782.

Friedman, Meyer, and Rosenman, Ray H. *Type A Behavior and Your Heart.* New York: Knopf, 1974.

Glass, David C. *Behavior Patterns, Stress, and Coronary Disease.* New York: Wiley, 1977.

Ishikawa, Hitoshi, et al. "Psychosomatic Study of Angina Pectoris." *Psychosomatics.* November–December, 1971, pp. 390–397.

Jenkins, C. David. "Psychologic and Social Precursors of Coronary Disease." *The New England Journal of Medicine.* February 11, 1971, pp. 307–317.

Jenkins, C. David. "Recent Evidence Supporting Psychologic and Social Risk Factors for Coronary Disease." *The New England Journal of Medicine.* May 6, 1976, pp. 1033–1038.

Keith, Robert Allen. "Personality and Coronary Heart Disease: A Review." *Journal of Chronic Disease.* Vol. 19, 1966, pp. 1231–1243.

Keith, Robert Allen, Lown, Bernard, and Stare, Frederick J. "Coronary Heart Disease and Behavior Patterns." *Psychosomatic Medicine.* Vol. 27, No. 5, 1965, pp. 424–434.

Kidson, Malcolm A. "Personality and Hypertension." *Journal of Psychosomatic Research.* Vol. 17, 1973, pp. 35–41.

Kobayashi, Tachio, Ishikawa, Hitoshi, and Tawara, Ineko. "Psychosomatic Aspects of Angina Pectoris." *Scandinavian Journal of Rehabilitative Medicine.* Vol. 2–3, 1970, pp. 87–91.

Lane, Frederick M. "Mental Mechanisms and the Pain of Angina Pectoris." *American Heart Journal.* April, 1973, pp. 563–568.

Lebovits, Binyamin Z. "Prospective and Retrospective Psychological Studies of Coronary Heart Disease." *Psychosomatic Medicine.* Vol. 29, No. 3, 1967, pp. 265–272.

Leigh, Denis. "Psychosomatic Aspects of Essential Hypertension." *The Practitioner.* July, 1971, pp. 28–35.

Lewis, Jerry M., et al. "Chest Pain, Personality and Coronary Arteriography." *Southern Medical Journal.* April, 1971, pp. 467–471.

Lind, Evy, and Theorell, Töres. "Sociological Characteristics and Myocardial Infarctions." *Journal of Psychosomatic Research.* Vol. 17, 1973, pp. 59–73.

Lown, Bernard, et al. "Basis for Recurring Ventricular Fibrillation in the Absence of Coronary Heart Disease and Its Management." *The New England Journal of Medicine.* March 18, 1976, pp. 623–629.

Matthews, Karen A., and Krantz, David S. "Resemblances of Twins and Their Parents in Pattern A Behavior." *Psychosomatic Medicine.* March–April, 1976, pp. 140–144.

McClelland, David C. *The Achieving Society.* New York: Van Nostrand, 1961.

McClelland, David C. "Sources of Stress in the Drive for Power." New York: The Kittay Scientific Foundation. 1975.

Mordkoff, Arnold M., and Parsons, Oscar A. "The Coronary Personality: A Critique." *Psychosomatic Medicine.* Vol. 29, No. 1, 1967, pp. 1–14.

Pilowsky, I., et al. "Hypertension and Personality." *Psychosomatic Medicine.* January–February, 1973, pp. 50–55.

Rahe, Richard H., and Lind, Evy. "Psychosocial Factors and Sudden Cardiac Death: A Pilot Study." *Journal of Psychosomatic Research.* Vol. 15, 1971, pp. 19–24.

Rime, Bernard, and Bonami, Michel. "Specificité psychosomatique et affections cardiaques coronariennes: essai de verification de la théorie de Dunbar au moyen du MMPI." *Journal of Psychosomatic Research*. Vol. 17, 1973, pp. 345-352.

Russek, Henry J. "Role of Emotional Stress in the Etiology of Clinical Coronary Heart Disease." *Diseases of the Chest*. July, 1967, pp. 1-9.

Siltanen, et al. "Psychological Characteristics Related to Coronary Heart Disease." *Journal of Psychosomatic Research*. Vol. 19, 1975, pp. 183-195.

Theorell, Töres, and Rahe, Richard H. "Psychosocial Factors and Myocardial Infarction—I. An Inpatient Study in Sweden." *Journal of Psychosomatic Research*. Vol. 15, 1971, pp. 25-31.

Thiel, Hans G., Parker, Donald, and Bruce, Thomas A. "Stress Factors and the Risk of Myocardial Infarction." *Journal of Psychosomatic Research*. Vol. 17, 1973, pp. 43-57.

Thomas, Caroline Bedell. "Precursors of Premature Disease and Death—The Predictive Potential of Habits and Family Attitudes." *Annals of Internal Medicine*. November, 1976, pp. 653-657.

Thomas, Caroline Bedell and Duszynski, Karen R. "Closeness to Parents and the Family Constellation in a Prospective Study of Five Disease States: Suicide, Mental Illness, Malignant Tumor, Hypertension and Coronary Heart Disease." *The Johns Hopkins Medical Journal*. May, 1974. pp. 251-270.

Thomas, Caroline Bedell, and Greenstreet, Richard L. "Psychobiological Characteristics in Youth as Predictors of Five Disease States: Suicide, Mental Illness, Hypertension, Coronary Heart Disease and Tumor." *The Johns Hopkins Medical Journal*. January, 1973, pp. 16-40.

Thomas, Caroline Bedell, et al. "A Prospective Study of the Rorschachs of Suicides: The Predictive Potential of Pathological Content." *The Johns Hopkins Medical Journal*. June, 1973, pp. 334-360.

Torgersen, Svenn, and Kringlen, Einar. "Blood Pressure and Personality: A Study of the Relationship Between Intrapair Differences in Systolic Blood Pressure and Personality in Monozygotic Twins." *Journal of Psychosomatic Research*. Vol. 15, 1971, pp. 183-191.

Waldron, Ingrid. "The Coronary-Prone Behavior Pattern, Blood Pressure, Employment and Socio-Economic Status in Women." *Journal of Psychosomatic Research*. Vol. 22, 1978, pp. 79-87.

Wardwell, Walter I., and Bahnson, Claus B. "Behavioral Variables and Myocardial Infarction in the Southeastern Connecticut Heart Study." *Journal of Chronic Disease*. Vol. 26, 1973, pp. 447-461.

Williams, Redford B., Poon, Leonard W., and Burdette, Linda J. "Locus of Control and Vasomotor Response to Sensory Processing." *Psychosomatic Medicine*. March-April, 1977, pp. 127-133.

Zyzanski, Stephen J., and Jenkins, C. David. "Basic Dimensions Within the Coronary-Prone Behavior Pattern." *Journal of Chronic Disease*. Vol. 23, 1970, pp. 781-795.

Chapter 3

Alp., M. H., Court, J. H., and Grant, A. Kerr. "Personality Pattern and Emotional Stress in the Genesis of Gastric Ulcer." *Gut*. Vol. 11, 1970, pp. 773-777.

Anon. "Mind and Ulcer." *British Medical Journal*. August 16, 1969, p. 374.

Apter, N., and Hurst, L. A. "Personality and Duodenal Ulcer." *South African Medical Journal.* November 10, 1973, pp. 2131-2133.

Atkinson, Roland M., and Ringuette, Eugene L., "A Survey of Biographical and Psychological Features in Extraordinary Fatness." *Psychosomatic Medicine.* Vol. 29, No. 2, 1967, pp. 121-133.

Ayers, Arthur W., Burr, Harry B., and Tuttle, William B. "Personality Concomitants of Peptic Ulcer Among Managerial, Supervisory and Presupervisory Personnel." *Journal of Occupational Medicine.* Vol. 5, 1963, pp. 252-258.

Bockus, H. L. "Reflections on Functional-Structural Interrelationships in Digestive Tract Disorders." *Canadian Medical Association Journal.* March 8, 1969, pp. 476-480.

Bonfils, S., and M'Uzan, M. de. "Irritable Bowel Syndrome Versus Ulcerative Colitis: Psychofunctional Disturbance Versus Psychosomatic Disease?" *Journal of Psychosomatic Research.* Vol. 18, 1974, pp. 291-296.

Bruch, Hilde. *The Golden Cage—The Enigma of Anorexia Nervosa.* Cambridge, Mass.: Harvard University Press, 1978.

Coddington, R. Dean. "Study of an Infant with a Gastric Fistula and her Normal Twin." *Psychosomatic Medicine,* Vol. 30, No. 2, 1965, pp. 172-192.

Coddington, R. Dean. "Peptic Ulcers in Children." *Psychosomatics.* January-February, 1968, pp. 38-43.

Crohn, Burrell B. "Psychosomatic Factors in Ulcerative Colitis in Children." *New York State Journal of Medicine.* May 15, 1963, pp. 1456-1457.

Eberhard, Göran. "The Personality of Peptic Ulcer—Preliminary Report of a Twin Study." *Acta Psychiatrica Scandinavica.* Vol. 203, 1968, pp. 131-133.

Eberhard, Göran. "Peptic Ulcers in Twins—A Study in Personality, Heredity and Environment." *Acta Psychiatrica Scandinavica Supplementum.* Vol. 205, 1968, pp. 3-120.

Ehrensing, Rudolph, and Weitzman, Elliott L. "The Mother-Daughter Relationship in Anorexia Nervosa." *Psychosomatic Medicine.* March-April, 1970, pp. 201-208.

Foltz, Eldon L. and Millett, Fay E., Jr. "Experimental Psychosomatic Disease States in Monkeys—I. Peptic Ulcer—'Executive Monkeys.' " *Journal of Surgical Research.* October, 1964, pp. 445-453.

Frazier, Claude A. *Psychosomatic Aspects of Allergy.* New York: Van Nostrand Reinhold, 1977.

Frazier, Shervert H. "Anorexia Nervosa." *Diseases of the Nervous System.* March, 1965, pp. 155-159.

Fullerton, Donald T. "Psychosomatic Diseases of the Colon in Adults." *California Medicine.* January, 1965, pp. 33-39.

Glen, A. I. M., and Coy, Alan G. "Psychological Factors, Operative Procedures and Results of Surgery for Duodenal Ulcer." *Gut.* Vol. 9, 1968, pp. 667-671.

Greenberg, Joel. "The Fat American." *Science News.* March 25, 1978, pp. 188-189.

Guiora, Alexander Z. "Dysorexia: A Psychopathological Study of Anorexia Nervosa and Bulimia." *American Journal of Psychiatry.* Vol. 124, No. 3, 1967, pp. 391-393.

Harper, Patrick. "Psychosomatic Medicine—Weight Disorders." *The Practitioner.* August, 1972, pp. 244-250.

Hock, Charles W. "Psychosomatic Aspects of Gastrointestinal Disorders." *The American Journal of Proctology.* April, 1965, pp. 133-136.

Hogan, William, Huerta, Enrique, and Lucas, Alexander R. "Diagnosing Anorexia Nervosa in Males." *Psychosomatics*. August–September, 1974, pp. 122–126.

Jackson, Don D. and Yalom, Irvin. "Family Research on the Problem of Ulcerative Colitis." *Archives of General Psychiatry*. October, 1966, pp. 410–418.

Jacobson, Eugene D., et al. "A Survey of Opportunities and Needs in Research on Digestive Diseases." *Gastroenterology*. November, 1975, pp. 1051–1165.

Klein, H. Sydney. "Notes on a Case of Ulcerative Colitis." *International Journal of Psychoanalysis*. July, 1966, pp. 342–350.

McKegney, F. Patrick. "Psychosomatic Gastrointestinal Disturbances—A Multifactor, Interactional Concept." *Postgraduate Medicine*. May, 1970, pp. 109–113.

McKegney, F. Patrick, Gordon, Robert O., and Levine, Stephen M. "A Psychosomatic Comparison of Patients with Ulcerative Colitis and Crohn's Disease." *Psychosomatic Medicine*. March–April, 1970, pp. 153–165.

McMahon, Arthur W. "Personality Differences Between Inflammatory Bowel Disease Patients and Their Healthy Siblings." *Psychosomatic Medicine*. March–April, 1973, pp. 91–103.

Miller, Neal E. "Animal Experiments on Emotionally Induced Ulcers." *Medical Psychology*. 1962, pp. 213–219.

Mutter, Arthur Z., and Schleifer, Maxwell J. "The Role of Psychological and Social Factors in the Onset of Somatic Illness in Children." *Psychosomatic Medicine*. Vol. 28, No. 4 (Part 1), 1966, pp. 333–343.

O'Connor, John F., et al. "Prognostic Implications of Psychiatric Diagnosis in Ulcerative Colitis." *Psychosomatic Medicine*. Vol. 28, No. 4 (Part 1), 1966, pp. 375–381.

Paulley, J. W. "Cultural Influences on the Incidence and Pattern of Disease." *Psychotherapy and Psychosomatics*. Vol. 26, 1975, pp. 2–11.

Pierloot, R. A., Wellens, W., and Houben, M. E. "Elements of Resistance to a Combined Medical and Psychotherapeutic Program in Anorexia Nervosa." *Psychotherapy and Psychosomatics*. Vol. 26, 1975, pp. 101–117.

Pipineli-Potamianou, A. "The Child, Vulnerable in the Mother's Desire." *Psychotherapy and Psychosomatics*. Vol. 26, 1975, pp. 211–218.

Salem, S. N., and Shubair, Kandel S. "Nonspecific Ulcerative Colitis in Bedouin Arabs." *The Lancet*. March 4, 1967, pp. 473–475.

Schmitt, Barton D. "Personality and Ulcerative Colitis." *The New England Journal of Medicine*. March 19, 1970, pp. 689.

Schucman, Helen, and Thetford, William N. "A Comparison of Personality Traits in Ulcerative Colitis and Migraine Patients." *Journal of Abnormal Psychology*. Vol. 76, No. 3, 1970, pp. 443–452.

Sharma, Shridhar, and Rao, Champa. "Personality Factors and Adjustment Patterns of Peptic Ulcer Patients in India." *Psychosomatics*. August–September, 1974, pp. 139–142.

Shields, Robert. "Psychosomatic Aspects of Ulcerative Colitis." *The Practitioner*. December, 1972, pp. 851–858.

Smith, Vernon M. "Psychosomatic Aspects of Gastrointestinal Diseases." *Psychosomatics*. March–April, 1963, pp. 85–90.

Weiner, Herbert, et al. "Etiology of Duodenal Ulcer. I. Relation of Specific Psychological Characteristics to Rate of Gastric Secretion." *Psychosomatic Medicine*. Vol. 19, 1957, pp. 1–10.

West, Ranyard. "Ulcerative Colitis." *British Medical Journal.* May 8, 1971, pp. 340–341.

Wolf, Stewart. "Stress and the Gut." *Gastroenterology,* Vol. 52, No. 2, 1967, pp. 288–289.

Chapter 4

Aitken, R. C. B., Zealley, A. K., and Rosenthal, S. V. "Psychological and Physiological Measures of Emotion in Chronic Asthmatic Patients." *Journal of Psychosomatic Research.* Vol. 13, 1969, pp. 289–297.

Anon. "NIAID Describes Immunologic and Biochemical Interactions That Precipitate Asthma Attack." *News and Features from NIH.* March, 1978, pp. 1–9.

Dally, P. J. "Allergy and Psychiatry." *The Practitioner.* Vol. 196, 1966, pp. 795–799.

Farr, Richard S. "Asthma in Adults: The Ambulatory Patient." *Hospital Practice.* April, 1978, pp. 113–123.

Frazier, Claude. *Psychosomatic Aspects of Allergy.* New York: Van Nostrand Reinhold, 1977.

Green, Richard. "Asthma and Manic Depressive Psychosis—Simultaneously Incompatible or Coexistent?" *The Journal of Nervous and Mental Disease.* January, 1965, pp. 64–70.

Jacobs, Martin A., et al. "Incidence of Psychosomatic Predisposing Factors in Allergic Disorders." *Psychosomatic Medicine.* Vol. 28, No. 5, 1966, pp. 679–695.

Kagan, Susan G., and Weiss, Jonathan H. "Allergic Potential and Emotional Precipitants of Asthma in Children." *Journal of Psychosomatic Research.* Vol. 20, 1976, pp. 135–139.

Kahn, J. P. "Allergic Children: Their Psyche and Skin." *Postgraduate Medicine.* February, 1969, pp. 149–152.

Khan, Aman U. "Present Status of Psychosomatic Aspects of Asthma." *Psychosomatics.* August, 1973, pp. 195–200.

Knapp, Peter H., Mushatt, Cecil, and Nemetz, S. Joseph. "Asthma, Melancholia, and Death." *Psychosomatic Medicine.* Vol. 28, No. 2, 1966, pp. 114–133.

Knight, James A. "Psychodynamics of the Allergic Eczemas." *Annals of Allergy.* July, 1967, pp. 393–396.

Lidz, Theodore. "Disruptions of Defensive Life Patterns and Psychosomatic Disorders." *Hopkins Medical Journal.* November, 1969, pp. 233–244.

Masuda, M., Notske, R. N., and Holmes, T. H. "Catecholamine Excretion and Asthmatic Behavior." *Journal of Psychosomatic Research.* Vol. 10, 1966, pp. 255–262.

Meijer, Alexander. "High Risk Factors for Childhood Asthma." *Annals of Allergy.* August, 1976, pp. 119–121.

Miklich, Donald R., et al. "A Preliminary Investigation of Psychophysiological Responses to Stress Among Different Subgroups of Asthmatic Children." *Journal of Psychosomatic Research.* Vol. 17, 1973, pp. 1–8.

Paley, Aaron, and Luparello, Thomas J. "Understanding the Psychologic Factors in Asthma." *Geriatrics.* August, 1973, pp. 54–62.

Peshkin, M. Murray. "The Emotional Aspects of Allergy in Children." *The Journal of Asthma Research.* June, 1966, pp. 265–277.

Pinkerton, Philip. "Psychosomatic Medicine. III. Psychosomatic Aspects of Asthma." *The Practitioner.* March, 1972, pp. 430–436.

Pinkerton, Philip. "The Enigma of Asthma." *Psychosomatic Medicine.* November–December, 1973, pp. 461–463.

Purcell, K., et al. "A Comparison of Psychologic Findings in Variously Defined Asthmatic Subgroups." *Journal of Psychosomatic Research.* Vol. 13, 1969, pp. 67–75.

Rees, W. Linford. "Stress, Distress and Disease." *British Journal of Psychiatry.* Vol. 128, 1976, pp. 3–18.

Rosenthal, S. V., Aitken, R. C. B., and Zealley, A. K. "The Cattell 16¼F Personality Profile of Asthmatics." *Journal of Psychosomatic Research.* Vol. 17, 1973, pp. 9–14.

Seiden, Richard H. "The Psychoanalytic Significance of Onset Age in Bronchial Asthma." *The Journal of Asthma Research.* June, 1966, pp. 285–289.

Stein, Marvin. "Experimental Studies of Psychosocial and Physiological Effects on Immune Processes." Presented at the American Association for the Advancement of Science Symposium, "Brain Functions and Physical Well-Being," January 27, 1975, pp. 1–6.

Stein, Marvin, and Luparello, Thomas J. "Psychosomatic Aspects of Respiratory Disorders." *Postgraduate Medicine.* May, 1970, pp. 137–141.

Stein, Marvin, Schiavi, Raul C., and Luparello, Thomas J. "The Hypothalamus and Immune Process." *Annals of the New York Academy of Sciences.* Vol. 164, 1969, pp. 464–470.

Thoren, Rolf. "Psychosomatic Approach to Bronchial Asthma." *Acta Allergologica.* Vol. 22, 1967, pp. 145–173.

Zealley, A. K., Aitken, R. C. B., and Rosenthal, S. V. "Asthma: A Psychophysiological Investigation." *Proceedings of the Royal Society of Medicine.* August, 1971, pp. 825–829.

Chapter 5

Alexander, Franz, French, Thomas M., and Pollock, George H. "Rheumatoid Arthritis." *Psychosomatic Specificity.* Chicago: The University of Chicago Press, 1968, pp. 12–13.

Amkraut, Alfred A., Solomon, George F., and Kraemer, Helena C. "Stress, Early Experience and Adjuvant-Induced Arthritis in the Rat." *Psychosomatic Medicine.* May–June, 1971, pp. 203–214.

Anon. "Can RA Factor + Anger = Arthritis?" *Medical World News.* September 26, 1969, p. 28.

Anon. "Social and Psychosomatic Aspects of Rheumatic Arthritis." *Acta Rheumatologica Scandinavica Supplementum.* Vol. 13, 1969, pp. 1–69.

Anon. "Understanding Inflammation—A Giant Step." *Annual Report of the Arthritis Foundation.* 1969.

Anon. "Was the Arthritis Caused by Worry?" *Medical World News,* March 17, 1972, p. 820.

Anon. *Rheumatoid Arthritis—A Handbook for Patients.* The Arthritis Foundation, 1976.

Anon. "Arthritis—What Really Relieves the Pain?" *Saint Vincent Hospital/ Worcester, Mass./ Outlook.* March, 1978, p. 2.

Bennett, Charles C. "Family Stress May Trigger Childhood Arthritis." *News release from The Arthritis Foundation.* March 16, 1978.

Booth, Gotthard. "Organ Function and Form Perception—Use of the Rorschach Method with Cases of Chronic Arthritis, Parkinsonism and Arterial Hypertension." *Psychosomatic Medicine.* November–December, 1946, pp. 367–384.

Cleveland, Sidney E., and Fisher, Seymour. "Behavior and Unconscious Fantasies of Patients with Rheumatoid Arthritis." *Psychosomatic Medicine.* July–August, 1954, pp. 327–333.

Cleveland, Sidney E., and Fisher, Seymour. "A Comparison of Psychological Characteristics and Physiological Reactivity in Ulcer and Rheumatoid Arthritis Groups." *Psychosomatic Medicine.* Vol. 22, No. 4, 1960, pp. 283–293.

Cobb, Sidney. "Contained Hostility in Rheumatoid Arthritis." *Arthritis and Rheumatism.* Vol. 2, 1959, pp. 419–425.

Cobb, Sidney, and Hall, William. "Newly Identified Cluster of Diseases— Rheumatoid Arthritis, Peptic Ulcer and Tuberculosis." *The Journal of the American Medical Association.* September 27, 1965, pp. 95–97.

Cobb, Sidney, et al. "The Intrafamilial Transmission of Rheumatoid Arthritis —VII and VIII." *Journal of Chronic Disease.* Vol. 22, 1969, pp. 279–293, 295–296.

Harburg, Ernest, et al. "The Intrafamilial Transmission of Rheumatoid Arthritis—IV." *Journal of Chronic Disease.* Vol. 22, 1969, pp. 223–238.

Hoffman, Agnes L. "Psychological Factors Associated with Rheumatoid Arthritis." *Nursing Research.* May–June, 1974, pp. 218–232.

Johnson, Adelaide, Shapiro, Louis B., and Alexander, Franz. "Preliminary Report on a Psychosomatic Study of Rheumatoid Arthritis. *Psychosomatic Medicine.* September, 1947, pp. 295–300.

Kasl, Stanislav V., and Cobb, Sidney. "The Intrafamilial Transmission of Rheumatoid Arthritis—V." *Journal of Chronic Disease.* Vol. 22, 1969, pp. 239–258.

King, Stanley H., and Cobb, Sidney. "Psychosocial Factors in the Epidemiology of Rheumatoid Arthritis." *Journal of Chronic Disease.* June, 1955, pp. 466–475.

Kirchman, Margaret M. "The Personality of the Rheumatoid Arthritis Patient." *American Journal of Occupational Therapy.* Vol. 19, No. 3, 1965, pp. 160–164.

Ludwig, Alfred O. "Rheumatoid Arthritis." *In Recent Developments in Psychosomatic Medicine.* Philadelphia, Pa.: Lippincott, 1954, pp. 232–244.

Ludwig, Alfred O. "Rheumatoid Arthritis—Psychiatric Aspects." *Medical Insight.* December, 1970, pp. 14–19.

Meyerowitz, Sanford. "The Continuing Investigation of Psychosocial Variables in Rheumatoid Arthritis." *Modern Trends in Rheumatology.* Vol. 2. New York: Appleton, Century, 1971.

Moldolfsky, Harvey, and Chester, W. J. "Pain and Mood Patterns in Patients with Rheumatoid Arthritis—A Prospective Study." *Psychosomatic Medicine.* May–June, 1970, pp. 309–318.

Moldofsky, Harvey, and Rothman, Arthur I. "Personality, Disease Parameters and Medication in Rheumatoid Arthritis." *Journal of Chronic Disease.* Vol. 24, 1971, pp. 363–372.

Moos, Rudolf H. "Personality Factors Associated with Rheumatoid Arthritis: A Review." *Journal of Chronic Disease.* Vol. 17, 1964, pp. 41–55.

Moos, Rudolf H., and Solomon, George F. "Psychologic Comparisons Between Women with Rheumatoid Arthritis and Their Nonarthritic Sisters." *Psychosomatic Medicine.* Vol. 27, No. 2, 1965, pp. 135–149.

Nalven, Fredric B., and O'Brien, John F. "Personality Patterns of Rheumatoid Arthritis Patients." *Arthritis and Rheumatism.* February, 1961, pp. 18–28.

Robinson, Harry. "A Psychological Study of Rheumatoid Arthritis and Selected Controls." *Journal of Chronic Disease.* Vol. 23, 1971, pp. 791–801.

Solomon, George F. "Emotions, Stress, the Central Nervous System and Immunity." *Annals of the New York Academy of Sciences.* Vol. 164, 1969, pp. 335–342.

Solomon, George F., and Moos, Rudolf H. "The Relationship of Personality to the Presence of Rheumatoid Factor in Asymptomatic Relatives of Patients with Rheumatoid Arthritis." *Psychosomatic Medicine.* Vol. 27, No. 4, 1965, pp. 350–360.

Thomas, Lewis. *New Directions in Arthritis Research.* The Arthritis Foundation, 1973.

Williams, Robert L., and Krasnoff, Alan G. "Body Image and Physiological Patterns in Patients with Peptic Ulcer and Rheumatoid Arthritis." *Psychosomatic Medicine.* Vol. 26, No. 6, 1964, pp. 701–709.

Chapter 6

Alden, Carl B., et al. "Headache," *New York State Journal of Medicine.* February 15, 1966, pp. 467–486.

Alfaro, Victor R. "Psychogenic Influences in Otolaryngology." *A.M.A. Archives of Otolaryngology.* January, 1960, pp. 11/1–17/7.

Arana, George. "Young Man with Headache: Syndrome, Psyche or Both?" *Headache.* October, 1975, pp. 173–176.

Aring, Charles D. "Emotion-Induced Headache." *Postgraduate Medicine.* September, 1974, pp. 191–194.

Barolin, Gerhard S. "Psychology and Neuropsychology in Migraine." *Research and Clinical Studies in Headache.* Vol. 3, 1972, pp. 126–153.

Bihldorff, John P., King, Stanley H., and Parnes, Leo R. "Psychological Factors in Headache." *Headache.* October, 1971, pp. 117–127.

Dalessio, Donald J. "Report from San Diego—Migraine Management." *Headache Update.* Spring, 1977, pp. 1–3.

Diamond, Seymour. "Psychosomatic Aspects of Headache." *Illinois Medical Journal.* February, 1969, pp. 153–156.

Friedman, Arnold, von Storch, Theodore J. C., and Merritt, Houston H. "Migraine and Tension Headaches—Clinical Study of Two Thousand Cases." *Neurology.* Vol. 4, 1954, pp. 773–788.

Gainotti, G., Cianchetti, C., and Taramelli, M. "Anxiety Level and Psychodynamic Mechanisms in Medical Headaches." *Research and Clinical Studies in Headache.* Vol. 3, 1972, pp. 182–190.

Garner, Harry H., et al. "Psychiatric Aspects of Headache." *Headache.* April, 1967, pp. 1–12.

Guthiel, E. "Analysis of a Case of Migraine." *Psychoanalytic Review.* Vol. 21, 1934, pp. 272–299.

Harris, C. M. "Psychosomatic Medicine—Tiredness and Headaches." *The Practitioner.* June, 1972, pp. 845–850.

Henahan, John F. "Headache!" *Science Digest.* September, 1976, pp. 46–54.

Hsu, L. K. G., et al. "Early Morning Migraine." *The Lancet.* February 26, 1977, pp. 447–450.

Ikemi, Yujiro, Kusamo, Tadayoshi, and Fukamachi, Ken. "Psychogenic Factors in Headache." *International Journal of Neurology,* Vol. 3, No. 1, 1962, pp. 368–375.

Kashiwagi, I., McClure, James N., Jr., and Wetzel, Richard D. "Headache and Psychiatric Disorders." *Diseases of the Nervous System.* October, 1972, pp. 659–663.

Kudrow, Lee. "Physical and Personality Characteristics in Cluster Headache." *Headache,* January, 1974, pp. 197–202.

Lance, James W. *Headache—Understanding Alleviation.* New York: Scribners, 1975.

Packard, Russell C. "What is Psychogenic Headache?" *Headache.* March, 1976, pp. 20–23.

Paulley, J. W., and Haskell, D. A. L. "The Treatment of Migraine Without Drugs." *Journal of Psychosomatic Research.* Vol. 19, 1975, pp. 367–374.

Prescott, H. F. M. *Mary Tudor.* New York: MacMillan, 1968.

Rees, W. Linford. "Personality and Psychodynamic Mechanisms in Migraine." *Psychotherapy and Psychosomatics.* Vol. 23, 1974, pp. 111–122.

Rees, W. Linford. "Stress, Distress and Disease." *British Journal of Psychiatry.* Vol. 128, 1976, pp. 3–18.

Ross, W. Donald, and McNaughton, Francis L. "Objective Personality Studies in Migraine by Means of the Rorschach Method." *Psychosomatic Medicine.* Vol. 7, 1945, pp. 73–79.

Selby, George, and Lance, James W. "Observations on 500 Cases of Migraine and Allied Vascular Headache." *Journal of Neurosurgery and Psychiatry.* Vol. 23, 1960, pp. 23–32.

Sperling, Melitta. "Further Contribution to the Psycho-Analytic Study of Migraine and Psychogenic Headaches." *International Journal of Psychoanalysis.* October, 1964, pp. 549–557.

Touraine, Grace A., and Draper, George. "The Migrainous Patient—A Constitutional Study." *The Journal of Nervous and Mental Disease.* Vol. 80, 1934, pp. 1–23.

Walters, Allan. "Psychogenic Regional Pain Alias Hysterical Pain." *Brain.* March, 1961, pp. 1–18.

Walters, Allan. "Psychogenic Regional Headache." *Headache.* October, 1973, pp. 107–116.

Wolff, Harold G. "Personality Features and Reactions of Subjects with Migraine." *Archives of Neurology and Psychiatry.* Vol. 37, 1937, pp. 895–921.

Chapter 7

Beck, Aaron T., Kovacs, Maria, and Weissman, Arlene. "Hopelessness and Suicidal Behavior." *Journal of the American Medical Association.* December 15, 1975, pp. 1146–1149.

Bhagat, M. "The Spouses of Attempted Suicides: A Personal Study." *British Journal of Psychiatry.* Vol. 128, 1976, pp. 44–46.

Blackburn, R. "An Empirical Classification of Psychopathic Personality." *British Journal of Psychiatry.* Vol. 127, 1975, pp. 456–460.

Blum, Howard. "Reexamination of Berkowitz Files Offers New Insights." *The New York Times,* May 17, 1978, pp. B1, B4.

Boekelheide, Priscilla Day. "Evaluation of Suicide Risk." *American Family Practitioner.* December, 1978, pp. 109–113.

Brill, Norman Q. "Schizophrenia: A Psychosomatic Disorder?" *Psychosomatics*. November, 1978, pp. 665–670.

Cadoret, Remi J. "New Approaches to Old Problems: Personality and Depression." *International Journal of Psychiatry*. Vol. 11, 1973, pp. 234–236.

Chodoff, Paul. "The Depressive Personality—A Critical Review." *Archives of General Psychiatry*. November, 1972, pp. 666–673.

Chodoff, Paul. "The Depressive Personality: A Critical Review." *International Journal of Psychiatry*. Vol. 11, 1973, pp. 196–217, 237–238.

Cohen, Earl, Motto, Jerome A., and Seiden, Richard H. "An Instrument for Evaluating Suicide Potential: A Preliminary Study." *American Journal of Psychiatry*. Vol. 122, 1966, pp. 886–891.

Donlon, Patrick T. "The Enigma of the Schizophrenias." *Psychosomatics*. July–August, 1972, pp. 272–275.

Farberow, Norman L., MacKinnon, Douglas R., and Nelson, Franklyn L. "Suicide: Who's Counting." *Public Health Reports*. May–June, 1977, pp. 223–239.

Greenberg, Joel. "Blueprint of a Killer's Personality." *Science News*. September 24, 1977, p. 201.

Greenberg, Joel. "Psychological Problems and Parental Loss." *Science News*. January 14, 1978, p. 21.

Greenberg, Joel. "The Stressful Price of Prosperity." *Science News*. March 18, 1978, p. 166.

Harrower, Molly, Thomas, Caroline Bedell, and Altman, Ann. "Human Figure Drawings in a Prospective Study of Six Disorders: Hypertension, Coronary Heart Disease, Malignant Tumor, Suicide, Mental Illness, and Emotional Disturbance." *Journal of Nervous and Mental Disease*. Vol. 161, no. 3, 1975, pp. 191–199.

Havens, Leston. "Five Possible Meanings of Predictive Criteria." *International Journal of Psychiatry*. Vol. 2, 1966, pp. 630–633.

Horn, Joseph M. "Factors Associated with Criminality." *Science*. May 12, 1978, pp. 647–649.

Huber, G., Gross, G., and Schüttler, R. "A Long-Term Follow-Up Study of Schizophrenia: Psychiatric Course of Illness and Prognosis." *Acta Psychiatrica Scandinavica*. Vol. 52, 1975, pp. 49–57.

Jacobson, Edith. "The Depressive Personality." *International Journal of Psychiatry*. Vol. 11, 1973, pp. 218–221.

Kane, Francis J. "Post-partum Psychosis in Identical Twins." *Psychosomatics*. September–October, 1968, pp. 278–281.

Kiev, Ari. "Cluster Analysis Profiles of Suicide Attempters." *American Journal of Psychiatry*. February, 1976, pp. 150–153.

Klerman, Gerald L. "The Relationships Between Personality and Clinical Depressions: Overcoming the Obstacles to Verifying Psychodynamic Theories." *International Journal of Psychiatry*. Vol. 11, 1973, pp. 227–233.

Kupfer, David J., Detre, Thomas P., and Koral, Jacqueline. "Relationships of Certain Childhood 'Traits' to Adult Psychiatric Disorders." *American Journal of Orthopsychiatry*. January, 1975, pp. 74–80.

Lamont, John, Fischoff, Stuart, and Gottlieb, Harold. "Recall of Parental Behaviors in Female Neurotic Depressives." *Journal of Clinical Psychology*. October, 1976, pp. 762–765.

Lo, W. H. "Aetiological Factors in Childhood Neurosis." *British Journal of Psychiatry*, Vol. 115, 1969, pp. 889–894.

Mendelson, Myer. "Some Second Thoughts on the Depressive Personality." *International Journal of Psychiatry*. Vol. 11, 1973, pp. 222–226.

Morgan, H. Gethin, et al. "Deliberate Self-Harm: Clinical and Socio-economic Characteristics of 368 Patients." *British Journal of Psychiatry*. Vol. 127, 1975, pp. 564–574.

Murthy, Vinoda Narayana. "Personality and the Nature of Suicide Attempts." *British Journal of Psychiatry*. Vol. 115, 1969, pp. 791–795.

Pallis, D. J., and Birtchnell, J. "Personality and Suicidal History in Psychiatric Patients." *Journal of Clinical Psychology*. April, 1976, pp. 246–253.

Panton, James H. "Personality Characteristics of Death-Row Prison Inmates." *Journal of Clinical Psychology*. April, 1976, pp. 306–309.

Pasnau, Robert O., and Russell, Andrew T. "Psychiatric Resident Suicide: An Analysis of Five Cases." *American Journal of Psychiatry*. April, 1975, pp. 402–405.

Paykel, Eugene S. "Life Stress, Depression and Suicide." *Journal of Human Stress*. September, 1976, pp. 3–11.

Rosenfeld, Megan. "The Brief Career of Becky Hanslin." *The Washington Post*, May 19, 1977, pp. A1., A6.

Sanborn, D. E., et al. "Suicide and Stress-Related Dermatoses." *Diseases of the Nervous System*. June, 1972, pp. 391–394.

Sendi, Ismah B., and Blomgren, Paul G. "Comparative Study of Predictive Criteria in the Predisposition of Homicidal Adolescents." *American Journal of Psychiatry*. April, 1975, pp. 423–427.

Smith, Selwyn M., and Hanson, Ruth. "Interpersonal Relationships and Child-Rearing Practices in 214 Parents of Battered Children." *British Journal of Psychiatry*. Vol. 127, 1975, pp. 513–525.

Sperling, Melitta. "Further Contribution to the Psycho-Analytic Study of Migraine and Psychogenic Headaches." *International Journal of Psychoanalysis*. Vol. 45, 1964, pp. 549–557.

Stabenau, James R., and Pollin, William. "Early Characteristics of Monozygotic Twins Discordant for Schizophrenia." *Archives of General Psychiatry*. December, 1967, pp. 723–734.

Thomas, Caroline Bedell. "Suicide Among Us: II. Habits of Nervous Tension as Potential Predictors." *The Johns Hopkins Medical Journal*. October, 1971, pp. 190–201.

Thomas, Caroline Bedell. "Precursors of Premature Disease and Death." *Annals of Internal Medicine*. Vol. 85, 1976, pp. 653–658.

Thomas, Caroline Bedell. "What Becomes of Medical Students: The Dark Side." *The Johns Hopkins Medical Journal*. May, 1976, pp. 185–195.

Thomas, Caroline Bedell, and Duszynski, Karen R. "Closeness to Parents and the Family Constellation in a Prospective Study of Five Disease States: Suicide, Mental Illness, Malignant Tumor, Hypertension and Coronary Heart Disease." *The Johns Hopkins Medical Journal*. May, 1974, pp. 251–270.

Thomas, Caroline Bedell, and Greenstreet, Richard L. "Psychobiological Characteristics in Youth as Predictors of Five Disease States: Suicide, Mental Illness, Hypertension, Coronary Heart Disease and Tumor." *The Johns Hopkins Medical Journal*. January, 1973, pp. 16–43.

Thomas, Caroline Bedell, et al. "A Prospective Study of the Rorschachs of Suicides: The Predictive Potential of Pathological Content." *The Johns Hopkins Medical Journal*. June, 1973, pp. 334–360.

Thornton, William E., and Pray, Bonnie J. "The Portrait of a Murderer." *Diseases of the Nervous System*. April, 1975, pp. 176–178.

Videbech, Th. "A Study of Genetic Factors, Childhood Bereavement, and Premorbid Personality Traits in Patients with Anancastic Endogenous Depression." *Acta Psychiatrica Scandinavica*. Vol. 52, 1975, pp. 178–222.

Wagner, Nathaniel N., and Stegman, Karen L. "The Schizoid Child and Adult Schizophrenia." *Mental Hygiene*. October, 1969, pp. 530–538.

Wright, Logan. "The 'Sick but Slick' Syndrome as a Personality Component of Parents of Battered Chidren." *Journal of Clinical Psychology*. January, 1976, pp. 41–45.

Chapter 8

Amkraut, Alfred O., Solomon, George F., and Kraemer, Helena C. "Stress, Early Experience and Adjuvant-Induced Arthritis in the Rat." *Psychosomatic Medicine*. May–June, 1971, pp. 203–214.

Anon. "NIAID Describes Immunologic and Biochemical Interactions That Precipitate Asthma Attack." *News and Features from NIH*. March, 1978, pp. 1–9.

Anon. "Cancer and the Mind: How Are They Connected?" *Science*. June 23, 1978, pp. 1363–1365.

Arehart-Treichel, Joan. "Emotions and High Blood Pressure." *Science News*. July 26, 1975, p. 58.

Arehart-Treichel, Joan. "The Mind-Body Link." *Science News*. December 20 and 27, 1975, pp. 394–395.

Aring, Charles D. "Emotion-Induced Headache." *Postgraduate Medicine*. September, 1974, pp. 191–194.

Barolin, Gerhard S. "Psychology and Neuropsychology in Migraine." *Research in Clinical Studies of Headache*. Vol. 3, 1972, pp. 126–153.

Bishop, Louis F., and Reichert, Philip. "Emotion and Heart Failure." *Psychosomatics*. November–December, 1971, pp. 412–415.

Bullock, Theodore Holmes. "Are We Learning What Actually Goes on When the Brain Recognizes and Controls?" *Journal of Experimental Zoology*. Vol. 194, 1975, pp. 13–34.

Coddington, R. Dean. "Study of an Infant With a Gastric Fistula and Her Normal Twin." *Psychosomatic Medicine*. Vol. 30, No. 2, 1968, pp. 172–192.

Coddington, R. Dean. "Peptic Ulcers in Children." *Psychosomatics*. January–February, 1968, pp. 38–43.

Cohen, Sanford I. "Psychoneurophysiologic Considerations of Emotions." *Postgraduate Medicine*. May, 1970, pp. 79–82.

Dally, P. J. "Allergy and Psychiatry." *The Practitioner*. Vol. 196, 1966, pp. 795–799.

Dongier, M. "Psychosomatic Aspect in Myocardial Infarction in Comparison With Angina Pectoris." *Psychotherapy and Psychosomatics*. Vol. 23, 1974, pp. 123–131.

Farr, Richard S. "Asthma in Adults: The Ambulatory Patient." *Hospital Practice*. April, 1978, pp. 113–123.

Finestone, Albert J. "The Psychophysiology of Stress." *Psychosomatics*. October, 1978, pp. 587–589.

Frazier, Claude A. *Psychosomatic Aspects of Allergy*. New York: Van Nostrand Reinhold, 1977.

Friedman, Stanford B., et al. "Effects of Psychological Stress in Adult Mice Inoculated With Coxsackie B Viruses." *Psychosomatic Medicine.* Vol. 27, No. 4, 1965, pp. 361–368.

Friedman, Stanley. "A Psychophysiological Model For the Chemotherapy of Psychosomatic Illness." *The Journal of Nervous and Mental Disease.* Vol. 166, No. 2, pp. 110–116.

Greenberg, Joel. "Stress May Damage Cell Immunity." *Science News.* March 11, 1978, p. 151.

Henahan, John F. "Headache!" *Science Digest.* September, 1976, pp. 45–54.

Hopson, Janet. "Social Stress and the Immune System," *Science News.* February 1, 1975, pp. 68–69.

Hsu, L. K. G., et al. "Early Morning Migraine." *The Lancet.* February 26, 1977, pp. 447–450.

Ishikawa, Hitoshi, et al. "Psychosomatic Study of Angina Pectoris." *Psychosomatics.* November–December, 1971, pp. 390–397.

Johns, M. W., et al. "Relationship Between Sleep Habits, Adrenocortical Activity and Personality." *Psychosomatic Medicine.* November–December, 1971, pp. 499–508.

Katz, Jack, et al. "Psychoendocrine Considerations in Cancer of the Breast." *Annals of the New York Academy of Sciences.* October 14, 1969, pp. 509–515.

Kavetsky, R. E., et al. "Induced Carcinogenesis Under the Influences on the Hypothalamus." *Annals of the New York Academy of Sciences.* October 14, 1969, pp. 517–519.

Khan, Aman U. "Present Status of Psychosomatic Aspects of Asthma." *Psychosomatics.* August, 1973, pp. 195–200.

Kissen, David M., and Reo, L. G. S. "Steroid Excretion Patterns and Personality in Lung Cancer." *Annals of the New York Academy of Sciences.* October 14, 1969, pp. 476–481.

Knobil, Ernst. "The Pituitary Growth Hormone: An Adventure in Physiology." *The Physiologist.* Vol. 9, 1966, pp. 25–41.

Lance, James W. *Headache—Understanding Alleviation.* New York: Scribners, 1975.

Lane, Frederick M. "Mental Mechanisms and the Pain of Angina Pectoris." *American Heart Journal.* April, 1973, pp. 563–568.

Lidz, Theodore. "Disruptions of Defensive Life Patterns and Psychosomatic Disorders." *Hopkins Medical Journal.* November, 1969, pp. 233–244.

Lipowski, Z. J., and Kiriakos, R. Z. "Psychosomatic Aspects of Central Serious Retinopathy." *Psychosomatics.* November–December, 1971, pp. 398–401.

Lund, Reimer. "Personality Factors and Desynchronization of Circadian Rhythms." *Psychosomatic Medicine.* May–June, 1974, pp. 224–228.

Mason, John W. "A Review of Psychoendocrine Research on the Pituitary-Adrenal Cortical System." *Psychosomatic Medicine.* September–October, 1968, pp. 576–607.

Mason, John W. "The Integrative Approach in Medicine—Implications of Neuroendocrine Mechanisms." *Perspectives in Biology and Medicine.* Spring, 1974, pp. 333–347.

Mason, John W. "Emotion as Reflected in Patterns of Endocrine Integration." In L. Levi, ed., *Emotions—Their Parameters and Measurement.* New York: Raven Press, 1975.

Mason, John W. "A Historical View of the Stress Field." *Journal of Human Stress.* March, 1975, pp. 6–16.

Masuda, M., et al. "Catecholamine Excretion and Asthmatic Behavior." *Journal of Psychosomatic Research*. Vol. 10, 1966, pp. 255–262.

McClelland, David C. "Sources of Stress in the Drive For Power." New York: Kittay Scientific Foundation, 1975.

McQuerter, Gregory. "Cancer: Clues in the Mind." *Science News*. January 21, 1978, pp. 44–45.

Miklich, Donald R. "A Preliminary Investigation of Psychophysiological Responses to Stress Among Different Subgroups of Asthmatic Children." *Journal of Psychosomatic Research*. Vol. 17, 1973, pp. 1–8.

Miller, Neal E. "Interactions Between Learned and Physical Factors in Mental Illness." *Seminars in Psychiatry*. August, 1972, pp. 239–254.

Miller, Neal E. "The Role of Learning in Physiological Responses to Stress." Kittay Scientific Foundation 3rd International Symposium, "Psychopathology of Human Adaptation," April 6–8, 1975.

Moriarty, C. Michael, et al. "Bioactive and Immunoactive ACTH in the Rat Pituitary: Influence of Stress and Adrenalectomy." *Endocrinology*. Vol. 96, No. 6, 1975, pp. 1419–1436.

Pelletier, Kenneth R. *Mind as Healer, Mind as Slayer*. New York: Delta, 1977.

Peshkin, M. Murray. "The Emotional Aspects of Allergy in Children." *The Journal of Asthma Research*. June, 1966, pp. 265–277.

Pettingale, Keith W., et al. "Serum IgA and Emotional Expression in Breast Cancer Patients." *Journal of Psychosomatic Research*. Vol. 21, 1977, pp. 395–399.

Prehn, Richmond T. "The Relationship of Immunology to Carcinogenesis." *Annals of the New York Academy of Sciences*. October 14, 1969, pp. 449–453.

Rees, W. Linford. "Stress, Distress and Disease." *British Journal of Psychiatry*. Vol. 128, 1976, pp. 3–18.

Riley, Vernon. "Mouse Mammary Tumors: Alteration of Incidence as Apparent Function of Stress." *Science*. August 8, 1975, pp. 465–467.

Russek, Henry I. "Role of Emotional Stress in the Etiology of Clinical Coronary Heart Disease." *Diseases of the Chest*. July, 1967, pp. 1–9.

Schmidt, Robert T. "Personality and Fainting." *Journal of Psychosomatic Research*. Vol. 19, 1975, pp. 21–25.

Solomon, George F. "Emotions, Stress, the CNS and Immunity." *Annals of the New York Academy of Sciences*. October 14, 1969, pp. 335–342.

Solomon, George F., and Moos, Rudolf H. "The Relationship of Personality to the Presence of Rheumatoid Factor in Asymptomatic Relatives of Patients With Rheumatoid Arthritis." *Psychosomatic Medicine*. Vol. 27, No. 4, 1965, pp. 350–360.

Solomon, George F., et al. "Early Experience and Immunity." *Nature*. November 23, 1968, pp. 821–822.

Southam, Chester M. "Emotions, Immunology and Cancer: How Might the Psyche Influence Neoplasia?" *Annals of the New York Academy of Sciences*. October 14, 1969, pp. 473–475.

Stein, Marvin. "Experimental Studies of Psychosocial and Physiological Effects on Immune Processes." The American Association for the Advancement of Science Symposium, "Brain Functions and Physical Well-Being," January 27, 1975, pp. 1–6.

Stein, Marvin, et al. "The Hypothalamus and Immune Process." *Annals of the New York Academy of Sciences*. October 14, 1969, pp. 464–470.

Stern, Elizabeth, et al. "Neuroendocrine Factors in Experimental Carcinogenesis." *Annals of the New York Academy of Sciences.* October 14, 1969, pp. 494–507.

Trotter, Robert J. "Stress—Confusion and Controversy." *Science News.* May 31, 1975, pp. 356–359.

Weiss, David W. "Immunological Parameters of the Host-Parasite Relationship in Neoplasia." *Annals of the New York Academy of Sciences.* October 14, 1969, pp. 431–447.

Williams, Ralph C. "Immunopathology of Rheumatoid Arthritis." *Hospital Practice.* February, 1978, pp. 53–60.

Wittkower, E. D., et al. "Psychosomatic Aspects of Endocrinologic Disorders." *Postgraduate Medicine.* May, 1970, pp. 146–150.

Wolf, Stewart. "Stress and the Gut." *Gastroenterology.* Vol. 52, No. 2, 1967, pp. 288–289.

Chapter 9

Alden, Carl B., et al. "Headache." *New York State Journal of Medicine.* February 15, 1966, pp. 467–486.

Anon. "Jogging May Keep Depressives off Therapist's Couch." *Medical World News.* March 20, 1978, p. 15.

Anton, John P. "Health, Harmony, and the Ancient Greeks." *Medicine at Emory.* Vol. 39, 1977, pp. 40–41.

Arana, George. "Young Man with Headache: Syndrome, Psyche or Both?" *Headache.* October, 1975, pp. 173–176.

Arehart-Treichel, Joan. "Muscle Tension and Biofeedback." *Science News.* February 16, 1974, p. 107.

Arehart-Treichel, Joan. "Asthma and Biofeedback Control." *Science News.* December 13, 1975, p. 377.

Arehart-Treichel, Joan. "Fighting Cancer with Mental Images." *Science News.* November 18, 1978, p. 328.

Arehart-Treichel, Joan, "The Current Fate of Cancer Patient Ron J." Personal communication with the U.S. Naval Academy, January, 1979.

Arieti, Silvano. "Psychotherapy of Severe Depression." *American Journal of Psychiatry.* August, 1977, pp. 864–868.

Aring, Charles D. "Emotion-Induced Headache." *Postgraduate Medicine.* September, 1974, pp. 191–194.

Barron, Jules. "Psychotherapy as Healing." *The American Journal of Psychoanalysis.* Vol. 37, 1977, pp. 147–153.

Bartle, Stuart H., and Bishop, Louis F. "Psychological Study of Patients with Coronary Heart Disease with Unexpectedly Long Survival and High Level Function." *Psychosomatics.* April–May–June, 1974, pp. 68–69.

Beary, John F., Benson, Herbert, and Klemchuk, Helen P. *Psychosomatic Medicine.* March–April, 1974, pp. 115–120.

Bensimon, Helen Frank. "The Heart." *The Magazine of Rush-Presbyterian-St. Luke's Medical Center.* Spring, 1977, pp. 3–27.

Benson, Herbert, Beary, John F., and Carol, Mark P. "The Relaxation Response." *Psychiatry.* February, 1974, pp. 37–46.

Bisbrouck, Véronique, "Le retour en forme ... ou presque." *Chercheurs/Université de Montréal.* January, 1978, pp 8–11

Blanchard, Richard B., and Young, Larry D. "Clinic Applications of Biofeedback Training." *Archives of General Psychiatry*. May, 1974, pp. 573–589.

Brown, Barbara. *Stress and the Art of Biofeedback*. New York: Bantam, 1978.

Bry, Adelaide, and Blair, Marjorie. "The Medicine of the Mind." *Cosmopolitan*. July, 1978, pp. 169–171, p. 266.

Calin, Andrei. "Rheumatoid Arthritis." *American Family Physician*. July, 1978, pp. 89–94.

Cromie, William J. "Faith Healers Help People Help Themselves, Say Experts." *Enterprise Science News*. August 31, 1977.

Dalessio, Donald J. "Migraine Management." *Headache Update*. Spring, 1977, pp. 1–3.

Dally, P. J. "Allergy and Psychiatry." *The Practitioner*. Vol. 196, 1966, pp. 795–799.

Davis, Margaret H., et al. "Relaxation Training Facilitated by Biofeedback Apparatus as a Supplemental Treatment in Bronchial Asthma." *Jounal of Psychosomatic Research*, Vol. 17, 1973, pp. 121–128.

De Araujo, Gilberto, et al. "Life Change, Coping Ability and Chronic Intrinsic Asthma." *Journal of Psychosomatic Research*. Vol. 17, 1973, pp. 359–363.

Dunkle, Mary. "Exercise Late in Life and Health." *News release from Pennsylvania State University*, January 4, 1979.

Eliot, Robert S., and Forker, Alan D. "Emotional Stress and Cardiac Disease." *Journal of the American Medical Association*. November 15, 1966, pp. 2325–2326.

Engle, Bernard T. "How Biofeedback Helps Prevent Heart Attacks." *Aging Tomorrow*. September–October, 1976, p. 13.

Feldman, Gary Michael. "The Effect of Biofeedback Training on Respiratory Resistance of Asthmatic Children." *Psychosomatic Medicine*. January–February, 1976, pp. 27–34.

Flynn, William E. "Managing the Emotional Aspects of Peptic Ulcer and Ulcerative Colitis." *Postgraduate Medicine*. May, 1970, pp. 119–122.

Frank, Jerome D. "Psychotherapy of Bodily Disease." *Psychotherapy and Psychosomatics*. Vol. 26, 1975, pp. 192–202.

Frazier, Claude A. *Psychosomatic Aspects of Allergy*. New York: Van Nostrand Reinhold, 1977.

Friedman, Meyer, and Rosenman, Ray H. *Type A Behavior and Your Heart*. New York: Knopf, 1974.

Fullerton, Donald T. "Psychosomatic Diseases of the Colon in Adults." *California Medicine*. January, 1965, pp. 33–39.

Geller, Jeffrey L. "Treatment of Anorexia Nervosa by the Integration of Behavior Therapy and Psychotherapy." *Psychotherapy and Psychosomatics*. Vol. 26, 1975, pp. 167–177.

Glass, David C. *Behavior Patterns, Stress and Coronary Disease*. Hillsdale, N.J.: Lawrence Erlbaum Associates, 1977.

Glueck, Bernard C., and Stroebel, Charles F. "Biofeedback and Meditation in the Treatment of Psychiatric Illnesses." *Current Psychiatric Therapies*. 1975, pp. 109–116.

Goetz, Patricia, et al. "Anorexia Nervosa in Children." *American Journal of Orthopsychiatry*. October, 1977, pp. 597–603.

Hackett, Thomas P., and Cassem, Ned H. "Psychological Management of the Myocardial Infarction Patient." *Journal of Human Stress*. September, 1975, pp. 25–38.

Henahan, John F. "Headache!" *Science Digest.* September, 1976, pp. 46–54.
Hertz, Dan G. "Rejection of Motherhood." *Psychosomatics.* August, 1973, pp. 241–244.
Hock, R. A., et al. "Medico-psychological Interventions in Male Asthmatic Children: An Evaluation of Physiological Change." *Psychosomatic Medicine.* May, 1978, pp. 210–215.
Hussey, Hugh H. "Anorexia Nervosa: Treatment by Behavior Modification." *Journal of the American Medical Association.* April 15, 1974, p. 344.
Hutschnecker, Arnold A. *The Will to Live.* New York: Cornerstone Library, 1977.
Jencks, Beata. *Your Body—Biofeedback at Its Best.* Chicago: Nelson Hall, 1977.
Katz, Jack, et al. "Psychoendocrine Considerations in Cancer of the Breast." *Annals of the New York Academy of Sciences.* October 14, 1969, pp. 509–515.
Khan, Aman U. "Acquired Bronchial Hypersensitivity in Asthma." *Psychosomatics.* October–November–December, 1974, pp. 188–189.
Kobayashi, Tachio, Ishikawa, Hitoshi, and Tawara, Ineko. "Psychosomatic Aspects of Angina Pectoris." *Scandinavian Journal of Rehabilitative Medicine.* Vol. 2–3, 1970, pp. 87–91.
Lane, Frederick M. "Mental Mechanisms and the Pain of Angina Pectoris." *American Heart Journal.* April, 1973, pp. 563–568.
LeShan, Lawrence. *You Can Fight for Your Life.* New York: Evans, 1977.
Lidz, Theodore. "Disruptions of Defensive Life Patterns and Psychosomatic Disorders." *Hopkins Medical Journal.* 1969, pp. 233–244.
Lodewegens, F. J., et al. "The Effect of Psychic Factors on the Spontaneous Cure of Secondary Amenorrhoea: A Comparison of Cases with and without Spontaneous Cure." *Journal of Psychosomatic Research.* Vol. 21, 1977, pp. 175–182.
Loebl, Suzanne. "Treating Arthritis Pain with Drugless Methods." *News release from the Arthritis Foundation,* June 2, 1978.
Lynch, James J., et al. "Human Contact and Cardiac Arrhythmia in a Coronary Care Unit." *Psychosomatic Medicine.* May–June, 1977, pp. 188–192.
MacLauchlan, Ruth. "He Conquered Cancer." *Anne Arundel Times.* June 10, 1976, pp. 1–8.
McMahon, Arthur W., et al. "Personality Differences Between Inflammatory Bowel Disease Patients and Their Healthy Siblings." *Psychosomatic Medicine.* March–April, 1973, pp. 91–103.
Meyerowitz, Sanford. "The Continuing Investigation of Psychosocial Variables in Rheumatoid Arthritis." *Modern Trends in Rheumatology.* New York: Appleton-Century, 1971, pp. 92–105.
Moore, Charlotte Dickinson. "Understanding Neurotic Disorder." *Department of Health, Education and Welfare Publication NO. (ADM) 78-614.*
Mordkoff, Arnold M., and Rand, Melvin A. "Personality and Adaptation to Coronary Artery Disease." *Journal of Consulting and Clinical Psychology.* Vol. 32, No. 6, 1968, pp. 645–653.
Niven, Robert G. "Psychologic Adjustment to Coronary Artery Disease." *Postgraduate Medicine.* November, 1976, pp. 152–157.
Ohno, Yoshiteru, et al. "The Treatment of Hysterical Blindness by Behavior Therapy." *Psychosomatics.* April–June, 1974, pp. 79–82.
Packard, Russell C. "What is Psychogenic Headache?" *Headache.* March, 1970, pp. 20–23.

Paley, Aaron, and Luparello, Thomas J. "Understanding the Psychological Factors in Asthma." *Geriatrics*. August, 1973, pp. 54–62.

Pattison, E. Mansell, Lapins, Mikolajs A., and Doerr, Hans A. "Faith Healing." *The Journal of Nervous and Mental Disease*. December, 1973, pp. 397–409.

Paulley, J. W., and Haskell, D. A. L. "The Treatment of Migraine Without Drugs." *Journal of Psychosomatic Research*. Vol. 19, 1975, pp. 367–374.

Pelletier, Kenneth R. *Mind as Healer, Mind as Slayer*. New York: Delta, 1974.

Peshkin, M. Murray. "The Emotional Aspects of Allergy in Children." *The Journal of Asthma Research*. June, 1966, pp. 265–277.

Peters, Ruanne K., Benson, Herbert, and Peters, John M. "Daily Relaxation Response Breaks in a Working Population: II. Effects on Blood Pressure." *American Journal of Public Health*. October, 1977, pp. 954–959.

Pierlott, A., Wellens, W., and Houben, M. E. "Elements of Resistance to a Combined Medical and Psychotherapeutic Program in Anorexia Nervosa." *Psychotherapy and Psychosomatics*. Vol. 26, 1975, pp. 101–117.

Pinkerton, Philip. "Psychosomatic Medicine. III. Psychosomatic Aspects of Asthma." *The Practitioner*. March, 1972, pp. 430–436.

Prociuk, Therry J., Breen, Lawrence J., and Lussier, Richard J. "Hopelessness, Internal-External Locus of Control, and Depression." *Journal of Clinical Psychology*. April, 1976, pp. 299–300.

Rees, W. Linford. "Personality and Psychodynamic Mechanisms in Migraine." *Psychotherapy and Psychosomatics*. Vol. 23, 1974, pp. 111–122.

Reinhart, John B., and Drash, Allan L. "Psychosocial Dwarfism: Environmentally Induced Recovery." *Psychosomatic Medicine*. Vol. 31, No. 2, 1969, pp. 165–172.

Rustin, R. M., et al. "Smoking Habits and Psycho-Socio-Biological Factors." *Journal of Psychosomatic Research*. Vol. 22, 1978, pp. 89–99.

Sampson, Paul. "People with Pets Fare Better After Serious Heart Disease." *News release from the American Heart Association*. No. 15, 1978.

Schaufler, Judith, et al. " 'Hand Gym' for Patients with Arthritic Hand Disabilities: Preliminary Report." *Archives of Physical Medicine and Rehabilitation*. May, 1978, pp. 221–226.

Schuster, Marvin M. "Biofeedback Treatment of Gastrointestinal Disorders." *Medical Clinics of North America*. July, 1977, pp. 907–912.

Schwartz, Leslie H., Marcus, Robert, and Condon, Robert. "Multidisciplinary Group Therapy for Rheumatoid Arthritis." *Psychosomatics*. May, 1978, pp. 289–293.

Segal, Julius. "Biofeedback as a Medical Treatment." *Journal of the American Medical Association*. April 14, 1975, p. 179.

Selye, Hans. *The Stress of Life*. New York: McGraw Hill, 1976.

Simonton, O. Carl, Matthews-Simonton, Stephanie, and Creighton, James. *Getting Well Again*. New York: Tarcher/St. Martin's, 1978.

Solomon, George F. "Psychologic Aspects of Response to Treatment in Rheumatoid Arthritis." *General Practitioner*. December, 1965, pp. 113–119.

Sperling, Melitta. "Further Contribution to the Psycho-Analytic Study of Migraine and Psychogenic Headaches." *International Journal of Psychoanalysis*, Vol. 45, 1964, pp. 549–557.

Stewart, Wendell K. "Hopelessness Following Illness in Middle Age." *Psychosomatics*. June, 1977, pp. 29–32.

Stonehill, Edward, Crisp, A. H. "Psychoneurotic Characteristics of Patients with Anorexia Nervosa Before and After Treatment and at Follow-up 4–7 Years Later." *Journal of Psychosomatic Research.* Vol. 21, 1977, pp. 187–193.

Suinn, Richard M., et al. "Behavior Therapy for Type A Patients." *The American Journal of Cardiology.* August, 1975, p. 269.

Sundsvold, Marit. "Muscular Tension and Psychopathology." *Psychotherapy and Psychosomatics.* Vol. 26, 1975, pp. 219–228.

Swaim, L. T. "The President's Address—Ninth Annual Meeting of the American Rheumatism Association." *Annals of Internal Medicine.* Vol. 19, 1943, p. 118.

Teiramaa, Esko. "Psychosocial and Psychic Factors in the Course of Asthma." *Journal of Psychosomatic Research.* Vol. 22, 1978, pp. 121–125.

Vachon, Louis, and Rich, Edwin S. "Visceral Learning in Asthma." *Psychosomatic Medicine.* March–April, 1976, pp. 122–130.

Chapter 10

Altman, Lawrence K. "Exertion Found to Ease Heart Risk." *The New York Times,* March 24, 1977.

Anon. "Long Trips, Easy Riders." *Medical World News.* May 5, 1975, pp. 7–8.

Anon. "Physician Says Stress Can be Good or Not Good." *The New York Times,* October 16, 1977, p. 15.

Anon. "Plain Talk About the Art of Relaxation." *Department of Health, Education and Welfare Publication No. (ADM) 78–632.* January, 1978.

Anon. "North Lies the Cradle of 'Lifestyle' Medicine." *Medical Tribune.* February 22, 1978, pp. 1, 12.

Anon. "Life on the Run with MD-author." *American Medical News.* August 25, 1978, pp. 13–15.

Anon. "Program on Bellydancers in the United States." ABC TV, August 30, 1978.

Arehart-Treichel, Joan. "Rats on the MTA." *Science News,* April 24, 1976, p. 266.

Arehart-Treichel, Joan. "How to Succeed at Failure." *Kiwanis Magazine.* September, 1976, pp. 28–29, 42.

Arehart-Treichel, Joan. "Bow-wow for Recovery." *Science News.* December 9, 1978, p. 408.

Arehart-Treichel, Joan. "Exercise Prevents Heart Attacks." *Science News,* December 9, 1978, p. 408.

Beck, Aaron T., and Weissman, Arlene. "The Measurement of Pessimism: The Hoplessness Scale." *Journal of Consulting and Clinical Psychology.* Vol. 42, No. 6, 1975, pp. 861–865.

Bensimon, Helen Frank. "The Heart." *The Magazine of the Rush-Presbyterian-St. Luke's Medical Center.* Spring, 1977, pp. 3–27.

Birren, James E. "Weathering the Years." *Health.* Summer, 1978, pp. 8–9, 24–25.

Brody, Jane E. "Studies Are Asking: Who's Happy?" *The New York Times,* January 16, 1979, pp. C1, C2.

Byrners, Michael A. "You Can Learn to Relax." *Story Ideas from Georgetown University.* November, 1976.

Cantwell, John D. "Running." *Journal of the American Medical Association.* September 22, 1978, pp. 1409–1410.

Cobb, Sidney. "Social Support as a Moderator of Life Stress." *Psychosomatic Medicine.* September–October, 1976, pp. 300–314.

Cohen, Ronald Jay, and Smith, Frederick J. "Socially Reinforced Obsessing: Etiology of a Disorder in a Christian Scientist." *Journal of Consulting and Clinical Psychology.* Vol. 44, No. 1, 1976, pp. 142–144.

Colligan, Douglas. "That Helpless Feeling: The Dangers of Stress." *New York.* July 14, 1975, pp. 28–32.

De Grâce, Gaston. "Effects of Meditation on Personality and Values." *Journal of Clinical Psychology.* October, 1976, pp. 809–813.

Deutsch, Ronald I. "Work Environment and People's Health." *News release from Stanford Research Institute,* August 20, 1974.

Dohrenwend, Barbara Snell, and Dohrenwend, Bruce P. "Some Issues in Research on Stressful Life Events." *The Journal of Nervous and Mental Disease.* Vol. 166, No. 1, 1978, pp. 7–15.

Dongier, M. "Psychosomatic Aspects in Myocardial Infarction in Comparison with Angina Pectoris." *Psychotherapy and Psychosomatics.* Vol. 23, 1974, pp. 123–131.

Engel, Geroge L. "Is Grief a Disease?" *Psychosomatic Medicine.* Vol. 23, No. 1, 1961, pp. 18–22.

Frankenhaeuser, Marianne. "Job Demands, Health and Wellbeing." *Journal of Psychosomatic Research.* Vol. 21, 1977, pp. 313–321.

Gal, Reuven, and Lazarus, Richard S. "The Role of Activity in Anticipating and Confronting Stressful Situations." *The Journal of Human Stress.* December, 1975, pp. 4–19.

Garrity, Thomas F., Marx, Martin B., and Somes, Grant W. "The Relationship of Recent Life Change to Seriousness of Later Illness." *Journal of Psychosomatic Research.* Vol. 22, 1978, pp. 7–12.

Goleman, Daniel J., and Schwartz, Gary E. "Meditation as an Intervention in Stress Reactivity." *Journal of Consulting and Clinical Psychology.* Vol. 44, No. 3, 1976, pp. 456–466.

Greenberg, Joel. "The Stress-Illness Link: Not 'If' but 'How.' " *Science News.* December 10, 1977, pp. 394–395.

Greenberg, Joel. "The Americanization of Roseto." *Science News.* June 10, 1978, pp. 378–379, 382.

Greenberg, Joel. "Adulthood Comes of Age." *Science News.* July 29, 1978, pp. 74–75, 79.

Greenberg, Joel. "The Great Depression: 40 Years After." *Science News.* September 23, 1978, p. 214.

Hacker, David W. "Living Dangerously? You Can ask a Computer." *National Observer,* March 12, 1977.

Hall-Smith, Patrick, and Ryle, Anthony. "Marital Patterns, Hostility and Personal Illness." *British Journal of Psychiatry.* Vol. 115, 1969, pp. 1197–1198.

Hill, A. B. "Personality Correlates of Dream Recall." *Journal of Consulting and Clinical Psychology.* Vol. 42, No. 6, 1974, pp. 766–773.

Hutschnecker, Arnold A. *The Will to Live.* New York: Cornerstone Library, 1977.

Irwin, Theodore. "How to Cope with Crises." *Public Affairs Pamphlet No. 464,* 1971.

Jacobs, Martin A., Spilken, Aron, and Norman, Martin. "Relationship of Life Change, Maladaptive Aggression, and Upper Respiratory Infection in Male College Students." *Psychosomatic Medicine.* Vol. 31, No. 1, 1969, pp. 31–44.

Kerr, Dorothy. "Meditate and Relax—It's Good for Your Health." *News release from the American Scientist,* August 3, 1977.

Lewis, Charles E., and Lewis, Mary Ann. "The Potential Impact of Sexual Equality on Health." *The New England Journal of Medicine*. Vol. 297, No. 16, 1977, pp. 863–868.

Luborsky, Lester, Todd, Thomas C., and Katcher, Aaron H. "A Self-Administered Social Assets Scale for Predicting Physical and Psychological Illness and Health." *Journal of Psychosomatic Research*. Vol. 17, 1973, pp. 109–120.

Marks, Joseph J. "It's Not Too Late to Get in Shape." *News release from the University of Missouri*, April 6, 1978.

McClelland, David C. "Sources of Stress in the Drive for Power." *The Kittay Scientific Foundation*, 1975.

McFadden, Robert D. "How the Layoffs Have Affected Some City Workers." *The New York Times*, July 28, 1975.

McNerney, Walter J., et al. "Stress." *Blue Print for Health*. Vol. 25, No. 1, 1974, pp. 1–96.

Mechanic, David. "Stress, Illness, and Illness Behavior." *Journal of Human Stress*. June, 1976, pp. 2–6.

Miller, Neal E. "Interactions Between Learned and Physical Factors in Mental Illness." *Seminars in Psychiatry*. Vol. 4, No. 3, 1972, pp. 239–253.

Miller, P. McC., Ingham, J. G., and Davidson, S. "Life Events, Symptoms and Social Support." *Journal of Psychosomatic Research*. Vol. 20, 1976, pp. 515–522.

Neumann, Charles P. "Success Today—Achievement Without Happiness." *Psychosomatics*. Vol. 16, No. 3, 1975, pp. 103–106.

Peale, Norman Vincent. *The Power of Positive Thinking*. New York: Fawcett Crest, 1956.

Pelletier, Kenneth R. *Mind as Healer, Mind as Slayer*, New York: Delta, 1977.

Rahe, Richard H., and Arthur, Ransom J. "Life Changes and Illness Studies: Past History and Future Directions." *Journal of Human Stress*. March, 1978, pp. 3–15.

Riley, Vernon. "Mouse Mammary Tumors: Alteration of Incidence as Apparent Function of Stress." *Science*. August 8, 1975, pp. 465–466.

Rosenman, Ray H., and Friedman, Meyer. "Modifying Type A Behavior Pattern." *Journal of Psychosomatic Research*. Vol. 21, 1977, pp. 323–331.

Schmeck, Harold M. "Preventive Medicine Reports Emphasize Economic Factors." *The New York Times*, June 10, 1975.

Solomon, George, F., and Moos Rudolf H. "The Relationship of Personality to the Presence of Rheumatoid Factor in Asymptomatic Relatives of Patients with Rheumatoid Arthritis." *Psychosomatic Medicine*. Vol. 27, No. 4, 1965, pp. 350–360.

Stoudenmire, John. "A Comparison of Muscle Relaxation Training and Music to the Reduction of State and Trait Anxiety." *Journal of Clinical Psychology*. Vol. 31, No. 3, 1975, pp. 490–492.

Tec, Leon. *The Fear of Success*. New York: Reader's Digest Press, 1976.

Thurlow, H. John. "Illness in Relation to Life Situation and Sick-Role Tendency." *Journal of Psychosomatic Research*. Vol. 15, 1971, pp. 73–88.

Vaux, Kenneth. "Religion and Health." *Preventive Medicine*. Vol. 5, 1976, pp. 522–536.

Waldron, Ingrid, and Johnston, Susan. "Why Do Women Live Longer Than Men?" *Journal of Human Stress*. June, 1976, pp. 19–30.

Yankelovich, Daniel. "The New Psychological Contracts at Work." *Psychology Today*, May, 1978.

Chapter 11

Alfaro, Victor R. "Psychogenic Influences in Otolaryngology." *A.M.A. Archives of Otolaryngology.* January, 1966, pp. 11/1–17/7.

Amkraut, Alfred A., Solomon, George F., and Kraemer, Helena C. "Stress, Early Experience and Adjuvant-Induced Arthritis in the Rat." *Psychosomatic Medicine.* May–June, 1971, pp. 203–214.

Anon. "Program Seeks to Identify 'Problem Pregnancies' Early." *Health Sciences Report of the University of Utah,* November, 1975, p. 8.

Anon. "High Blood Pressure May Originate in Childhood." *News release from the Medical and Pharmaceutical Information Bureau,* September 24, 1976.

Anon. "School Problems Only One of Many for Minimal Brain Dysfunction Child." *News release from the Medical and Pharmaceutical Information Bureau,* October 2, 1976.

Anon. "Bereft, Burdened and Bewildered." *Emergency Medicine.* November, 1978, pp. 105–107.

Arehart-Treichel, Joan. "Smoking Imperils the Unborn." *Science News,* January 27, 1979, p. 55.

Brody, Jane E. "Studies Are Asking: Who's Happy?" *The New York Times,* January 16, 1979, p. C1, C2.

Booth, Gotthard. "General and Organic-Specific Object Relationships in Cancer." *Annals of the New York Academy of Sciences,* Vol. 164, 1969, pp. 568–575.

Bortner, Rayman, Rosenman, Ray H., and Friedman, Meyer. "Familial Similarity in Pattern A Behavior." *Journal of Chronic Disease.* Vol. 23, 1970, pp. 39–43.

Butensky, Arthur, et al. "Elements of the Coronary Prone Behavior Pattern in Children and Teenagers." *Jounal of Psychosomatic Research.* Vol. 20, 1976, pp. 439–444.

Cameron, James R. "Parental Treatment, Children's Temperament, and the Risk of Childhood Behavioral Problems." *American Journal of Orthopsychiatry.* January, 1978, pp. 140–147.

Cobb, Sidney. "Social Support as a Moderator of Life Stress." *Psychosomatic Medicine.* September–October, 1976, pp. 300–314.

Coddington, R. Dean. "The Significance of Life Events as Etiologic Factors in the Diseases of Children." *Journal of Psychosomatic Research.* Vol. 16, 1972, pp. 7–18.

Crase, Dixie R., and Crase, Darrell. "Death and the Young Child." *Clinical Pediatrics.* August, 1975, pp. 747–750.

Dunn, Judith F. "Mother-Infant Relations over the First 14 Months." *Journal of Psychosomatic Research.* Vol. 20, 1976, pp. 273–277.

Fann, William E., and Sussex, James N. "Late Effects of Early Dependency Need Deprivation: The Meal Ticket Syndrome." *British Journal of Psychiatry.* Vol. 128, 1976, pp. 262–268.

Fox, Matthew. "Teaching Joy." *The National Catholic Reporter.* December 22, 1978.

Frazier, Shervert H. "Anorexia Nervosa." *Diseases of the Nervous System.* March, 1965, pp. 155–159.

Friedman, Stanford B., Glasgow, Lowell A., and Ader, Robert. "Psychosocial Factors Modifying Host Resistance to Experimental Infections." *Annals of the New York Academy of Sciences.* Vol 164, 1969, pp. 381–391.

Gardner, Richard A. "Easing the Damage of Divorce or Death." *Blue Print for Health,* Vol. 26, No. 1, 1976, pp. 42–48.

Glass, David C. *Behavior Patterns, Stress and Coronary Disease.* Hillsdale, N.J.: Lawrence Erlbaum Associates, 1977.

Greenberg, Joel. "Mother-to-be's Anxiety Linked to Autism." *Science News.* December 3, 1977, p. 374.

Greenberg, Joel. "Genius and Parental Loss." *Science News.* April 22, 1978, p. 245.

Greenberg, Joel. "Holocaust: Parents 'Transmit' Effects." *Science News.* May 20, 1978, pp. 323.

Greeenberg, Joel. "Prenatal Influences on Newborn." *Science News.* September 16, 1978, pp. 201.

Hall, Fae. "Prenatal Events and Later Infant Behavior." *Journal of Psychosomatic Research.* Vol. 21, 1977, pp. 253–257.

Henoch, Monica Jean, Batson, Jean W., and Baum, John. "Psychosocial Factors in Juvenile Rheumatoid Arthritis." *Arthritis & Rheumatism.* March, 1978, pp. 229–233.

Hicks, Nancy. "Family Stress Called a Menace to Health." *The New York Times,* October, 1976.

Jacobs, Martin A., et al. "Incidence of Psychosomatic Predisposing Factors in Allergic Disorders." *Psychosomatic Medicine.* Vol. 28, No. 5, 1966, pp. 679–695.

Johnson, Charles Felzen. "Why Children Fail." *Medical Times.* December, 1976, pp. 81–83.

Klagsbrun, Francine. "Preventing Teenage Suicide." *Family Health/Today's Health.* April, 1977, pp. 21–24.

Levin, Sidney. "A Brief Note on the 'Undoing' of Childhood Traumatic Experiences Through Environmental Manipulation." *Bulletin of the Menninger Clinic.* Vol. 38, 1974, pp. 365–368.

Matthews, Karen, and Krantz, David S. "Resemblances of Twins and Their Parents in Pattern A Behavior." *Psychosomatic Medicine.* March–April, 1976, pp. 140–144.

McMahon, Arthur W., et al. "Personality Differences Between Inflammatory Bowel Disease Patients and Their Healthy Siblings." *Psychosomatic Medicine.* March–April, 1973, pp. 91–103.

Meijer, Alexander. "Sources of Dependency in Asthmatic Children." *Psychosomatics.* June, 1978, pp. 351–355.

Mutter, Arthur Z., and Schleifer, Maxwell J. "The Role of Psychological and Social Factors in the Onset of Somatic Illness in Children." *Psychosomatic Medicine.* Vol. 28, No. 4 (Part 1), 1966, pp. 333–343.

Pelletier, Kenneth R. *Mind as Healer, Mind as Slayer.* New York: Delta, 1977, pp. 105–106 (re: how parents teach children to withhold anger).

Pipineli-Potamianou, A. "The Child, Vulnerable in the Mother's Desire." *Psychotherapy and Psychosomatics.* Vol. 26, 1975, pp. 211–218.

Pollitt, Ernesto, Eichler, Aviva Weisel, and Chan, Chee-Khoon. "Psychosocial Development and Behavior of Mothers of Failure-to-Thrive Children." *American Journal of Orthopsychiatry.* July, 1975, pp. 525–537.

Rahe, Richard H., and Arthur, Ransom J. "Life Change and Illness Studies: Past History and Future Directions." *Journal of Human Stress.* March, 1978, pp. 3–15.

Reinhart, John B., and Drash, Allan L. "Psychosocial Dwarfism: Environmentally Induced Recovery." *Psychosomatic Medicine.* Vol. 31, No. 2, 1969, pp. 165–172.

Rixse, Robert, et al. "Attempted Suicide in Adolescence." *Clinical Proceedings—Children's Hospital National Medical Center,* May, 1975, pp. 81–88.

Salk, Lee. "Growing Up Emotionally." *Blue Print for Health.* Vol. 26, No. 1, 1976, pp. 42–48.

Salk, Lee, et al. "Growing Up Mentally Fit." *Blue Print for Health.* Vol. 25, No. 1, 1974, pp. 16–33.

Scharf, Laura. "Teenage Suicides on the Rise." *News release from Margaret Larson,* June 15, 1976.

Segal, Julius. *A Child's Journey—Forces that Shape the Lives of Our Young.* New York: McGraw Hill, 1978.

Solomon, George F. "Early Experience and Immunity." *Nature.* November 23, 1968, pp. 821–822.

Sontag, Lester. "Fetal Environment and Adult Personality." *Annals of the New York Academy of Sciences.* Vol. 134, 1966, pp. 782–786.

Tec, Loen. *The Fear of Success.* New York: The Reader's Digest Press, 1976.

Trotter, Robert J. "Changing the Face of Birth." *Science News.* August 16, 1975, pp. 106–108.

Trotter, Robert J. "Leboyer's Babies." *Science News.* January 22, 1977, p. 59.

Wessel, Morris A. "A Death in the Family—the Impact on Children." *Journal of the American Medical Association.* November 24, 1975, pp. 865–866.

Wilson, Elaine Blume. "How to Protect Your Child Against Cancer, Mental Illness and Heart Disease." *Harper's Bazaar.* October, 1976, pp. 122, 184C, 199.

Yahraes, Herbert. "Developing a Sense of Competence in Young Children." *Department of Health, Education and Welfare Publication No. (ADM) 78-643,* 1978.

Chapter 12

Anon. "Emotional Factors Seen by Physicians as Most Important Cause of Declining Health of Retirees." *News release from Richard Weiner,* March 11, 1977.

Anon. "Clergyman Longevity Linked to Good Health, Lifestyle." *Medical Tribune.* July 9, 1978, pp. 1, 11.

Anon. "The Life of Multibillionaire Howard Hughes." CBS-TV, August 29–30, 1978.

Anon. "Feature on Black Ragtime Pianist Eubie Blake." NBC-TV, February 5, 1979.

Arehart-Treichel, Joan. "It's Never Too Late to Start Living Longer." *New York.* April 11, 1977, pp. 38–40.

Atlas, Donald H. "Longevity in Symphony Conductors." *Forum on Medicine.* November, 1978, pp. 50–51.

Benet, Sula. *How to Live to Be 100.* New York: Dial Press, 1976.

Comfort, Alex. *A Good Age.* New York: Crown, 1976.

Davies, David. *The Centenarians of the Andes.* New York: Anchor Press/ Doubleday, 1975.

Hutschnecker, Arnold A. *The Will to Live.* New York: Cornerstone Library, 1977.

Peale, Norman Vincent. *The Power of Positive Thinking.* New York: Fawcett Crest, 1956.

Pelletier, Kenneth R. *Mind as Healer, Mind as Slayer.* New York: Delta, 1977.

Rosenfeld, Albert. "Is There Life After Life?" *Horizon.* Autumn, 1976, pp. 43–47.

Selye, Hans. *Stress Without Distress.* Philadelphia, Pa.: Lippincott, 1974.

Wren, Christopher. "Soviet Centenarians Say It's Diet, Work and Family—Not Yogurt." *The New York Times,* September, 9, 1977.

INDEX